Second Edition

QUALITY LEADERSHIP SKILLS

Standards of Leadership Behavior

Richard W. Leatherman, Ph.D.

Published by: International Training Consultants, Inc.
P.O. Box 35613
Richmond, VA 23235-0613

1-800-998-8764

First Printing

ISBN 0-9674325-1-0

To my son, Matt Leatherman

May he have many "Turtle Days" with his sons, Tanner and Trevor

Preface

Traditionally, human resource departments focused on providing leadership training for only supervisors and managers. And in that training they talked a lot about "participative" leadership. But more often than not, the supervisors and managers left the training department to enter a world of work that did not encourage or allow participation! So we paid mere lip service to good leadership practices, and vast segments of this country's businesses became noncompetitive in the world market.

Now, however, significant shifts in organizational focus have taken place. Many organizations now utilize work teams that in the past were usually led by traditional managers. Today, they are more likely to be self-directed teams. These employee involvement teams have such names as "Total Quality Performance," "Total Quality Management," or "Continuous Quality Improvement." These teams are cross-functional groups as well as department teams in the marketing, service, and operations areas.

Today's organizations are emphasizing quality, effectiveness, and productivity! To help them do so, they are downsizing, reducing the middle management population ("flattening"), delegating responsibility downward, and giving the responsibility for quality to front-line employees.

In a growing number of organizations across the country, the President says, "Executive Vice President Jones, we are going to win that quality award for excellence!"

The Executive VP replies, "Right, boss."

Vice President Jones then calls in the Senior VP of Human Resources and says, "The chief wants us to win that award for excellence. What do we have to do to make it happen?"

The Senior VP replies, "I don't know, boss. But I'll find out."

So, the Senior VP calls in his VP of Training and Development and states, "The chief wants us to win that prize for excellence! What do we need to do?"

The Training Department VP responds, "Let our supervisors and managers do what they have been trained to do—create an environment that supports participative management practices. And while you're at it," he continues, "give the non-exempts training in how to take on the new responsibility that participative management creates."

"But what about the budget?" cries the Senior VP of HR. "Where are we going to get the money to continue our regular supervisory and management training—and train all the employees at the same time?"

"Use one of the oldest teaching tools in the trade," replies the training manager. "Buy them a book!"

"You're nuts!" snorts the Senior VP. "You mean you expect me to tell my boss to buy books for our supervisors and managers?"

"Yes," replies the training manager. "I do."

This book, *Quality Leadership Skills*, is part of the answer to today's need for quality performance. It is a practical how-to-do-it manual that explains the basic leadership tasks in a simple, step-by-step manner. As such, it is an important update for those who have been trained and retrained—and trained again—in leadership principles. It is also a key manual for new and future leaders.

And it's easy to use. Would you like to know how *really* to empower your employees so that they will take greater charge over their own careers? To teach your employees how to take more responsibility for their performance appraisal interviews? To learn how to effectively delegate work to employees? Do you understand that the old saying, "You can't delegate responsibility, only authority," is 99% myth?

In the chapters that follow, you will find clear directions on how to develop your employees. And the exciting thing about it is that you and your employees will produce more, better, and faster—and enjoy doing it, too!

Table of Contents

Introduction

1. Leadership in the 21st Century — 5
2. Values—the Foundation — 11
3. Motivating Employees — 17

Leadership Skills for Improving Performance

4. Establishing Employee Performance Standards — 55
5. One-On-One Training Skills — 69
6. Improving Employee Performance Through Coaching — 87
7. Improving Employee Performance Through Counseling — 131
8. Handling Employee Complaints — 153

Processes of Leadership

9. Delegation — 167
10. Problem Solving — 201
11. Decision Making — 241
12. The Importance of Planning — 267
13. Developing Objectives with Employees — 285
14. Conducting Effective Performance Appraisals — 299

Personal Leadership Skills

15. Managing Our Time — 329
16. Managing and Conducting Meetings — 343
17. Interviewing and Selection — 377

Leading Transitions

18. Career Counseling — 423
19. Leading Change — 447

The Close

20. Leading Your Employees — 463

Introduction to Leadership

Introduction

A machine is easy to run. Hit this button, and it starts! Push that one, and it stops. And it usually produces more, better, and faster than a manual worker could ever hope to do. We have automated most of our highly skilled jobs in a continuous effort to make everything bigger, better, and faster.

But there is one high-skill area that can never be automated—interactions between people—especially those between a leader and his or her team members.

We know that it often takes more skill than we have to deal with the great variety of employee needs and problems we encounter. Remember your feelings of discomfort when you had to handle that discipline problem? You're not alone! Most of us have had those same feelings in dealing with employee situations.

The fact is that it's good that we experience these uncomfortable feelings, because they serve as motivation—motivation to learn more about leading our employees effectively.

A number of years ago I felt like a very lucky supervisor. I had not just one, but four very competent employees. It was fortunate for them that they were outstanding—because I was the original "gutless" supervisor!

I found it very easy to praise my employees on their good work. But it was extremely difficult for me to tell them how I felt they could improve.

So, I didn't! I didn't give them feedback on improvement because it made me feel uncomfortable. And as a result, they were deprived of important opportunities to develop and grow—because they didn't receive accurate information from me.

Then one day my manager asked me if one of these employees was ready for a promotion. "Not yet," I replied. "There are a couple of areas she needs to work on. Let's give her another year."

The next morning, the employee stood in my office doorway and said, "Can I see you for a minute, Dick?"

"Sure," I replied.

She stepped inside—and shut my door. "Dick," she asked, "did you turn me down for a promotion?"

"Well . . . yes," I replied.

"Why?" she asked.

"Because," I said, "I felt you weren't ready."

"Why not?" she responded.

"Well, there are two particular areas I feel you need to work on." And I lamely spelled out the problems.

"But you never told me this," she replied. And she was right!

Two months later, she quit our organization.

At that point in my career, I had a great need to know how to truly lead my employees. Much of what I have learned since then has come the hard way, by making and learning from my mistakes.

I have also watched other leaders closely—both good ones and poor ones. Further, I regularly attend leadership programs and read books on leadership. And I've learned much from 30 years of teaching leadership skills.

This book is my learning process—put into writing for you. It is for leaders who want common sense ideas on how to handle the often-bewildering array of employee problem situations they face.

It is a very special "how-to" book, with step-by-step instructions, a book that gives practical advice, not just theories. Throughout, it presents clear standards of performance for every leader. The chapters show you how to handle the many day-to-day interactions that are key to empowering your employees—to helping them be more productive, and fulfilled!

Leadership in the 21st Century

If you did not hold a position of authority, if your name was not on the door, would anyone follow you for what you believe in, who you are as a person, and where you want to go?

Bruce E. Thom
Navigation Through the "Heart of Darkness"

Today, we see incredible changes occurring in our organizations. Organizations are in transition—downsizing, rightsizing, merging, and acquiring. They change to enhance their value to stockholders. They change in order to survive in today's competitive world markets. And they change the internal structure of the organization to reduce department boundaries in order to enhance creativity and communication.

But, as a result of all these organizational changes, we also see corresponding changes in our workforce.

First, how employees see their life's work has changed. The good employees, the ones the organization wants to keep, no longer see anything wrong with leaving the organization to take what they see is a better job. Few employees, if any, look forward to the gold watch and retirement party. And it's not because today's employees are any less loyal than the employees of yesterday. They are loyal. They are usually loyal until the organization gives them reason to leave.

Think about it. No employee remembers the Great Depression and what it was like to be grateful to have a job—any job! The following generation, whose only links to that life-changing time were the stories they heard from their parents, are themselves now retired. Our younger generation has lost the fear of not being able to find work. Now, the perception of most employees is that employment is readily available. And they're right—organizations are hungry for good people. So, when good employees feel dissatisfied in their jobs or the way that they are treated, they quit and find work someplace else.

One of the major sources of dissatisfaction for employees is to have what they consider are incompetent leaders. Years ago, they were more willing to put up with an incompetent boss—today, they leave! Therefore, in order to keep high-quality employees, it is now mandatory that organizations provide high-quality leaders for them.

Employees are also more willing to leave because it is now socially acceptable. There is little or no stigma today attached to an individual who leaves one company to work for another. With the destruction of the psychological employee/organization contract, an employee's loyalty today is more often to his or her profession, not to the organization.

Second, as a result of organizational change, we see wider spans of control. More and more people work for fewer and fewer bosses. The more people a leader has, the more he or she needs to delegate, motivate, and create teams that can take responsibility for their own work—in short, they must lead.

With the implementation of teams, organizations need people to lead these teams. In some cases, these teams need leaders, but not in the typical sense of being a supervisor or manager. They might simply need individuals who can step forward and take over the role of team leadership.

Third, the organization's old internal boundaries are disappearing. Departments no longer work as silos, focused only on their own narrow view of the organization's mission. We want our employees to work across functions and the department borders. This requires leadership. It requires leaders who are able to create a vision for their employees—a vision of what they are about and where they are going. And it requires employees who realize they must cooperate with others in the organization in order to complete the mission.

Fourth and last, we used to promote employees to positions of leadership because they were competent at doing the department's tasks. But with the rapid changes in technology which lead to changes in the way we do the work, employees may now know more about the tasks to be done than their leaders. Therefore, the supervisor's or manager's authority comes not from his or her detailed and competent knowledge of the section's jobs, but in his or her ability to lead a talented team of diverse employees.

Strengths, in today's organization, come from many diverse individuals, not just one person. Our workforce is no longer made up of predominately male Caucasians. We are of all ethnic backgrounds, races, faiths, and both men and women. To manage today's employees, we need leadership, not just management.

Unfortunately, we don't prepare our employees to take on the role of leadership. We just promote them and somehow expect them to know what to do. We teach them to complete paperwork. We teach them how to manage. But we don't teach them how to lead. It used to be that the manager had the time to mentor the new supervisor in the mostly unconscious skills of leadership. Today, it is difficult for most managers to find the quality time required to help his or her supervisor make the transition from employee to leader. Furthermore, many of our managers are not themselves good leaders, so how are they going to teach the new supervisor to lead. And some of our managers know how to lead, but don't know how to teach others what they know.

In addition, today many employees are reluctant to take on the title and role of a supervisor. They feel, with some justification, that to do so is just not worth the hassle of dealing with problem employees, a never-ending flow of paperwork, a diverse workforce, sexual-harassment problems, and their own lack of knowledge in how to lead.

Professor Kotter, noted leadership author and Professor of Organizational Behavior at Harvard, wrote in the Harvard Business Review, "Leadership is about coping with change. Doing what was done yesterday, or doing it 5% better, is no longer a formula for success. Major changes are more and more necessary to survive and compete effectively in this new environment. More change always demands more leadership."

So, how do we teach this thing called "Leadership"?

Dr. Kotter offered us one way of looking at leadership by comparing it to management. He said that management is made up of the activities of planning and budgeting, organizing and staffing, and controlling and problem solving. He states that leadership, however, is about setting a direction, a vision, aligning people to the organization's vision, and then motivating and inspiring employees to achieve their vision.

Management	**Leadership**
Planning & Budgeting	Setting a Direction, a Vision
Organizing and Staffing	Aligning People
Controlling and Problem Solving	Motivating and Inspiring

Unfortunately, the graduates we hire that have had a traditional four-year liberal arts program receive little or no training in leadership. And graduates with bachelor's degrees in business administration receive the majority of their training in accounting, economics, statistics, and finances. Good management stuff, but not leadership! Even graduates in a typical MBA program receive little in the way of leadership education and training. We are thus left to "grow our own" leaders.

Professor Kotter also wrote, "Most U.S. corporations today are over managed and under led. They need to develop their capacity to exercise leadership. Successful corporations don't wait for leaders to come along. They actively seek out people with leadership potential and expose them to career experiences designed to develop that potential. Indeed, with careful selection, nurturing, and encouragement, dozens of people can play important leadership roles in business organizations."

J. Thomas Wren, Professor at the Jepson School of Leadership, wrote in his book, The Leader's Companion, "Many dismiss the subject [of leadership] with the confident assertion that 'leaders are born not made.' Nonsense! Most of what leaders have that enables them to lead is learned. Leadership is not a mysterious activity. It is possible to describe the tasks that leaders perform."

And if we can describe it, we can learn it! We can study famous leaders. We can examine the latest research that has practical, on-the-job application for leaders. We can learn how the environment that surrounds the organization affects leadership. We can study ethics. And we can learn the skills of leadership.

2

Leadership
Values——the Foundation

Leadership is not a person or a position. It is a complex moral relationship between people, based on trust, obligation, commitment, emotion, and a shared vision of the good.

Joanne Ciulla
Ethics, The Heart of Leadership

So, what do values have to do with leadership? Everything! Our underlying values guide our actions. We can learn the key behavioral steps required for any given leader/employee situation, but if our values aren't aligned with the needed behaviors, we likely won't consistently say or do what needs to be said or done. For example, I know that "walk around leadership" is important. Taking the time to stop working on a particular task, leave my office, and schmooze with my staff is worthwhile. I know it, but I don't consistently do it. I don't stop work to talk to my staff because I tend to be task driven and become almost unconscious to the outside world. I know how to do it, I even know I'm "supposed" to do it. But it is rare that I just walk around and talk to people. Nice causal conversations like, "How's everything going?" "What's happening in your life?" "How's your family?" "What concerns do you have about your job?" If I walked up to a member of my staff and started asking what I feel are "chit-chat" kinds of questions, he or she would wonder if I had been taken over by aliens. Not that they wouldn't like me to do it—they would! It would seem a bit unusual at first, but if I consistently took time out of my day to visit my staff, it would have a positive effect on the workforce. It is a bit embarrassing to write this, but creating strong interpersonal relationships with my staff is just not at the top of my list of things to do. Talking one-on-one with others is not something I learned to do as a child nor am I comfortable doing it. It's funny, I love teaching groups or making presentations (one-way communications), but taking the time from my busy schedule of doing the things I like to do (like writing this book) to reach out to others doesn't "feel" right for me. It is just not a deep-seated value for me—even though it "ought" to be!

We aren't born with values. We learn them, mostly in early childhood. We learn what's right and not right. We learn how to behave, and how not to behave. We learn values from our parents, teachers, good bosses and bad bosses, and other significant people in our lives. These values are mostly subconscious. We rarely if ever take the time to say to ourselves, "What are my basic values about leadership?" As I think about my own leadership values, I realize how difficult it is to articulate them. I know that I value 1) integrity, 2) the Golden Rule, 3) respect for all individuals who work for and with me, and 4) helping others who need assistance.

As I read back over the four items above, I realize that I also value hard work, tolerance for others' mistakes, and life-long learning. But, is "hard work" a leadership value? I think so. It does affect the way that I relate to individuals on my staff in two ways. First, I tend to invest more of my time in mentoring employees who work hard. I also cut them more slack when they make mistakes. And, I would more likely reward a hard worker with salary increases and promotions. This strong value of mine, however, also gets in my way as a leader. I tend not to be as understanding of individuals who may be just as productive, but because they put their childcare or family life ahead of their job, they take time off when they are needed on the job or they are not available to volunteer for special and important work projects on the weekend. "Wow," you might think, "this guy Leatherman is not much of a leader!" You may be right. In some ways, I am not. What this personal example illustrates is that our values about leadership, especially those that are core to our being, can also be detrimental to good leadership—especially when taken to excess. And there is no question that I take the value of "hard work" to an extreme.

Any of our values can get us in trouble when taken to extreme. For example, "integrity" is, for many leaders, an important value. But I have met leaders who take pride in always being brutally honest, seem to get pleasure in verbally destroying an employee with "truth," and justify their behavior by saying, "I was only being honest."

It is important to clearly know our values so that we understand why we do the things we do as leaders. Understanding them allows us to guard against excesses when we project our values onto others and helps guide our future actions. For example, knowing that I strongly value hard work and desire that others do also allows me to monitor my own behavior when dealing with subordinates who don't value what I value.

Our core values seldom change over time. What we choose to do (the actions we take as we lead) can change and do change. But the personal core values rarely change. These values help us to examine how we should treat our followers, and bring to light how we really treat them. Then, they enable us to look at the gap that may exist between how we treat employees and how we should treat them, help us figure out why we do what we do, and point out what action may be needed.

I strongly encourage you to take a few minutes and consider your values. Can you list below your top five leadership values?

1. _Be a good listner_
2. _respected_
3. _honest_
4. _fair_
5. _be able to Motivate others_

After considering your personal leadership values, you may also want to think about the leadership values of the organization for which you work. If your values and your organization's values are similar, then the culture of your organization supports the way that you lead your employees. If not, then you have a problem.

Suppose, for example, that one of your values is "truth-telling." Further suppose that you have an employee who is technically very competent and almost irreplaceable. This employee is also very ambitious and strongly desires a promotion into a leadership position. Unfortunately, he wants a promotion for the wrong reasons: he wants the prestige, money, and recognition that would come with a promotion. These are not good long-term reasons for wanting to be a leader. In addition, this employee does not have the personality necessary to lead others. He is abrupt, authoritative, and autocratic when dealing with others, and is basically a loner who prefers to work alone.

In preparing for your annual performance appraisal interview with this employee, you discuss the situation with your boss. He tells you that in order to keep this employee in his important job, let him think that he has a future chance at being a supervisor. At this point, your key value of honesty is in direct conflict with your boss's wishes. Most of us would try to convince our boss that he or she needs to see the long-term problems that are created when we don't tell the employee the truth. But if the boss isn't convinced, we have a problem. When faced with an ethical dilemma such as this, leaders must make the decision that is right for them. In this case, the right decision is to tell the truth—no matter the personal consequences.

Working in an environment that is opposed to our core values is a disaster in the making. The chances are that not only are we unhappy with the organization where we work, the organization is also unhappy with us. Thus, if we can't change the environment, we may need to find a new place to work that matches our values.

When we are young, decisions to move to another job because of major differences between our values and the organization's are somewhat easier. We usually have fewer outside responsibilities (we're not paying for our children's college tuition—yet), our level in the organization is not as high as in later years, and as a result, we have less to lose by leaving one job for another. But as we get older, it may be more risky to leave one job in order to find another. In other words, the consequence of quitting a job as a matter of principle becomes much more difficult. Therefore, it is very, very important that you think through your personal values early in your career, and ensure that they do in fact match those of your organization.

In the following chapters, you will see models of leadership behavior for a number of different leadership tasks. But remember that these are models that fit my beliefs and values. You may need to adapt or modify a particular model to be better aligned with your core beliefs and values. If, however, there is something about the model that bothers you, don't discard the whole model. First, figure out what part of it bothers you, why that particular step in the model doesn't work for you, and then what you would do or say in place of that step. Or, you may discover that the underlying reason for completing a particular step in a model is so strongly needed that you will choose to do it in spite of your discomfort.

My beliefs about leadership that underlie the behaviors in the following chapters are as follows:

1. Both leaders and employees can learn new and better ways of working together.
2. Leaders show respect for all employees.
3. Leaders trust their employees to do the right thing unless proven otherwise.
4. Leaders trust their employees with information about the organization's mission, vision, and strategic and tactical plans.
5. Leaders talk *with* employees, not *at* them.
6. Both authority and responsibility can be delegated and shared with employees—individually or in teams.
7. With the complexity of today's jobs, it is likely that employees know more about their jobs than their leaders—and thus may have better ideas.
8. Creativity is widely dispersed in the organization—not just the providence of leaders.
9. Employees are involved in problem solving, decision making, and planning.
10. Quality discussions with employees take time—time to prepare and time to conduct. Effective leaders are willing to take the necessary time.
11. Leaders have an unlimited opportunity to provide positive feedback to employees.
12. Employees should be allowed to take appropriate risks, make mistakes, and learn from them.
13. It is almost always better to tell the truth.

3

Leadership
Motivating Employees

Effective leaders recognize that "motivation" is not something that they do to an employee. Their challenge is to create an environment where motivation naturally occurs.

R. W. Leatherman

Theories of Motivation

Employees are motivated to excel for many different reasons. Thus it is difficult to establish hard and fast motivational rules. But because people are similar in so many ways, we can make some general statements about motivating our employees.

For example, if your boss informs you that she is going to give you a big raise because of your outstanding contributions during the past year, you will probably feel—at least for the moment—highly motivated.

However, suppose you are already making big bucks in your job, yet you feel unappreciated because your boss never takes the time to tell you how much she appreciated your work. Odds are that a sincere compliment might mean just as much—maybe even more—than a somewhat bigger paycheck.

Yet, some people feel uncomfortable receiving compliments. For these employees, something different, like a more challenging job, or even a different job, might be a better motivator. In short, employees are motivated by their needs, not ours.

So how do we motivate our employees? First, we motivate by knowing something about the dynamics of motivation, and second, by using this knowledge appropriately. Let's look, then, at some general theories of motivation.

Of the many persons who have contributed to our knowledge about motivation, Douglas McGregor, Abraham Maslow, and Frederick Herzberg have been particularly helpful. These three individuals began the search for answers to the "How in the heck do I motivate my employees?" question. Although parts of their theories don't hold up in light of modern-day research, they still offer us the best way of looking at the issue of motivation. The figure below suggests how the three main theories contribute to our understanding of motivation.

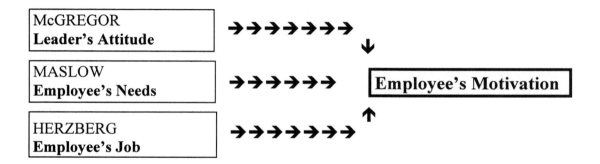

Douglas McGregor studied the relationship between a **leader's attitude** toward his or her employees and the resultant employee behavior. Maslow investigated **employee needs**. And Herzberg looked at how the **employee's job** affects his or her motivation. All three of these factors—the leader's attitude, the employee's needs, and the job itself—greatly affect employee motivation.

The Leader's Attitude

McGregor believed that there are two types of leaders. One type believes that an employee works hard only because he or she has to and will goof off if given a chance. McGregor labeled this type of leader "X." He also felt there is a second group of leaders who believe that employees work productively because they enjoy their work. He labeled these leaders "Y."

McGregor emphasized that a leader's attitude toward employees affects the way he or she manages. For example, if I believe that my people work only because they are made to work, I will probably be a very controlling boss. That is, I will establish strict job standards, set up job controls, observe and monitor my people carefully, and let them know that they are being watched.

On the other hand, if I believe that my employees can be trusted to do their jobs, I will tend to be less controlling. I won't need to control my people because they will control themselves. Now whether or not my employees need to be controlled is not the point—it's whether or not I believe they do. What we believe to be true tends to result in our employees becoming what we expect. It's a little like raising children. If we expect children to be dishonest and therefore treat them as if they were dishonest, they often become dishonest.

The same thing is true with adult workers. If we believe that employees have to be watched, monitored, controlled, and forced to work, then they tend to become that way. But if we expect our people to do their work, then they usually will. A lot of what happens in terms of an employee's morale is simply due to our attitude about him or her.

Let's look at an example. Suppose, one day, an employee takes excessive time for his morning break. An "X" type leader will say to this employee, "You're late. Don't you know that breaks are only ten minutes? Get back to work—and in the future, I'll be watching you!" Here, the leader believes that he or she has to keep a close eye on this employee in order to prevent future problems. In short, there is a lack of trust that employees will behave appropriately on the job. This lack of trust is due to the way this particular leader views his or her employees. As a result, the employee, not feeling trusted, is more likely to behave in untrustworthy ways in the future.

A less controlling leader might say to this employee, "I'm surprised that you are late from break. What happened?" Here, the implication is that there may be a legitimate reason why the employee was late returning from break, and that the employee is self-motivated in wanting to return to his job on time. The leader has clearly communicated his or her standards ("I'm surprised that you are late from work?") and has demonstrated his or her concern for the employee's situation ("What happened").

In order to see how "Theories X and Y" can be applied to the work world, read Part 1 of the following case. When you have finished reading Part 1, answer the questions at the end of the case before turning to Part 2.

The Case of the Disappearing Profits

Part 1

The Natural Taste Company's sales and distribution facility is located in Pamplin City, Virginia. It's early Monday morning and George Dishberger, NTC's vice president of sales and distribution, is waiting for Joyce Havinstock, NTC's senior vice president of marketing in New York, to arrive.

George is not a happy man. Things have not been going well for the organization during the past year. Sales are down, and costs are up. George is afraid that Joyce is coming to either fire him, demote him, or "straighten him out" in some unpleasant way or another.

The intercom buzzes, and with a deep sigh, George picks up his phone.

"Ms. Havinstock is here," his receptionist reports.

"Send her in," George replies. He sighs again, straightens his tie, and stands to greet Joyce as she breezes into the office.

"Good morning, Joyce," he says, with a strained smile.

"I wish it was a good morning," she replies. "Unfortunately, you have serious problems and I'm here to see that they get fixed! Your sales are miserable and your costs are even worse. Frankly, George, your job is on the line. Now, why don't you fill me in on what's going on?"

"Well, Joyce," he replies, "You're right about sales being down a bit, but our competition is a lot tougher than it used to be. And costs are up a little because our labor costs are higher."

"That is just an excuse for incompetent management," Joyce grimly replies. "Sales are down a lot more than a 'bit' and your costs have risen more than 11% during the past two years!"

"Look, Joyce, you really need to look at what we are facing here. Most of our telemarketers are just college kids. We hire them, they work for a year or two, and when they graduate, they quit. You know that high turnover is normal for our type of business."

"Yes, George," she says, "you've always had high turnover but your operating costs used to be much lower . . .."

"But," he interrupts, "we used to be the only major employer within 20 miles of Pamplin City. Now there are three other organizations that compete with us in the same labor market."

"So what's your excuse for the decrease in sales?" she replies.

"It's the competition, Joyce. Look, walk out with me to the sales area and see for yourself what they face every day."

"OK, George. Let's take a look at how your people are doing."

As they walk back to the telemarketing area, he fervently hopes that his people will be at their best. For the most part, they are great employees. But because this was the first job for most of them, they don't all have good work habits. If they have had to stay up studying for a tough exam, they might be a little late coming in the next morning. *Let them all be there*, he thinks.

Oh, no! There are three empty stations. Maybe she won't notice. And where is Betty, the supervisor?

"Joyce, let me introduce you to one of our more experienced telemarketers, Dan Williams. Dan, this is Joyce Havinstock, our senior VP of marketing from New York."

"Nice to meet you, Dan."

"Likewise, Ms. Havinstock."

"Well Dan, how do you like working for NTC?" she asks.

"It's great," he replies. "They really treat you well. When I have too much class work—you know, a tough report that's due—they give me extra time off to take care of it. And when it's exam time, nobody fusses if we come in late after studying all night. This is a nice place to work. It's like working for my own family."

"I see," says Joyce. "And how do you like the work you do?"

"Well, uh . . .," he stammers, "I guess it is OK."

"What do you mean, OK?" she asks.

"It's just that," Dan replies, "who gets excited about making phone calls all day to people who feel like you are intruding on their time? It makes it hard to keep up your enthusiasm day after day."

"I see," says Joyce.

"Say, Dan, where is Betty?" asks George.

"I don't know, boss," he replies. "I think she went to call Randy at home to find out when he is coming in. She should be back in a few minutes."

"OK," George says, "tell her I stopped by."

"You bet, boss. Nice to have met you, Ms. Havinstock."

As they walk away from the section, Joyce says, "I saw several stations empty. Where is everybody?"

"I don't know," George says. "There's Betty. She'll know."

"Betty, I'd like you to meet Joyce Havinstock. She is our senior V.P. of marketing. Joyce, this is Betty Thurston, the supervisor of the telemarketing department."

"Hi Betty."

"Pleased to meet you, Ms. Havinstock."

"Betty," George says, "we noticed a few people missing. What seems to be the problem?"

"Oh, no problem, boss. I think there was a fraternity party over at the college last night and some of our people were probably up pretty late. They'll be along."

"Good, good," George says.

"Tell me," says Joyce, "Don't you have set schedules for your people?"

"Not exactly," replies Betty. "Oh we do have a schedule, but we let the telemarketers keep their own hours because of their studies. We had a strict schedule at one time, but it was too hard to keep good students, especially in their junior and senior years."

"Oh, excuse me, Mr. Dishberger, but could I see you when you are free?" asks Paul Otts.

"Paul, this is Joyce Havinstock, NTC's vice president of marketing. Joyce, this is Paul Otts. He takes care of our computers for us."

"Hi, Ms. Havinstock, it's nice to meet you."

"It's nice to see you, too," Joyce replies.

"It was nice to meet you also," Betty says, as she turns to leave. "But I need to get back to the section. See you later, boss."

"Bye, Betty," replies George.

"Now, what seems to be the problem, Paul?"

"Mr. Dishberger, there is a serious problem with the computer network, and I don't know what's wrong with it. Frankly, I think there is something wrong with the basic system. Could you call in a technical representative from the Computer Company and see if they can find out what's wrong? We need to fix it as soon as possible because section B's out of business. They are having to write up all of their calls longhand."

"Sure, Paul. Leave a note on my desk and I'll get somebody out here right away."

"Thanks, Mr. Dishberger. Let me know what you find out. Nice to meet you, Ms. Havinstock."

"Yes," replies Joyce.

As Paul leaves, she turns to George and asks, "Why do you have a computer technician who obviously doesn't know his job?"

"Well, Joyce, he is the son of our old shipping and receiving manager who died last year. So, when Paul needed a job, we felt it was important to find him a place. Actually, it turned out pretty good. He's got a lot to learn, but he is coming along fine."

"Well," replies Joyce, "I'm beginning to see why your profits are down and your costs are up. You keep people who can't do their jobs out of respect for the deceased. You let a bunch of college kids run amok and do whatever they want, when they want. You're not running a business, you're running a resort! You need to fire your computer technician, and get somebody who knows what they are doing. You need to set up standards and controls to make sure your people come to work on time. And you need a new management team that can keep a close eye on your people. But most important, you need to get tough. And you need to do it all yesterday!"

"Wait a minute," says George. "How long do you think it will take for all my people to leave and join the competition? You just can't treat people like they did 100 years ago!"

"No, you wait a minute," replies Joyce. "These people don't work because they like doing what they are doing. They work so they can afford to party at their fraternities. Do you actually think that people work because they're in love with their jobs?"

George hesitates a minute, and says, "No, I guess not."

After reading the preceding story, how would you classify the leadership style of Joyce Havinstock:

☒ Theory "X"?
☐ Theory "Y"?

What did Joyce say or do that made you classify her as you did?

She believed they need controls set up and watched all the time.

How would you classify the leadership style of George Dishberger:

☐ Theory "X"?
☑ Theory "Y"?

What did George say or do that made you classify him as you did?

Because George was not controlling he trusted his people.

END OF PART ONE

Now, turn the page and read the discussion about this case.

Did you find it easy to classify Joyce as an archetypal Theory X manager? Was it more difficult to classify George? If you reluctantly wrote that George was a Theory Y manager, you are not alone. Others who have read this case also rated him a Theory Y manager.

But stop and remember that George and his employees actually made the following statements:

1. One of George's employees said, "This is a nice place to work. It's like working for my own family."

2. George agreed to call in an outside computer expert rather than encourage the employee to make the call. In other words, George reinforced the employee's dependency on him and didn't use this situation as an opportunity to empower his employee.

3. But the strongest indictment of all occurred when Joyce asked, "Do you actually think that people work because they're in love with their jobs?" Do you remember how George answered that question? He said, *"No, I guess not."* What do you think that George's answer would have been if he had in fact been a Theory Y manager? He would have said, "YES!"

As you have probably guessed, George exhibits just another form of Theory X leadership. In his own way, he is just as paternalistic as Joyce.

At this point, you can see that McGregor's work was not as simplistic as you might have imagined. In fact, it is even more complex. Read the next page (Part 2 of the case) and again answer the questions at the end.

The Case of the Disappearing Profits

Part 2

Let's pretend that it is one week before the Monday that Joyce Havinstock is scheduled to visit George Dishberger. As George drives to work, a black cloud forms above his car. Suddenly, a bolt of lightning flashes down and strikes his car, instantly changing George to a *true* theory "Y" manager. At that moment, he has new insight into his job and a whole new way of looking at his people.

When he arrives at work, his receptionist hands him a phone message from Joyce Havinstock. She is planning to visit next week and wants to meet with him to discuss sales, costs, and profits.

George walks into his office, sighs, and pulls out a legal pad, and begins to make some notes on what must be done before Joyce arrives. He knows his job is on the line.

END OF PART 2

If you were George Dishberger, what would you do to prepare for Joyce's imminent visit? Remember that poor George has only five working days to get ready for Joyce!

Tell employees Joyce is coming

Address attendance problems

Let the computer person get what he needs -

Now, read the following list of actions and see if any of them match yours:

1. Set production targets for the employees.
2. Establish and publish attendance requirements.
3. Review selection procedures to ensure that only people who want to work are hired.
4. Tell the computer person to take a course in computer maintenance.
5. Call a meeting to inform the employees of all the changes.
6. Tell the employees that Joyce is coming and to look sharp when she is around.

But if you examine this list, would you say that the style of leadership is participative, Theory Y, or more directive, Theory X? In other words, which way does the communication flow in each of the above examples, up the organization or down from the boss?

Right—down. Most of George's listed actions flow from him down to his people. If George had really been changed to a Theory Y leader, he might have listed the following kinds of actions:

1. Ask his supervisors and managers to meet with their employees and set production targets.
2. Meet with the key employees and determine the problems Joyce might see, what the causes of those problems are, and obtain the group's input on possible solutions.
3. Ask the supervisor of the telemarketing department to meet with her employees and determine ways to make their jobs more challenging.
4. Meet with the supervisor of the telemarketing department and several of her key employees to analyze ways of reducing the attendance problem.
5. Ask the computer person what he needs to do the job.

It is easy to nod wisely when we talk about McGregor's theories. But as we have seen, when the stakes are high and the pressure is on, many people begin to operate as Theory X leaders because 1) participation takes time and 2) it is difficult to delegate in crisis.

But our attitudes and beliefs about how our employees feel about work is only part of the motivational puzzle. Another piece of the puzzle involves our employees' needs and how they are motivated to fulfill those needs.

Employee Needs

Abraham Maslow studied highly motivated people to determine why they are successful. He discovered that individuals have a series of needs, and that they can be arranged in a hierarchy of ascending order. These are physiological needs, safety needs, the need to belong and/or be loved, esteem needs, and self-actualization needs.

Let's look at these needs in more detail.

Physiological needs are the most basic. They include the needs for food, water, sleep, warmth, and sex. Maslow suggested that employees are motivated to meet these primary needs before they are motivated by the needs at the next level. For example, if you are walking across a desert and haven't had water in two days, you are going to be most strongly motivated to satisfy your thirst. Until you obtain water you are not going to be interested in other needs. On the job, physiological needs can be satisfied by paying employees fair salaries that enable them to pay their water bills, purchase food, and keep their houses warm.

Safety needs include both the need to be free from imminent danger and the need for security. On the job, safety needs include a work environment that is not hazardous, safe equipment, and freedom from worry about losing one's job. If you are genuinely worried about losing your job, you are not likely going to be motivated by higher-level needs. Conversely, if you are dying from a lack of water (a physiological need), you are probably not going to be very concerned about losing your job.

Belonging and/or love needs include the need to feel a part of a group, to receive affection from others, and to be in a loving relationship. For example, do you remember what it was like when you first came to work for your organization? Remember the feelings of uneasiness when you arrived? No one knew you, and you didn't feel included as a part of the work group. The lack of belonging produces strong needs that most people are motivated to fulfill. Maslow believes that all individuals will try to satisfy the need to belong—but only when their physiological needs and safety needs have already been satisfied.

Esteem needs are at the top of Maslow's hierarchy. He states that all people have a need for the esteem of others, as well as a need for self-esteem. On the job, this need is usually met by different forms of recognition. Examples are giving an employee a sincere compliment for a task well done, awarding him or her the "Employee of the Month" parking place, asking an employee's advice, or assigning him or her to a special task group.

Esteem given by others, especially when received in the employee's formative years, usually results in self-esteem. If an employee did not receive positive feedback as a child, then he or she may become either a person who is never able to get enough compliments, or one who seems uncomfortable receiving compliments. In either case, it is necessary for a leader to attack such a deficiency with sincere positive feedback.

Self-actualization is seen by Maslow as the highest or "peak" experience. This level results from having all of our other needs met while we are engaged in a satisfying job.

As an example, at the turn of the century there were a number of companies that still manufactured old-fashioned pump organs. But as pianos became more and more popular, pump organs in the "parlor" went out of style. Today you would be hard-pressed to buy a new pump organ.

But there was a man in Virginia's Shenandoah Valley who made pump organs—one at a time. He cut his own walnut, and spent hours sanding, rubbing, and finishing each by hand. This man was happy doing what he did. In other words, he was "self-actualized" because his work was personally interesting, rewarding, challenging and important to him.

When our employees come to work because they take joy in what they do, they can also become self-actualized. Part of our job as leaders is to make sure, as much as possible, that our employees' other need levels are being met so they can operate at this peak level of being.

One last point: Employees don't arrive one day at their highest level of functioning and simply remain there forever. Suppose you are in the middle of an exciting, challenging and joyful task. The phone rings, and it's your boss. She is not happy. She wants to see you in her office—now! Suddenly, you no longer feel self-actualized. You are now concerned about your safety needs.

The Employee's Job

Herzberg interviewed many employees. First, he asked them to think of the times that they were happy on the job and to describe the events that made them feel happy. Next, he asked them to think of times when they had been unhappy on the job and again, to describe the events that produced those feelings.

From these interviews Herzberg discovered something remarkable: the things that people did on the job that made them happy were not necessarily the same things that made them unhappy! Herzberg learned that employees listed five factors as those that caused the most happiness and satisfaction on the job. He called them "Satisfiers."

Satisfiers were:

1. Achievement
2. Recognition
3. Work itself
4. Responsibility
5. Advancement

But the factors that caused the most unhappiness on the job were, except in the area of "Recognition," different. Herzberg called these "Dissatisfiers." They were:

1. Poor organizational policy and administration
2. Technically incompetent supervisors
3. Lack of recognition
4. Salary perceived as being unfair
5. Poor interpersonal relations with supervisors

Thus, Herzberg discovered that having good organizational policy, technically competent supervisors, and a fair salary didn't of themselves make people happy. Having these items satisfied just kept them from being unhappy. He believed that it is necessary to improve the way that the employee is treated, eliminating dissatisfiers, so using the satisfiers can motivate the employee.

Note that the items that employees said made them happy were those that had to do with the job—i.e., achievement in the job, recognition for a job well done, the job itself, more responsibility, and advancement to a higher level. But the items that made people unhappy had to do with how they were treated. Only "Recognition" appeared in the top five of both lists as a factor causing happiness, or, in its absence, unhappiness. That is why, as we will see later, employee recognition is a very powerful motivational tool.

Application

These early theories of motivation can give us important clues as to how to motivate our employees and ourselves. In the following section you will see how to apply motivational theory to the question of what you as a leader can do to increase employee motivation, with reference to the employees' jobs, the organization, and your actions toward your employees.

The Employee's Job

We can have a significant positive impact on the morale of our employees by matching their jobs to them as much as possible. An effective leader modifies jobs to fit people, not people to fit jobs. Small changes in a job can result in large changes in motivation! We can look for ways to make our employees' jobs more interesting, create challenging and responsible jobs for them, reduce the stress level as much as possible, protect their status, organize the work so one task is completed before another is started, and make sure that their jobs provide visible feedback of results.

1. Create interesting jobs for our employees. Granted, there are restrictions as to what we can do in restructuring an employee's job. But if we believe that there is nothing we can do to make a job more interesting for an employee, then that is exactly what will happen to his or her motivation—nothing. So we need to take the time to talk with our employees to learn the kinds of things they like, or don't like, to do. We may find that it is quite possible to enhance an employee's job and make it more interesting.

Sometimes we can reverse specialization by combining tasks previously done by several people into one job. We can also consider cross-training people within our section or department to jobs that, because of their newness, are more interesting. A key question to ask is, "What can this employee do uncommonly well?" Chances are that what an employee does well is also something that he or she enjoys doing. If we can modify a job so that the employee can better utilize his or her strengths, we can probably produce a motivated employee.

2. Create challenging jobs for our employees. It is possible to have an interesting job that is not especially challenging. A job tends to be interesting because it is something that the employee likes to do. A job is challenging when it allows the employee to work to his or her full potential. The best job for an employee is both interesting and challenging. To create a challenging job, we can assign tasks that provide opportunities for growth and development.

3. Create responsible jobs. We need to do everything we can to make the job of each employee in our section or department appear special in the eyes of all employees. Never refer to an employee's job as being "simple," or "a job that anyone can do," or a "no-brainer job"! To the employee, the job may not be simple at all.

We think through the reasons why each employee's job is important to the organization. Then we make sure the employee understands those reasons and, thus, the real importance of his or her job.

4. Reduce the level of stress in our employees' jobs. Impossible deadlines, excessive workloads, and constant interruptions all create unhealthy stress for our employees. If we are part of the stress problem, then it is up to us to become part of the solution.

We can make sure that deadlines are realistic. If the workload is excessive, we can document the need for additional people, or say "No!" to unrealistic demands that ask our employees to do more than is possible. We can help our people to manage interruptions by having them keep a log of when and how they are interrupted. Then we can examine this log to determine if there are patterns that can be changed to help the employee reduce unnecessary interruptions.

In the long run, continuous stress is extremely unhealthy for our employees. It is up to us to monitor them to make sure that their job requirements are reasonable.

5. Protect our employee's status. Reprimanding an employee in private for something he or she did is bad enough. Chewing out an employee in public is even worse—for it affects his or her status. If an employee does something we think is especially bad, it is sometimes difficult not to reprimand him or her on the spot. But unless there is a safety problem, it is usually better to wait until we can talk with the employee in private. When we do, we should take the time to find out why the employee behaved as he or she did before issuing a reprimand. We may discover that, from the employee's point of view, there was a legitimate reason for doing what was done. Leaders who don't take time to actively listen seriously undermine an employee's morale.

Another way to diminish an employee's status is to give him or her a task to do, and then step in and do it ourselves. If we take over a previously delegated task, we are demonstrating to his or her fellow workers that we lack confidence in this employee.

6. Organize the employee's work so that he or she can complete one task before moving on to another. One of the things that gives an employee good feelings on the job is to complete a task before moving on to another. If the work is set up so that this rarely happens, a great opportunity for motivation is lost. As much as possible we should try to arrange the workflow so that our employees can complete each task before moving on to the next one.

7. Provide visible feedback on the results of task completion. We should try to structure the workflow so that our employees can see the results of their completed tasks. If an employee does not receive visible and immediate feedback on his or her efforts, it is not only detrimental to the employee's morale, but it also prevents the employee from correcting his or her behavior.

The Organization

The organization and its policies and procedures have a great impact on our employees' motivation. Following are some suggestions that are often helpful in reducing the impact of organizational problems that hinder morale.

1. Make the value of organizational benefits clear. Although there is not much that we can do about our organization's benefits, the way that they are presented has a great deal to do with how they are viewed by our employees. Do you know how much employee benefits cost your organization? Do your employees understand what their benefits are worth? Most employees don't really know how much it costs today to fund their retirement and pay for their vacation time, holidays, sick time and medical insurance.

In most cases it is fairly easy for us to find out what employee benefits cost. We can talk to our personnel people, add up the figures, and make sure that our employees know exactly what their benefit costs are per year. It is usually true that employees won't fully value what they don't know the cost of.

2. Enhance opportunities for salary increases for deserving employees. We may not have complete control over our employees' salaries, but there are ways to compensate. We can carefully evaluate our people and develop them in areas where improvement may be needed. Then as much as possible, we make sure that they are paid fairly for their developed talents. And even where there is not much chance to obtain additional money for a specific employee, the fact that we tried will enhance this employee's feelings of worth.

One of the best ways to ensure that our employees are paid fairly is to document their accomplishments. We can keep an anecdotal file for each employee as a place to record key accomplishments during the year. Then, at the end of the year, we will have the information necessary to conduct a fair analysis of the employee's performance, and we will be able to suggest an appropriate salary increase.

The anecdotal file will also help us to explain to our employees why they did or did not receive raises, to justify the amount of salary increase, and to suggest areas for needed improvement. Remember that it isn't so much the amount of the employee's pay increase that is important as it is the employee's perception of the fairness with which he or she has been treated. It is far easier for the employee to accept less than what is expected if there are clear reasons why it is less, and if the employee is not taken by surprise.

3. Encourage technological growth in the employees' jobs. In recent years there has been tremendous growth in job technology. Innovation is rampant with new, faster computers, computer networking, robotics, electronic networking systems tied to computers, miniaturization, telecommuting, and e-commerce. These are just some of the changes that are having a major impact on our employees' jobs. Not only are the tools they use to do their jobs changing, but their jobs are changing, too.

One of our key tasks as a leader is to ensure that our employees are involved in lifelong learning. This means that we need to be lifelong trainers! Not that we will always have to do the training, but we will need to manage the employees' training.

For example, we can make sure that our employees receive journals that publish articles relevant to their jobs. We can send people off site for training when appropriate, bring in technical representatives and set up mini-training sessions where needed, or get help from our training department to obtain needed resources. Whatever it takes, we can try to keep our employees up-to-date on the changes that they will encounter in their jobs.

4. Help our employees make a difference in the organization. The basic question that must be answered here, and then communicated to our employees is, "How does each person's contribution affect the organization's success?" Do our people clearly know how their jobs help make the organization prosperous? It makes no difference if the end result is a product or a service. Our employees must feel that what they do or don't do makes a real difference. Our job as a leader is to determine the relationship between our employees' jobs and the organization's final output—and then to share this information with each employee.

5. Ensure that coworkers are friendly and supportive. We can work to establish a friendly and supportive work climate. For example, with new employees, we can first determine their outside interests or hobbies. Then when we introduce them to their coworkers, we can establish "interest" links between the new employees and their fellow employees. We can set up a "buddy" system by assigning each new employee to a senior employee. We can also ask our people to play a part in the selection of new employees who will be a part of their work team.

With existing employee groups, we develop their team spirit by working with them to create overall team goals. When individuals within a team work together to produce their group's goals, they become much more motivated to succeed. We can also train our employees in interpersonal communication skills. Of course it is nice when we can get the training department to conduct a half-day communications program for us. But if we can't, then we do it ourselves! We can select any good book on interpersonal communications skills that has information on asking questions, paraphrasing, summarizing, and listening skills. After studying these techniques, we can look for opportunities to teach them to our employees, either individually or in small groups.

Last, for truly effective work teams, make sure that they are taught problem-solving and decision-making skills. Problem-solving skills like situational and causal analysis, and decision-making skills such as determining alternatives, force-field analysis, the herringbone technique, and potential problem avoidance are all tools that can help our teams work together more cooperatively and effectively.

We need to remember that long-term happiness and high morale are as much the result of what our employees experience with each other as how we treat them. We can't just say, "Be happy!" Instead, we must create a climate where they can support and help one another. And we must teach them the skills to do so.

6. Arrange acceptable working hours. Today's work force is vastly different from what it was in the past. Single-parent families, parents who work outside the home, and different values all add up to the need for more flexible work hours. We may not be able to change the working hours of our employees or allow them to work out of their homes using computers and modems because of our organization's policies. But if we can, it may make our job easier—and also more difficult. It is easier because it can reduce the amount of our time spent in direct supervision, lessen overcrowding in our section or department, and provide us with employees we may not have been able to hire before.

But it is harder because it will be very difficult for us to observe both good performance and problem areas. In addition, employees who work out of their homes need solid work habits and self-discipline to maintain productivity. Employees also have social needs, and when they work alone these unmet needs may result in lower morale.

7. Provide good physical working conditions. Inadequate temperature control, excessive noise level, unpleasant surroundings, and an unsafe environment are just a few of the things that can create poor morale in our section or department. Even though working conditions are really an "organizational" factor, we can often effect improvements that may be needed. With strong legal penalties for unsafe working conditions and much organizational experience in creating pleasant environments for employees, it is often fairly easy to obtain funding for better working conditions. But it is still up to us to make this happen! We are the ones who will need to write up problems for upper management to consider. And we are the ones who will need to follow up to make sure that things get done. We need to remember that improving the area where people work will not make them happy, it will only keep them from being unhappy.

8. Help employees obtain deserved promotions. It doesn't take long for the word to get around that a leader is concerned about the future promotional opportunities of his or her employees. It also doesn't take long for them to learn that the leader would rather not have them promoted because he or she might lose them to another section or have to train their replacements.

So, we can spend time meeting one-on-one with each of our employees and determine their job goals. If promotion is a realistic goal for a particular employee, then our job is to do everything possible to help him or her to achieve that promotion.

There are many things we can do in the present to help prepare employees for the future. We can assign them to special tasks such as leading one of our meetings, training a new employee, or being the team leader on a special project. If organizational exposure is important in order to obtain a promotion, we can "volunteer" an employee to serve on a special organizational task force or committee. We can also assign special jobs to the employee that require him or her to interact with people in other departments in the organization.

Organizational restrictions on promotions may keep us from promoting an employee even if he or she deserves a promotion. But if we have demonstrated a genuine concern for the employee's future by doing what we can do, we will find that the employee is much more accepting of the realities of the organization's restrictions.

The Leader's Direct Actions

Our direct actions toward our employees have a tremendous effect on their motivation, often more than the job or organizational modifications described above.

1. Share expectations. Employees will tend to live up to our expectations. If we expect a lot, we will usually get a lot. On the other hand, if we don't expect much from an employee, that's what we will probably get! If we feel that our employees are not very creative, we're not likely to ask for their suggestions or ideas. But if we expect them to have ideas about their jobs, we are more likely to get good ideas—simply because we ask for them. Leaders who ask for better ideas develop employees who think of better ideas.

2. Be fair. Employees expect to be treated fairly. And what's fair in their view is defined by them, not us. The problem of fairness is complicated by the tension between the need to treat all employees the same, while recognizing that all employees are different. Nonetheless, there are important things we can do to increase the chances that we will be perceived as fair. Look at two examples:

    a) Joe works for you. He is one of the nicest people you know. He has been with the organization about two years, and he has a very positive attitude about his job, the organization, and you. You find that it is easy to give him much of your time and attention, because he is so nice to be around.

    b) Betty works for you. She has worked for your organization for 35 years, and she is nearing retirement. You find it is similarly easy to give her special time and attention, since she has been a loyal and dedicated employee for so many years.

In examining these two examples, you may feel that your actions in both cases are fair. Your other employees may feel that your conduct in the first case is unfair, while they accept your preferential treatment of the 35-year veteran.

Some basic principles underlie the preceding examples:

    a) A leader simply cannot treat everybody the same. People are different. They have different needs. We need to give to each what we perceive he or she needs at the time, without playing favorites! This means, "Give to each what he or she needs," not "Give to each what we need." Playing favorites to meet our needs is, in fact, discrimination.

We communicate the rationale to our group when we are giving particular individuals what may appear to be preferential treatment. We can't get trapped by the employee's question, "Well, you did it for Mary. Why can't you do it for me?" Mary, in all likelihood, has different needs, and different needs require different treatment.

b) When resources are limited, we use the laws of probability to determine who gets a desired resource. For example, we flip a coin, draw straws, or pull slips of paper out of a box to find out who will receive a desired assignment, who has to work overtime, or who has to operate the phones on Christmas or Hanukkah.

c) Rules and policies are created to help make jobs easier. But they may have to be temporarily altered in order to be truly fair to particular employees in specific circumstances.

3. Involve employees in goal setting. Effective leaders usually set goals *with* their employees, rather than *for* them. If we know that our employees like what they do for a living, then we will more likely feel comfortable allowing them to determine some of their own goals. But, if we believe that our employees don't like to work, then we will be more apt to set goals for them.

This doesn't mean that it isn't perfectly appropriate for us to set goals for an employee occasionally. If, for example, our employee is new to his or her job and doesn't have enough experience to create his or her own goals, then we will probably need to write them. Or we may choose to write goals for a problem employee who has demonstrated an unwillingness or inability to write his or her own. In fact, we may need to give our employees goals that are required by the organization. But the best underlying philosophy is that employees can be trusted to work toward their full potential if given a chance. There is considerable payoff when we allow our employees to develop their own goals. First, we will find that they are more committed to fulfilling their own goals than those given to them. And second, motivated employees will often write better and more challenging goals than their leader.

4. Keep employees informed. Some leaders believe that since information is power, giving information to their employees is giving away power. But this is not true. In fact, the benefits to us of sharing as much information as possible with our employees are enormous.

Consider these facts: 1) employees who know what is going on make better decisions; 2) they are more accepting of present and future actions that management may be required to make; 3) they are more prepared for future changes; and, 4) most importantly, they feel more a part of the organization. For these reasons, let your people know what is going on in their organization.

5. Listen to employees. It isn't enough just to keep our employees informed. We also need to listen to them. And when we listen, we listen without interrupting. Unfortunately, this basic rule of communication and courtesy is often violated. In conversation, we may be so interested in what we want to tell the employee that we don't also listen to what he or she is saying.

By listening actively, we not only communicate to the employee the fact that we care about him or her, we also obtain new information. We may discover what works or doesn't work—and why. We can locate problems and solicit suggestions for solving them. Helpful information can then be spread to other levels of management that need it.

If we don't learn the power of listening, we will not get needed information. Remember, it is the listener who controls the conversation, not the speaker.

6. Consult employees about decisions that affect them. This powerful way of leading not only improves the quality of decisions, but also increases our employees' acceptance of those decisions. The quality of our decisions are likely to be enhanced for several reasons: our employees may well see additional decision alternatives beyond the one that we proposed; they will often identify additional factors that need to be considered while evaluating a decision; and they can often identify unanticipated risks in choosing a particular action. Employees naturally like to feel that they are a part of decisions that affect them. Asking for their input before making a decision will usually increase their acceptance of it when it is made.

7. Delegate appropriately to employees. Delegating work to our employees has many advantages. It will enrich our employees' jobs, develop better employees, give us more time for tasks that only we can do, and, most importantly, increase the morale of our employees.

Considering these clear advantages, you might wonder why most of us are not already excellent delegators. The main reason seems to be that we don't delegate because we don't want to! Delegation may heighten our fear of losing control, of giving up parts of our job that we like doing, of spending additional time training employees to do delegated tasks, or of burdening our employees with additional work.

We can overcome our fear when we realize that delegating a specific task doesn't mean that we have lost control of that job. Although we won't be physically doing a job that we delegated, we will still be able to provide quality follow-up with our employee to ensure that the job is properly completed.

It is true that in delegating we may be giving up parts of our job that we enjoy doing. But the payoff in terms of employee morale makes it well worth it. In addition, we will find that we have extra time to spend on other quality tasks that will provide even more payoffs than the one that was delegated.

Delegation will require much of our time at first. Odds are that we will soon receive a return on the time we invest that far exceeds the amount of time invested.

If we are concerned about delegated tasks becoming a burden to our employees, note the word "appropriately" used in the heading of this section. Delegating appropriately means being concerned not only about our needs, but also about our employees' needs. Placing excessive work on an employee, or simply giving more routine work to him or her, is not delegation.

To delegate, we need to evaluate our job, first by listing the major tasks in it. Then, we determine our authority level in each of the tasks.

> "A" = We have complete authority to do the task
> "B" = We can do the task but we must then report
> what we did
> "C" = We need to obtain permission from our boss
> before doing the task

When we have listed each task in our job and determined our level of authority for each one, we may be able to delegate a number of our "A" tasks. Some of these "A's" will be opportunities for both our employees and us.

After determining which tasks can be delegated, we need to evaluate our people to see which of them would benefit most by assuming the responsibility for specific tasks on our list. Finally, we can set up mini-training programs for the tasks that we have delegated.

8. Avoid over-supervising employees. Here are some examples of over-supervising:

a) Delegating a task—and then doing it yourself.

b) Training an employee in exactly how to do a task, and then continually monitoring him or her.

c) Giving an employee too much detail about how to do a task.

d) Asking for too many—or unnecessary—reports.

As a leader, we walk a fine line between being available for our employees and over-supervising them. If we delegate a task, we need to let the employee do it! Instead of giving an employee too much detail on how to do a task, we can define the end goals or results, and then ask the employee how he or she plans to complete the task. We avoid asking for unnecessary reports, or too many reports.

9. Conduct career counseling sessions with the employees. A key component of any system for motivating an employee is the career-counseling interview conducted by the leader with his or her employees. In years past, if an employee was willing to work hard, success would come almost automatically because of the many opportunities that existed within most organizations.

Today, this is largely no longer true. The idea that "hard work will ensure success" has become more myth than truth. Unfortunately, our employees expect the same opportunities for advancement that their parents enjoyed. But this is not going to happen in the way, or with the same frequency, that it used to. Therefore, we need to manage differently. And one solution is to conduct career-counseling sessions with our employees.

In providing career counseling, we will need to help the employees explore their strengths, areas of needed improvement, knowledge, skills, likes and dislikes, values, and career goals. A counseling interview should be conducted to discover what the employee wants to do in the future, what needs to be done by the employee to get there, and how well the employee's goals meet the needs of the organization.

10. Provide honest ongoing recognition for tasks well done. As Frederick Herzberg's research demonstrated, recognition is a major motivator. Conversely, lack of recognition is a powerful demotivator. And recognition becomes even more important to an employee when regulations and policy restrict other rewards, like pay.

The Power of Positive Feedback

We all know that recognition is important to most people. Yet, some of us still don't take the time to give our employees a needed pat on the back. Of course we have nice words for our superstar performers. But very few people are superstars! Most employees fall somewhere in the middle of the performance range.

The key to motivating our employees is their natural need for recognition. If they don't receive recognition in their work, they will usually put their energy into seeking it elsewhere—often to the detriment of their jobs.

Fortunately, there are three ways to provide recognition for our employees.

a) An employee's performance is never absolutely consistent. Like everyone, he or she has good and not-so-good days. We need to be alert to those times our employees are performing at an above-average level, and provide rapid recognition for such performance.

b) An employee's job is normally made up of a series of small operations, and the employee is likely to perform certain of these tasks better than others. Here, we offer positive feedback on the operations the employee does well.

c) We can give recognition for strengths that may not be directly related to the job. An employee who is only an average performer may consistently arrive early, may be good at orienting new employees, or at maintaining his or her area in a clean and orderly way. Our job is to reinforce the habit of excellence with positive recognition wherever we see it.

Remember: an employee may be only "average," but there is nearly always something that the employee does well. Genuine recognition given for whatever that employee does well produces greatly improved motivation and self-esteem.

You might ask here, how should I handle the recognition of slight improvement in a problem employee? Suppose you recently counseled an employee who has a job-related problem and, as a result, the employee makes minimal improvement—to a "just acceptable" level. Do you immediately tell this employee how pleased you are with his or her present performance?

Some leaders will answer, "No! Why should I give an employee a pat on the back when his performance is only barely acceptable? Besides, it was only last week that I chewed him out for his sloppy work. It's still too soon to tell if he has really changed."

Two questions are being raised here. One deals with the amount of improvement necessary before feedback is given, and the other, with when the feedback should be given. Let's look at the first point.

Suppose we turn the question around and ask, "Will recognition increase the chances that this employee will keep up improved performance?" The answer to this question is probably yes, simply because sincere recognition is one of the strongest motivators affecting most employees.

To reduce the chances that a marginal employee will lapse into unacceptable performance, an insightful leader recognizes that it is not so much the amount of change that is required before giving an employee positive feedback, but rather the direction of that change. If it's a change for the better, positive feedback will tend to maintain improvement.

The second point raised concerns timing. When should we give positive feedback? If an employee did something poorly, we wouldn't wait several months to tell him or her about it. The same is true with positive feedback. If we want to reinforce an employee's positive behavior, we should give feedback as soon as we see positive change. An effective leader hopes for improvement, expects improvement, and, at the first sign of improvement, quickly reinforces the positive change in the employee's performance.

What if we give immediate positive feedback to a marginal employee who has improved slightly, and he or she gets worse? Now we are really disappointed—and maybe even angry! We gave the employee positive recognition, and the employee let us down. Sometimes this is going to happen, but not usually. So we don't let one or two negative results prevent us from improving our "career average" as a motivating leader. We can continue to provide positive recognition to our low performance employees when they show small improvements. If we do it as soon as we see change, we will see our batting average start to climb.

Providing Positive Recognition

The way that we recognize employees is also very important. For example, general compliments like, "You did a good job" or "I'm proud of your improvement" are not in fact the best motivators. A better way is shown in the following step-by-step method.

1. Describe the positive situation in detail.

Overly general compliments are sometimes perceived as being insincere. We need to be specific by describing in detail the positive behaviors we observed. We don't just say, "You did a good job." Instead, we need to spell out what we mean by "a good job"—and then watch the employee smile.

This approach works because the employee most likely knows he or she did well—and our recognition of the specifics will be perceived as observant, accurate, and genuine. For example: "Your desk looks great! All the extra files are put away, there's nothing out of place, and your whole desk looks organized."

 2. Tell why the positive effort is important.

We can add meaning to a compliment by emphasizing why what was done is important. The opportunity for high-impact recognition is lost if we say only, "You did a good job," not only because we aren't being specific, but also because we haven't said why the positive performance was important.

There are three reasons we can mention as to why a positive effort was significant.

- Why the performance is important to the employee

- Why it is important to the section, department, or organization

- Why it is important to you as the leader

 3. State that we have confidence in his or her ability.

An employee who works for two different leaders will often exhibit two different levels of performance. One reason for this discrepancy has to do with what the leader expects. Leaders with high levels of expectation usually obtain better overall employee performance. When we tell an employee that we have confidence in his or her ability, we are communicating strongly our future expectations. By expressing confidence in an employee's ability following improved performance, we increase the employee's motivation to continue to fulfill our growing expectations.

4. Ask what we can do.

When employees do something better today than in the past, they have made some changes in what they are doing, whether it is a matter of coming to work on time, organizing their work more efficiently, or something else. And when an employee changes, even for the better, there is a likelihood that he or she will encounter some new problems—even that of getting teased by coworkers over his or her improvement!

All kinds of problems can arise with changes, and an alert leader anticipates problems. We need to check out the situation by asking the employee if there is anything we can do to help in supporting his or her progress.

 5. Emphasize our appreciation.

We conclude by expressing clearly and warmly the appreciation we feel. We all respond to others' feelings. If we feel good about what an employee has done, we should say so! We can say, "I really appreciate your efforts!" or "Thanks! I'm very pleased with your progress!" This reinforces what has been expressed and ends the discussion on the desired positive note. After the meeting, we need to be sure to make a note of our conversation with the employee, and place it in the employee's anecdotal file.

On the following pages are some aids to help you apply the concepts of motivation to your job as a leader.

First is a "Leader's Checklist" that will help you provide recognition to your employees.

Next is an "Employee Survey" that you can use with your people. It asks an employee to rate you in the three major areas covered in the preceding pages. After you receive the completed surveys from your people, examine them to determine if a particular employee has important areas of motivational need. Then tally each of the responses to see if there are any group needs. After evaluating the results, refer to the text for ideas on how to take action to improve the morale of your area of responsibility.

Finally, there is a "Motivating Others" worksheet that will allow you to systematically plan the actions you will take.

Motivating Employees
Leader's Checklist

☑ **1. Describe the positive situation in detail.**

- Focus attention on the employee
- Be specific: Who, What, Where, When, How

☑ **2. Tell why the positive effort is important.**

- Why the performance is important to the employee
- Why it is important to the section, department, or organization
- Why it is important to us as the leader

☑ **3. State that we have confidence in his or her ability.**

"It's a good feeling to know that I can count on your efforts in the future."

☑ **4. Ask if there is anything we can do to support his or her efforts.**

"What can I do to help you further?"

☑ **5. Emphasize our appreciation.**

"I just want you to know how much I appreciate your efforts."

EMPLOYEE SURVEY

Your Leader: _____   Your Section or Department: _____

Date: _____

Indicate the **importance** of each of the following to you:

Indicate the degree to which this need is **satisfied** in your job:

Your Job:

	Not Impt.	Some-What Impt.	Impt.	Very Impt.	Not Appl.		Not Sat.	Some-What Sat.	Sat.	Very Sat.	Not Appl.
Is interesting											
Is challenging											
Is a responsible job											
Involves low stress											
Provides status											
Allows you to complete a task before moving on to the next one											
Provides visible results when a task is done											

Your Organization Provides:

	Not Impt.	Some-What Impt.	Impt.	Very Impt.	Not Appl.		Not Sat.	Some-What Sat.	Sat.	Very Sat.	Not Appl.
Benefits (retirement, health, vacations, sick leave, etc.)											
Opportunities for salary increases											
Technological growth											
A chance to make a difference											
A contribution to society											
Friendly & supportive coworkers											
Good working hours											
Good working conditions (safety, temperature, noise, appearance)											
Chance for promotion											
Security											

Your Leader:

	Indicate the **importance** of each of the following to you:					Indicate the degree to which this need is **satisfied** in your job:				
	Not Impt.	Some-What Impt.	Impt.	Very Impt.	Not Appl.	Not Sat.	Some-What Sat.	Sat.	Very Sat.	Not Appl.
Has high expectations of you										
Is fair										
Gives you a chance to have a say in how you do your job										
Keeps you informed about what is going on										
Listens to you										
Consults you about decisions that affect you										
Delegates tasks appropriately to you										
Doesn't supervise you too closely										
Conducts career counseling sessions with you										
Gives you ongoing recognition for tasks that you do										

How would you rate your immediate supervisor's morale (your leader)?   (Place an "X" in the appropriate box.)

Very Low	Low	Somewhat Low	Neither High or Low	Somewhat High	High	Very High	Don't Know

How would you rate your overall morale?

Very Low	Low	Somewhat Low	Neither High or Low	Somewhat High	High	Very High	Don't Know

51

MOTIVATING OTHERS

Directions: List the people who report to you on this page (Column 1) and identify areas in which they have motivational needs (Column 2). Next, in Column 3, identify specific actions that you will take during the next two weeks to enhance each employee's morale. When you have completed your action for a specific employee, insert a completion date in Column 4. Then, in Column 5, make a brief note of the employee's reaction. At the end of the two-week period, discuss the results with your leader. If no one reports to you, you can select 1) peers, your boss (he or she needs motivation also), or 2) spouse, children, close friends, and/or children. Remember, this project is about MOTIVATION, not counseling!

1. Employee's Name (You may use initials)	2. Motivational Need (Per Maslow)	3. Actions to be Taken	4. Date(s) Completed	5. Employee's Reaction(s)

Leadership Skills for Improving Performance

4

Leadership
Establishing Standards
of Performance

. . . before any improvement is undertaken, it is essential that the current standards be stabilized and institutionalized. In the kaizen philosophy, there can be no improvement where there are no standards.

Michael Tushman and Philip Anderson
Managing Strategic Innovation and Change

Sometimes an employee may quite honestly say, "I didn't know I was supposed to do that!" When this happens, someone has let the employee down by not communicating exactly what was expected.

Or an employee may continually run into problems because the leader has failed to communicate what the employee should not do. This results in a worker who begins to "play it safe" by not seeking out additional tasks or responsibilities.

In addition, most employees are constantly faced with questions such as, "What is a good job?" or, "When am I not doing this job well enough?" and, "Am I spending too much time and energy on this task?" A leader must be able to state specific performance standards for each part of an employee's job. This key task is called "communicating standards of performance."

Why Standards?

Performance standards are useful for a number of purposes. They can help to:

Plan and Schedule Work

When standards properly define how much work is to be produced by an employee, it is possible to plan total output by combining the output of several employees. For example, maintenance work can be scheduled based on downtime of standby equipment, which, in turn, may be based on production output over time.

Estimate Budget Needs

Quantity of materials and labor can be estimated by knowing the amount of work to be produced by using data from performance standards. Then budgetary needs can be estimated by applying labor and material costs to quantity.

Handle Disciplinary Problems and Grievances

Information obtained from standards that is compared with actual performance can provide proof that an employee is performing below standard.

Provide Feedback to the Employee on His or Her Performance

The comparison of what's expected—the performance standards—to actual employee performance provides job performance feedback to both the leader and employee. The leader can use the information to provide positive feedback to employees who exceed standards, and the employee can use the information to monitor his or her performance.

Find the Cause of a Performance Problem

Because performance standards address each task, the leader can isolate a problem to one or two tasks. Task isolation will provide a starting point for problem analysis; it helps a leader to avoid vaguely worded observations such as, "You're not doing as well as you should," or "Your production is not satisfactory."

Compare and Evaluate Changes in Methods

Suggestions for improving methods often result in improved quantitative and qualitative output over time. If standards are in effect, we can compare each suggestion to the standard and obtain information on the relative value of that suggestion to the standard.

Determine Staffing Needs

Standards frequently indicate how much one employee can produce in a given time. If increased output or workload is desirable, this is pertinent when considering additional staffing needs.

Conducting Performance Standards Meetings with Employees

Now let's look at a step-by-step approach that will help you and your employees communicate in establishing performance standards. This method involves meeting with each employee at least once each year, at which time together you analyze the employee's job and mutually agree upon appropriate standards of performance. Here's how to use this approach:

 1. Plan and conduct an initial discussion with the employee.

The better prepared the employee is before a performance standards meeting, the easier it will be for him or her to discuss the job. Approximately one week before the standards meeting, we meet briefly with the employee to:

- Explain what performance standards are, and why they need to be established.

- Ask the employee to provide information needed to establish such standards and measure performance.

- Help the employee begin by:
    - selecting a critical job task
    - determining the standards that will measure performance, expressed in quality, quantity, cost, or time
    - analyzing any problems that may prevent optimum performance
    - explaining the employee's authority level to complete this task

- Give the employee a copy of the *Job Standards Worksheet* shown on the last page of this chapter, and ask him or her to complete it before the standards meeting.

The objective in this pre-standard meeting is to make sure both the leader and the employee have the needed information for the next meeting. Ideally, the employee should propose these standards. The employee should know what tasks the job includes and what he or she can do. The last part of this preparatory step is to set a time and place for the actual standards meeting.

☑ **2. Complete our copy of the *Job Standards Worksheet*.**

We also need to complete a copy of the *Job Standards Worksheet* before the standards meeting, describing our perceptions of the employee's job. This will help us to provide more specific input during the meeting and to relate the employee's job standards to our own standards or unit objectives.

☑ **3. Review the job summary.**

We begin the performance standards meeting by discussing and then agreeing upon the general description and content of the job. An agreement upon such a job summary is necessary before we can analyze and specify individual job tasks—the next step.

☑ **4. Ask the employee to describe each job task.**

We need to ask the employee to identify the first job task and its relationship to the total job, how this task might be measured, any problems he or she may have with the task, and his or her perceived authority to do the task. This step is the heart of establishing performance standards. The employee is telling us what he or she should do, how much, and how well.

Here is the employee's opportunity to tell us how he or she perceives the job. So we let the employee do the talking! But as the employee talks, we need to listen carefully to make sure that suggested standards are stated clearly. We eliminate vague or unclear terms. We are especially attentive when the employee identifies quantity or quality and assist him or her in being as specific as possible.

If the employee has problems while completing a task, our job is to help him or her develop solutions. Sometimes employees bring up an internal problem— i.e., one that is under the leader's control. For example, if the employee says, "I'm supposed to consolidate the manpower reports, but I can't figure out how to do it," we are dealing with a lack of knowledge. This is an internal problem that we can do something about. In the other case, the problem may be external: e.g., "The other department sends its reports in late every month. That means I can't make my deadline." Here we are dealing with a problem-solving/decision-making situation. We may have to delay establishing this standard, or temporarily set one lower than we wish.

A leadership maxim states, "Try to get the decision making done by the person who has the most information." The message is: listen carefully to what our employee says about authority level. The employee may be telling us that he or she can and wants to make some decisions without having to get our prior approval. And that may be a good idea! Sure, it's difficult at times to give up control. But remember we are also responsible for training and developing our employees. By letting an employee take on more responsibility, we are encouraging him or her to become more valuable to the organization.

 5. Share our perceptions of the task identified by the employee.

Now is our opportunity to provide input by discussing and resolving any differences in the way we both see the task. Our job is to reduce the employee's tension and to create a good climate for mutual development of standards, joint problem solving, and common agreement throughout the process. Here, we are both are attempting to answer these questions clearly:

- What are the job tasks?

- Which tasks are most important?

- How will each task be measured?

- What problems impede task completion?

- What are possible solutions for these problems?

- Who has what authority in each task?

 6. Reach a consensus.

Consensus greatly increases the chance that the employee will feel that the performance standards are fair and will be motivated to achieve them. It also tells the employee that if he or she meets a standard, then performance on that task is satisfactory.

We need to try and picture ourselves as a troubleshooter, guide, coach, or facilitator. We can't get trapped in an evaluative, judgmental role. That will make the employee feel defensive, frustrated, and deceived. He or she will feel that, in spite of our request for input, we really have our own preset agenda—and it doesn't make any difference what he or she says. A successful leader once stated: "When it gets right down to it, I feel my job is to make it easier for my people to do their jobs."

So, we can help our employee in these ways:

- Identify any job tasks, particularly critical ones, that the employee may have omitted.

- Make sure that performance is measured quantitatively or qualitatively, preferably both.

- Clarify vague terms.

- Ask the employee for his or her thoughts and recommendations on problems that are identified.

- Clarify any confusion about authority levels.

We need to look at and listen to the employee carefully. Notice nonverbal communication—frowning, nervousness, hesitation, or relief and relaxation. Such nonverbal signals can tell us quite clearly whether or not we are really reaching agreement.

 7. Ask the employee to make a composite of both worksheets after the meeting.

Here, we can give the employee a copy of our *Job Standards Worksheet* and ask the employee to make a composite of his or her worksheet and ours after the meeting. This puts the collaborative information into final form, as well as fostering a sense of ownership by the employee.

 8. Thank the employee for his or her efforts.

Since the employee has likely invested significant time, energy, and concern in preparing for this meeting, we should end the meeting by sincerely thanking the employee for his or her efforts. By thanking him or her, we are expressing deserved appreciation, as well as reinforcing productive future behavior.

 9. Follow up by reviewing the composite worksheet with the employee.

We should obtain a copy of the employee's composite worksheet, and briefly review it with the employee. This is an important opportunity for any final clarification and adjustment. And we should both keep copies of the final agreement.

☑ **10. Agree upon a trial period.**

Finally, we agree upon a trial period and set a future meeting date and time for a review of the employee's standards. This allows:

a. A reduction in potential tension if the employee feels irrevocably committed to an untried plan of action that he or she feels unsure about

b. A correction of any problems that may surface between the employee and ourselves, before they become serious

c. A specific meeting date and time to communicate to the employee that standards are important to us, and that we will be following up

On the following pages are 1) a meeting checklist that you can use to assist you in conducting a standards meeting, and 2) a *Job Standards Worksheet* that you can copy and use to set standards with your employees.

Establishing Standards Meeting Checklist

The following suggestions describe what you might say to an employee in a performance standards meeting. They are just that—suggestions.

Prior to the Performance Standards Meeting

 **1. Plan and conduct an initial discussion with the employee.**

- Explain what performance standards are and why they need to be established.

    "A performance standard is simply a statement that describes a job task and how well it is to be performed. I'd like you to propose the standards for your job. We'll discuss and agree on them at the next meeting."

- Explain the *Job Standards Worksheet* by analyzing one key job task, explaining criteria for good performance standards, and discussing authority levels.

    "This form will make it easier for you to write your standards. Notice that I've written one job task as an example. Let's go through this task completely to give you a better idea of how to develop the rest of your standards."

 2. Complete our copy of the *Job Standards Worksheet*.

During the Performance Standards Meeting

 3. Review the job summary.

"Let's go over this paragraph that sums up the job. Do you feel it is accurate? Is there anything you would like to add or change?"

4. Ask the employee to describe each job task.

> *"OK, read your first critical job task."*

- Ask the employee to state how he or she sees the task being measured.

> *"How do you think we ought to measure performance?"*

- Ask the employee to list problems he or she may have with the specific task.

> *"Are there any problems that are causing slowdowns or trouble?"*

- Ask the employee to state perceived authority levels.

> *"Do you think this task is one that requires my prior approval, or one whose completion should be reported to me?"*

5. Share our perceptions of the task identified by the employee.

- How we see the task measured and its relationship to the job

> *"This task might be difficult to measure. What are some of the indications that the job is done the way it ought to be done?"*

- Problems and possible causes that might prevent the task from being completed

> *"A concern that I have is . . .."*
> *"Another possible cause of this problem might be . . .."*

- Possible solutions to any problems

> *"Here is an idea you might consider."*

- Differences in our perception of authority

> *"In this task, I feel that you have complete authority to do the task, but I would like to know how it turns out for you."*

6. Reach a consensus.

> *"If you agree that you can achieve this standard, I'll consider it satisfactory performance."*

 7. Ask the employee to make a composite of both worksheets after the meeting.

> *"Please put what we've agreed to on a single Job Standards Worksheet. When you have completed it, please see that I get a copy for my records."*

 8. Thank the employee for his or her efforts.

> *"Thanks for your efforts. I'm looking forward to seeing the composite."*

After the Performance Standards Meeting

 9. Follow up by reviewing the composite worksheet with the employee.

 10. Agree on a trial period.

> *"OK, we'll use these standards for one month. Do you think that will give us enough time to test them thoroughly? We'll get together, say the 16th at 10:00 AM, to see if any changes are needed. Will that time be convenient for you?"*

Job Expectations Worksheet

Job Summary: _____
_____
_____
_____

Authority Levels

1. **Complete Authority**
2. **Act then Report**
3. **Act after Approval**

List the main tasks of your job.	Which are most important? "A" = Highest Priority "B" = Medium Priority "C" = Lowest Priority	What specific standards are used to measure performance? Quality/Cost/Time/Satisfaction	What problems exist that hamper optimum performance?	Authority Level for each task

5

Leadership
One-on-One
Training Skills

When my supervisor explains something to me, she knows the work so well. I wish she could get it across to me. She rattles it off and I am not sure I have it.

Very little training because the work was heavy. I really wasn't trained—just a quick "do this and here's how."

I got off to a bad start. I came when they were really busy, so I just sat there and read books.

Three employees talking about their
initial training experiences.

We can call it JIT (Job-Instructional-Training), OJT (On-the-Job-Training), or even a form of Behavior Modeling. We can call it whatever we want, one-on-one training is probably the oldest kind of education today. Parents have taught their children in this way for thousands of years, and senior employees long have used it to teach new employees their crafts.

The Beginning of Formalized One-on-One Training

During World War I, there was a critical need for almost half a million new workers. Charles R. Allen, a Massachusetts vocational instructor, was asked to develop a process for training urgently needed shipbuilders. In 1917, Allen developed "four-step, on-the-job training" (OJT), consisting of 1) showing, 2) teaching, 3) doing, and 4) checking. This method is still used today, suggesting that either our training is terribly out-of-date or the method is tried and true.

It's the latter! Time and again, this basic system has effectively trained new employees in all kinds of organizations. The four-step process works because it is just plain common sense.

Six Steps in Effective One-on-One Training

I would like, however, to update Allen's process. Modern behavioral science indicates that there are the following six steps for effective one-on-one training:

☑ 1. **Preparing** for the training

☑ 2. **Asking** questions to determine the trainee's experience

☑ 3. **Telling** the trainee about the task

☑ 4. **Showing** the trainee how the task is done

☑ 5. **Encouraging** the trainee to do the task

☑ 6. **Following up** to ensure that the trainee can do the task

On the following pages, each step is described in some detail.

☑ **1. Preparing for the training.**

One of the basic problems with one-on-one training is that we often do not take the time to prepare properly for the training session. In his article on the "Tyranny of the Urgent," Charles E. Hummel said, "We live in a constant tension between those things that are urgent and those things that are important." The problem is that training preparation is important, but it often doesn't seem "urgent." And because urgent tasks must be done today, important tasks like preparation for good training frequently are postponed until later. But never forget that appropriate preparation ensures that our training is concise and realistic, and it will usually ensure a positive experience for the leader and his or her trainee.

Even though most of us conduct one-on-one training, we aren't necessarily effective trainers. A major problem resulting from lack of preparation, for instance, is that we tend to talk too much! Our tendency is to tell the employee everything we know about the task, rather than just those things the employee needs to know. Wasted time, bored trainees, and frustration for everyone result from all this talking. To be effective trainers, we need to

    A. Analyze the job that will be taught by using task listing

    B. Determine what we want the trainee to be able to do by using task detailing

    C. Develop our training plans and strategies

Analyzing the Job (Task Listing)

By analyzing the job, we separate what the employee must know from what it would be nice for the employee to know. By listing the key tasks for the job, and putting those tasks in some sort of order, we can then make intelligent decisions about what should be taught, what shouldn't be taught, and what can be postponed until later.

For example, if we analyzed our job as a leader, it would probably look something like this:

Task Listing

Job: Leader

A. Task Listing
1. Assigns work
2. Counsels problem employees
3. Makes decisions
4. Writes goals and objectives for section
5. Develops employees
6. Conducts yearly performance appraisals
7. Gives positive feedback to employees
8. Writes exception reports
9. Holds meetings
10. Assists in selecting new employees
11. Records daily time cards
12. Coordinates work with other sections
13. Etc.

If you were a new leader and it was my responsibility to train you, I would prepare for the training by making a list of the major activities for your new job. Chances are that you would already be familiar with some of those activities. For example, if you had worked in my department, you would already have set your goals and objectives under Task 4. Therefore, I wouldn't need to spend time to teach you this task. But Task 5, "Develops employees," is one task you would not have had a chance to learn in your previous job, so I would teach this task.

Determining What We Want the Trainee to Be Able to Do (Task Detailing)

By detailing the key tasks, I can see fairly quickly the specific topics that need to be covered and those that don't. For example, let's imagine that you are an absolute whiz at managing your time. Now, let's really jump off the deep end and pretend that I'm a whiz at scheduling my time. If I don't take the time to think, "I don't have to teach him how to schedule his time because he's already a whiz at it," chances are that I'll bore you silly for two hours telling you how important managing your training time is!

Task detailing can also remind me to cover a key topic in our one-on-one training sessions. It tells me exactly what you and I need to do, because each task I've detailed which you don't already know how to do automatically becomes a training objective for us.

In the example that follows, I have selected Task 5, "Develops employees," from the preceding list of tasks, and then detailed all the sub-tasks you will need to do in developing employees.

Task Detailing

Job: Leader

    A. Task Listing
      5.   Develops employees

    B. Task Detailing
      1.   Determines training needs of individual employees
      2.   Schedules time for training
      3.   Completes task listing on employee's job
      4.   Completes task detailing on listed tasks of the employee's job
      5.   Develops training plans
      6.   Locates or devises training aids
      7.   Trains
      8.   Follows up to determine whether training is successful
      9.   Develops revised training plan to meet any needs that still exist
     10.   Etc.

Next, I will take each of the detailed tasks that you don't already know how to do and plan how the training will be done.

Training Plans and Strategies

In this part of my preparation, I take each topic that we'll cover and develop my training strategies or plan for that topic. In other words, just as I broke down each step of the Task Listing in detail, resulting in the Task Detailing, I'll use each step of the Task Detailing to guide me in creating a training plan for your new job. Planning is something you probably already know a good deal about, so I won't spend time here describing planning processes (I'll try to practice what I preach!) But I will illustrate Step 7, "Trains," from the task detailing of "Develops employees," in order to show what I would do in this step if I were going to train you to be a new leader.

Training Plans and Strategies

Job: Leader

    A. Task Listing
        5. Develops employees

    B. Task Detailing
        7. Trains

    C. Plans (strategies)
        1. Check the library for books on one-on-one training
        2. Write out the best step-by-step training model I can find
        3. Develop a skit to use to demonstrate how a new employee is trained
        4. Reserve the video equipment to use while practicing
        5. Reserve the conference room
        6. Etc.

This type of preparation—task listing, task detailing, and planning—will help to provide a smooth and effective training program. And note that all this essential work has been done with paper and pencil. I haven't even started the training yet!

 2. Asking questions to determine the trainee's experience.

Today, most one-on-one training models include the original "Show, Tell, Do, and Check" steps of the Allen training model—along with additional steps such as preparation and introduction. However, there still seems to be little reference to determine the employee's previous experience, as shown in Step 2 of this model.

Reasons for Asking Questions

In conducting training, I include Step 2—determining the trainee's experience—for the following reasons:

- It demonstrates a caring attitude on the part of the trainer, since he or she expresses interest in the trainee by asking questions and listening.

- It may reduce training time by revealing what the trainee already knows.

- It can reveal previous experience that might interfere with new learning.

  For example, having been in the business world for over forty years, I found it disconcerting when I turned my business over to my children and became a college professor. Having been my own boss for the past twenty-five years, working for someone else was a major adjustment. Because of my past experience, when I saw something that needed to be done my tendency was to just do it. It took some significant effort on my new boss's part to "teach" me that there were good reasons for not just "doing it" without checking with ten people first—including him!

- It may disclose prior experience to which new learning can be related.

How to Ask Questions

The idea is not just a quick "What have you experienced before?" and "OK, that's not the way to do things here!" The leader must have a sincere desire to probe for any possible past experience that can be linked to the new information.

If, for example, I were teaching an adult how to make PowerPoint® transparencies, I might ask first, "What's your experience with overhead transparencies—or 'viewgraphs,' as some people call them?" Either I will obtain new information, or I won't. If I do, then I can use this past experience to help explain new information.

If I don't get useful information, I will probably stop this particular line of questioning. I might ask, "What kinds of programs, if any, have you attended where PowerPoint® or overheads were used?" Or, "What are some of the things you like about overheads?" And, "What were some of the things you don't like about overheads?" Or, "What don't you like about PowerPoint® presentations?"

Whatever information I obtain, I listen actively, nodding my head and saying, "I see" or "Uh-huh" at appropriate points. In addition, I don't interrupt. And I will ask clarification questions such as "Can you be more specific?" "Could you give me an example?" or "How was that done?"

Types of Questions

Generally, the best questions to use are "open questions" which start with "What?" or "How?" In addition, there are questions that are perceived by the employee as requests for more information—although, technically, they are "closed questions" that can be answered with "Yes" or "No." Closed questions such as "Can you be more specific?" or "Could you give me an example?" may serve the same function as open questions.

Other open questions that start with "When?" or "Where?" obtain specific details and thus are less desirable for general probing of the trainee's experience. For example, if I am asking for a trainee's experience with overheads or PowerPoint®, I first inquire, "What experience have you have with overheads (or PowerPoint®)?" rather than, "When did you encounter overheads (or PowerPoint®)?"

The least desirable questions seem to be personal "Why?" questions—as in *"Why* did *you* do it that way?" A "Why" combined with "you" can produce defensive behavior, since it focuses upon personal motives. However, "Why did *they* do it that way?" does not normally challenge the trainee, since it asks for an opinion about a third party.

 3. Telling the trainee about the task.

"Telling" is a step any leader should be able to do well—right? Wrong! Because it's easy to tell our employees everything they might ever want to know about a specific task (after all, we are the experts!), we sometimes tend to talk, talk, and talk. As already discussed, part of this problem is solved by careful preparation in Step 1, when we delete every task the trainee already knows how to perform. We can also help to avoid "talking problems" by carefully asking key questions to determine the trainee's experience (Step 2 above). But Step 2 can also set the stage for the talking problem! It's as if we say, "OK, I listened to you in Step 2. Now it's my turn to talk." Never forget—talking too much can get the leader and the trainee into deep trouble.

So, remember the answers to those questions about past experience we asked in Step 2? We wanted to find out what the trainee already knows. How is that going to help us? In three ways! We can learn what the trainee

- Already knows—and doesn't need to relearn
- Doesn't know—and needs to learn
- Knows—that can be related to the new task, thus helping him or her in learning it

Explaining the Job or Job Task

While explaining the job or job task, we provide an umbrella of knowledge by giving the trainee an overview of *what* is to be done. Then we tell the *who, where,* and *when* of the job—to define the job's environment. Next, we tell *why* the job should be done, providing reasons that make sense. And here, we stay away from the old, "We do it because it's organizational policy." Policies are not written by a deity, but by people *for* people. If we don't know the *why,* we need to find out! Reasons for doing a task supply the trainee with motivation to do it.

Last, we provide specific information that describes *how* the task is to be done. We can use sketches, pictures, and even illustrations with rough drawings as we describe how the task should be done. We can deliberately structure pauses in our explanation to give the trainee an opportunity to interrupt and ask questions. If our trainee chooses not to interrupt, we interrupt ourselves by asking the trainee questions about what we have said. For example, we can get important feedback from our trainee by asking:

"How is this like your old job?"
"What problems do you see in doing this?"
"What questions do you have at this point?"

"Hey, Stupid, Do You Have Any Questions?"

We avoid the time worn, "Well, do you have any questions . . .?" The unspoken word the trainee hears at the end of this question is "dummy"! If I am your employee, then, of course, you as my boss, surely explained the task thoroughly and wisely—and I'm obviously not too bright if I have any questions! So I'll just nod wisely and we'll both get in trouble later. Instead, we ask, "What questions do you have?" The "What" implies that questions are expected! We can also ask questions about what we are going to explain next. But we don't set up the trainee for failure by asking things that he or she has no way of knowing about. Instead, during this "telling" portion of training, we ask questions that most people would be able to answer through common sense application.

For example, if I were teaching you the key steps for effective one-on-one training, I might ask, "OK, now that we have discussed how to tell the employee what to do, what do you think is the next step?" Even if you responded by saying, "Let the employee do it," I would not say, "Wrong! Wrong!" Rather, I would reply, "Great! Letting the employee do it is definitely another step in the one-on-one training process. But it's not the next step. If we tell the employee what to do, and plan to let him or her do it later, what should we do before we let the trainee do it?" Here the trainee will almost always say, "Show how," or "Demonstrate it."

It's important that we are not trapped into doing all the talking, even during the "telling" portion of the training. We need to strike a careful balance between telling and listening. And in order to listen, we will encourage the trainee to ask questions, to make comments, and to respond to our questions.

Everything New Is Difficult

One important point: we don't make comments such as, "This is really simple. You'll catch on in no time." When we say this, the message the trainee hears is, "If it's all that simple, I can't fail. So if I fail, I'm not very smart!" Even with the best of motives—trying to relax the trainee—we accomplish exactly the opposite, and the trainee's tension and anxiety increase. Remember, few things that are new are "simple." Usually, they're difficult at first!

 4. Showing the trainee how the task is done.

First, note that "showing" in Step 4 is not the same as showing a drawing or picture to illustrate what has been described in Step 3. In the Step 4, we model the job to be done. And, as we demonstrate the task, we give verbal clues to the trainee. We "talk our thoughts," so that the trainee both hears and sees how it is to be done, and where, when, and why it is done.

One idea to consider is to have the trainee talk us through the task. As the trainee tells us what to do, step-by-step, we demonstrate how the task is done. This technique gets the trainee involved in the learning process and also tells us exactly what the trainee has—or hasn't—learned. Showing the employee how the task is done through modeling may feel a little awkward in the beginning. But making a mistake or two ourselves simply makes us more human. A little humor here goes a long way, and we'll usually find the employee to be more relaxed when it's time for him or her to practice.

☑ **5. Encouraging the trainee to do the task.**

We can read books about riding a unicycle, watch someone ride one—and even write an article on "The Joys of Unicycle Riding." But we can't learn to ride a unicycle until we actually ride that thing! And our employees can't learn how to do a task by reading about it, and they can't learn skills by watching us or anybody else. They have to do the task themselves—and receive feedback on their performance. That's our job as a trainer. We watch them perform in a practice session, and then provide helpful, constructive feedback.

Feedback Should Be Tactful

In some cases, this will be the employee's first job. He or she may be nervous and unsure. It's up to us not only to look for lack of comprehension, but also for opportunities to give positive feedback on what he or she has done correctly! When lack of understanding is evident, we should avoid using phrases such as

"You did that wrong."

"You made an error."

"There were too many mistakes in your work."

"You'll just have to try harder in the future."

"You failed!"

Instead, we direct our remarks to what was done improperly, and how it can be corrected. We try hard to stay away from the personal attack (the "You" in the above statements). If needed, we can simply repeat Step 4, covering the areas where the trainee had difficulty.

Ask Questions

One of the best ways to help trainees develop task skills is to have them tell us what they are going to do before they do it. This allows us the opportunity to correct them before they make a mistake, and helps them perform the task properly the first time. If they still start to do something incorrectly, we ask them to stop, and then ask questions to help them think through the correct procedure. For example, suppose we observe a troubled trainee taping a transparency, and stretching the transparent tape too tightly. "Too tight!" we tautly tell the trainee.

But a better (less tongue-twisting) approach would be to stop the trainee and ask, "What could happen to this flimsy transparency's frame if the tape is stretched too tightly?" "Oh," says the trainee, "could it bend the frame?" "You bet! So, how could you make sure it's not too tight?" we ask. "Maybe if I relaxed it before I stuck it down," replies the trainee. "Excellent! Why don't you try it?" we respond.

Note that in the first question in the above paragraph, we "loaded" the question with a clue for the trainee—the word "flimsy." In this way, we set the employee up for a successful answer and at the same time, the employee gains confidence in his or her own ability to figure things out. This enhances the trainee's self-image, as well as better retention of the correct way to perform the task.

☑ **6. Following up to ensure that the trainee can do the task.**

Following up does not mean concluding with the familiar statement, "My door is always open. If you have any questions, don't hesitate to stop by, and I'll help you any way I can." Trainees who are apprehensive about their job and job environment may not feel comfortable enough to come to us with their questions.

Following up means *we* follow up. *We're* the ones who need to take the initiative and visit the trainee on a regular basis. We must make time in our schedule to visit our trainees. Good intentions don't count much here—action does!

We can view this step as an interview with several objectives. First, we find out what the trainee is feeling and thinking about the job. Second, we determine how well the job task is being done and if there are any areas that need improvement.

In order to obtain information, we again use questions. We ask our trainees how they feel about the task, what they like about it, what they don't like, and what concerns they may have.

Then, we have the trainee complete the key tasks to ensure that he or she is performing them correctly. When we see positive performance, we say so! And we avoid "parental" responses such as, "I'm proud of you!" Instead, we say, "That's exactly right." "Excellent!" "That's good work!" Then we carefully analyze the performance, and identify areas that need improvement.

Leader's Checklist
One-On-One Training Skills

☑ **1. Prepare for training.**
- Task listing
- Task detailing
- Develop training plans and strategies

☑ **2. Ask questions to determine the trainee's experience.**
Examples:
> *"What experience have you had with jobs like this?"*
> *"What have you done in the past that was similar to this?"*

☑ **3. Tell the trainee about the task.**
Examples:
> *"This is what you will be doing."*
> *"While completing this task, these are the people you will be dealing with . . .."*
> *"This is where the job will be done."*
> *"This job should be done when . . .."*
> *"The reasons for doing this job are . . .."*

Then ask:
> *"What questions do you have at this point?"*
> *"What concerns do you have about doing this?"*

☑ **4. Show the trainee how to do the task.**
Example:
> *"Watch me as I do this task, I'll talk my way through it for you."*

☑ **5. Encourage the trainee to do the task.**
Example:
> *"Now, you do it as I watch. And why don't you tell me what you are going to do just before you perform each step?"*

☑ **6. Follow up to ensure that the trainee can do the task.**
Example:
> *"Why don't we get back together tomorrow and see how you are doing? I'll stop by your area right after break, say at about ten o'clock."*

Training Worksheet

☑ **1. Prepare for the training.**

    A. List one task: _____

    B. One detailed task of the task listed above: _____
         _____

    C. Plans and strategies:

         _____
         _____
         _____
         _____
         _____
         _____
         _____
         _____

☑ **2. Ask questions to determine trainee's experience.** Answer the questions:

    "What does the employee already know that will (1) aid learning and (2) hinder learning?" What information do we need in order to teach this employee the specific unit of knowledge selected from our task-detailing sheet? _____

    _____
    _____
    _____
    _____
    _____
    _____
    _____

☑ **3. Tell the trainee about the task.**

    What specific unit of knowledge are we going to give this employee? (Taken from our task detailing and planning work sheets.) Briefly, what will you say? (Don't try to write out a "script." This should be in the form of notes.)

    _____
    _____
    _____
    _____
    _____
    _____

☑ **4. Show the trainee how to do the task.**

What will you do?

_____
_____
_____
_____

☑ **5. Encourage the trainee to do the task.**

What specific parts of the task do you think the employee will be able to perform correctly?

_____
_____
_____
_____

When the employee performs the above item successfully, what will you say?

_____
_____
_____

A. Describe what you saw:

_____
_____

B. Tell why it was important:

_____
_____

C. Express your feelings:

_____
_____

What specific part of the task may be difficult for the employee?

_____
_____

What will you say if the employee does this incorrectly?

_____
_____

☑ **6. Follow up to ensure that the trainee can do the task.**

What does the employee need to know about complicated, preventive, or corrective tasks, and/or housekeeping, that affects the performance of the task learned?

_____
_____
_____
_____
_____
_____
_____
_____
_____

What kinds of specific follow-up action will be necessary for you to take?

_____
_____
_____
_____
_____
_____
_____
_____
_____
_____
_____

6

Leadership
Improving Employee Performance Through Coaching

There is all the difference in the world between saying, "Keep your eye on the ball!" and asking, "Which way does the ball spin after it hits the ground?" or, "Exactly where does the tennis ball hit your racket?" Both are used to coach. Only one method is effective.

Paraphrased by Dick Leatherman
from *Coaching for Performance*
by John Whitmore

The words *coaching* and *counseling* are often used synonymously. In my opinion, coaching and counseling are two very different actions. Coaching is helping a person become even more effective. Counseling is a skill used to correct an individual's problems.

For coaching to be effective, it is necessary to make three assumptions. First, a good coach is in *partnership* with others. The coach wants peak performance from the people he or she has responsibility for. The "coachee" wants the rewards that come from personal effectiveness, both extrinsically in the form of recognition and intrinsically as a result of feeling competent. Both people have an investment in accomplishment.

Coaching experienced and motivated people requires a different set of leadership skills than those needed for counseling. The superior/ subordinate role may be appropriate for counseling, but coaching requires something different.

This leads to the second assumption—that people are *motivated* to improve and that they have a stake in accomplishing the task the best way possible. Good coaching requires neither the carrot nor the stick. It requires leadership.

Third, people have *experience* that can be used by the coach to assist them in their growth and development. This implies that coaches don't just tell people what to do and how to do it. Instead, effective coaches ask for input, listen to what is said, and hold discussions for mutual benefit.

In addition to the confusion evident between the terms "coaching" and "counseling," coaching is also confused with several other functions, such as one-on-one training, mentoring, and career counseling. Let's look briefly at each of these functions so that you'll know 1) what coaching is and 2) what it is not.

Coaching is a one-on-one interaction between a coach and another person; the coach creates in the other individual an awareness of the possibility of change, explores with him or her various change alternatives, assists in selecting a key area for attention, and helps create action plans to accomplish the desired changes.

Counseling is a workplace interview, initiated and conducted by a leader with his or her employee in order to correct a problem. In most cases, the employee is not meeting acceptable standards of attendance, work habits, or job performance. The leader then analyzes the situation with the employee by describing what is happening and what is expected, determining the probable cause(s), developing solutions, and implementing an action plan for improvement.

One-on-one training is similar to coaching in that it is an interaction between two people. The outcome of coaching and one-on-one training is also much the same—improved performance. But what is done and how it is done are decidedly different. One-on-one training teaches a trainee a new task. Coaching improves an individual's performance in an existing task. An individual can be a satisfactory performer and still be "coached" to be even better. On the other hand, one-on-one training is conducted when the trainee does not know how to do a task.

We can also look at how "directed" the trainer's actions are. As the figure below illustrates, the trainer initiates and maintains the interaction while training a person to do a new task; the trainer *tells* the trainee exactly what to do, shows him or her how to do it, and then has him or her do it. In this case, we would not see the trainer and the trainee "brainstorming" ideas on how best to teach this trainee. But with more experienced people who already know how to do the task, a coach could, in most cases, talk *with* the other person to create better ways to do the task.

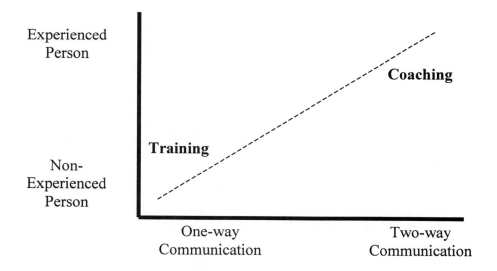

When we watch parents with their children, we notice that most parents have a tendency to spend too much time telling their children what to do and how to do it and not enough time asking questions. Think about what happens to a child's self-esteem when the parent assumes that he or she knows best and always tells the child what to do. Then consider parents who treat their children with respect, listen to what the children say, and then ask good questions to guide them to the discovery of their own answers to some of life's questions. Yet we often see parents who keep on "talking and telling" while the child is jumping up and down with excitement and exclaiming, "I can do it! Let me do it myself!"

Mentoring is a personal, one-on-one workplace connection between a respected leader or other senior person (not necessarily the direct boss) and an employee. It is a word used to describe a person's actions when he or she helps an employee 1) become sensitive to the organization's politics; 2) establish networks with other key people within the organization; 3) see the "big picture" in terms of the organization's culture and values; and 4) develop an awareness of what executive management expects. Coaching, as we will see later, can be used in the mentoring process, but coaching has outcomes very different from mentoring.

Finally, leaders conduct *career-counseling* interviews with employees in order to determine where they are, where they want to go, and how they are going to get there. This requires that leaders assist employees in determining their strengths and areas of need, to establish realistic career goals, and to create action plans that achieve their objectives.

What makes coaching, counseling, one-on-one training, mentoring, and career counseling seem similar is that they

- Are all personal interactions between two people
- Require sincerity in helping others

On the other hand, coaching require that coaches

- Talk *with* the individuals, not *at* them, as is often done in one-on-one training
- Make extensive use of the others' existing experiences instead of teaching new jobs
- Focus on present performance rather than on future career goals or the political climate
- Help people become more effective rather than deal with their performance problems
- View others as capable contributors, or respect their knowledge and abilities

Coaching: Why Bother?

"No one really believes that satisfactory, or average, performance is good enough. In a world of international competition, if managers accept satisfactory performance, they inevitably accept a loss in competitiveness, a decline in market share, stagnant capital growth, and decreasing profitability."

Dennis C. Kinlaw
Coaching for Commitment

Organizations are downsizing, rightsizing, restructuring, and reengineering. Whole layers of management have disappeared in many organizations. "Lean and mean" are the operational words in today's firms. Often, leaders are required to deal with wider spans of control (more employees report to them), increased workloads that were delegated to them from their bosses, and overworked employees who need to be even more productive.

In addition, employees' jobs are becoming more technical and complex. According to recent reports, the growth of technical workers as a job class has tripled compared to the workplace as a whole. This means that leaders are now required to supervise employees who, in all likelihood, know a great deal more about their jobs than their leaders do. Helping highly skilled employees who know more about their jobs than their leaders do will require that leaders use coaching skills with their employees in order to enhance productivity. So it's no wonder that astute leaders are looking for (make that *hungry* for!) new ways to manage.

Finally, all of us need the life skills of coaching. We coach each other, not only on the job, but off as well. We coach our children. We coach our spouses. And we coach volunteers. Coaching is just a great way to relate with others!

A New Way

The art and skill of coaching by using questions is both old and new. Socrates used questions to pursue Truth with the youth of ancient Greece. And Plato, who was a disciple of Socrates, also used this method of communicating. It became known as a dialectic discussion, *dia* from the

Greek word meaning "two" and "across," and *lectic* meaning "to lecture." In other words, two people would arrive at new knowledge by talking together and asking questions. Today, we use the word "Socratic" to describe this method of communication.

Although many of us know what the words *Socratic* or *dialectic* mean, not many of us have had a chance to acquire the skills to use the technique. We may have been taught to make presentations or give speeches, and we may have even been taught how to teach. But few of us ever had a class about helping someone become more effective by asking questions.

First, any discussion *between* two people can create far better ideas than a coach's or other person's monologue. For example, in the figure below there are things that the other person knows that the coach doesn't. If the coach simply tells the other person what to do and how to do it without engaging in a dialogue, then the other person's ideas may be lost. Likewise, if the other person doesn't bother to utilize his or her coach's experience and wisdom, then the coach's ideas may be lost. But if both can talk with each other, the end result is often greater than either thought possible.

What they both know	**What the coach knows and the other person doesn't**
What the other person knows and the coach doesn't	**What neither know**

In order to discover what the other person knows, the coach can use a questioning process to enhance understanding for both of them. Then both the coach and the other person can use questions to talk to others to discover what neither knows in the present.

But why questions? Why not just share ideas?

?

?

Coaching by using questions will

- Help develop self-sufficient people

- Produce, in the person being coached, a sense of ownership of the ideas and solutions that will result in a commitment to follow through with action

- Increase motivation in the people who are being coached

- Create better ideas and solutions

- Give both the coach and the employee a sense of personal satisfaction at being competent

- Make the coach's job more interesting, challenging, and even fun

- In the long run, help create self-sufficient and motivated people who will allow the coach to have a greater span of control

- Allow the coach to lead and develop people who know more technically about the task than the coach

Coaching Is a Process

Coaching is a process—it has a beginning, a middle, and an ending, with a common theme of using questions in a very special way. I'm not talking about something as simplistic as *open* and *closed* questions. Although coaching by asking questions may sound simple, it's not simple at all. In fact, it is subtly complex.

In the next section, we'll look at *how* coaches can use questions when they coach.

Using Questions to Coach

Trust is built by letting someone know you truly want to hear what he or she has to say and to understand his point of view. Beginning with the other person's view, rather than your own, is a powerful way to build that trust.

Trainer's Workshop
"Coaching, Counseling and Feedback"
American Management Association

Most leadership tasks start with preparation. We have likely spent a significant amount of time preparing to conduct a selection interview with a new applicant, thoroughly preparing to train a new employee, or devoting hours to preparing for a performance appraisal meeting. But coaching often occurs on the run, and there usually isn't time for extensive planning. For example, a coach may observe someone doing a task and take a moment to talk with that person about how the task could be done more effectively, or the person may ask for help with a particular task from the coach. So this coaching model doesn't start with preparation—it starts with questions.

Ask, Don't Tell

It sounds easy: just ask questions. But, as you will find, it is a difficult skill to use. It's fairly easy to learn the different types of questions to ask, but *knowing* the questions and actually *using* them are altogether different matters.

Let me give you a real example. I was an independent consultant for a number of years before starting my business. During that time, I wrote an article entitled, "So You Want to Be a Consultant, or It Isn't As Easy As It Looks!" In it, I shared all of the things that I had learned about starting a successful consulting business. As you might imagine, a number of fledgling consultants called for additional advice. I would talk, talk, talk, and talk, and they would become terribly impressed about how much I knew. But I talked *at* them, not *with* them.

I am now a little older and, perhaps, wiser. The last couple of people who have wandered into my office to talk about becoming a consultant weren't talked to, they were talked with. I asked questions, a lot of questions. And when they left, they had their own answers, not mine.

I recently talked with an individual who was in the process of being "reengineered" out of her job, and was considering becoming an independent consultant. One of the many questions I asked was, "How long do you think it will take you to begin generating revenue?" Her answer was, "about four months."

But rather than just telling her that I thought her schedule was unrealistic, I asked, "Considering the time it takes to market your services, schedule work to meet the client's timetable, invoice the customer after the job is completed, and finally get paid, how do you see that happening in less than six months?" Her answer: "Oh, I didn't think of the collection problems. Maybe six months is more realistic." Based on my own experiences, this seemed like a much more realistic view of the time it takes to become a consultant.

Next, I asked questions like, "How do you plan to survive the six months it will take you to begin generating revenue?" "What is your fallback position in case you haven't quite produced enough income to meet your needs?" "Who are your prospective clients?" "How will you identify them?" "How do you plan to reach these clients once you have identified them?"

Each succeeding answer stairsteps to another question. The follow-up question is focused on what the other person wants or needs rather than on what we think he or she might need. If others have answers to your coaching questions—and they might—you both may learn something.

Guidelines for Asking Questions

It is better to know some of the questions than all of the answers.

James Thurber

Before we look at a step-by-step model of how to ask questions, let's first look at some general guidelines that we can use to help us be better coaches.

- **Ask "Who?" "What?" "Where?" "When?" "How?" and sometimes "Why?" questions.**

  Questions that start with "What" or "How" yield the most information and help the individual think in detail about the situation under discussion. "Who," "Where," and "When" questions are useful for obtaining more specific details but are less helpful for acquiring general information. The question that can get us in trouble begins with the word "Why." For example, to ask "Why are you having trouble doing this particular task?" will likely result in the person's becoming defensive. The "Why" combined with the "you" focuses on personal motives and is more difficult to answer than the less threatening, "What are your major concerns about this particular task?" However, if the "Why" question focuses on the future instead of the past or present, it is usually less of a challenge to the other person. For example, to ask, "Why is that step in your plan important to you?" probes for a motive and would likely not make the other person feel uncomfortable. Or, "Why" questions could be used as a follow-up to determine facts and feelings.

- **Answer questions with questions that contain clues about possible answers.**

     This is not a manipulative device to get people to come up with *our* answer, but, rather, a complex way of communicating that helps people think of new possibilities that they might not have seen otherwise. We need to include enough additional information in our question to broaden the other person's vision, but not so much as to limit his or her answer to our question. Too many clues in our question will sound insulting to most listeners and may make our coaching effort counterproductive.

- **Maintain silence after asking a question to give the other person an opportunity to respond.**

     If we think we know what the other person should say or do, it is difficult to maintain silence. But we must keep our mouths shut! The objective here is to give people time to come up with their own ideas rather than ours. This fosters ownership and commitment. Ten seconds can feel like an eternity, but try counting to ten before asking another question or offering your ideas. Do, however, provide non-verbal responses (eye contact, head nods, and the like) to indicate to the other person that he or she has our undivided attention.

- **Avoid running two questions together. Ask one question and wait for a response before asking another question.**

     Sometimes as we ask one question we immediately think of a better one, or even a better way of asking the first one. But before we restate our question, or in our impatience ask a second one, we need to give people an opportunity to think about the first question we asked. Then, we take our cue from the other person as to whether we need to ask the same question in a different way.

- **If the other person has difficulty answering, we can say, "Let me rephrase the question," and ask another question that provides additional clues.**

     It is a balance between being too ready to jump in to lead others to the "right" answer and waiting too long for an answer. If we maintain a comfortable silence after asking a question and they are still unable to respond, then we simply ask the question in a different way to provide additional information concerning the original question.

- **If another person seems unable to provide an answer to a question, ask permission before directly providing information.**

  Prefacing a suggestion on our part by asking permission keeps the other person in control of the conversation. If I ask, "Could I make a suggestion?" the individual might respond by saying, "Wait. Let me think about it for a minute." Or he or she could well say, "Sure." Either way, the other person takes responsibility for the direction of the discussion.

Coaching Is Not Interrogation

Coaching is a conversation that is led by the coach's questions. If all the coach does is ask question after question, the other person may soon begin to feel that he or she is being interrogated. There are two things that a coach can do to prevent this.

Responding. When the other person begins to answer a question, a coach can respond both while the individual is talking and when the individual has finished. As the other person speaks, the coach can maintain eye contact, nod to indicate listening, and say "I see," "Uh-huh," or "OK." And when the other person stops talking, the coach can respond in several ways.

If the other person covered a lot of information in his or her response to the coach's original question, the coach can respond by *summarizing*. Summarizing is simply making a statement that attempts to reflect accurately the content of what was said by the other person. This will indicate to the other person that the coach really did listen to what was said and will help ensure that what was said was also understood.

Or, the coach may choose to pay more attention to the *feelings* expressed than to the content of what is said. For example, if the other person has strong feelings about what he or she says, the coach might choose to *recognize and affirm those feelings* by saying, "I can see why you might feel that way," or "You seem to have some strong feelings about that." Note that this is not agreement! It is only an empathetic statement by the coach that legitimizes the other person's right to have feelings. Statements such as "You shouldn't feel that way" or "I don't understand why you would feel like that" discount the other person and result in barriers to the conversation.

Self-Disclosure. Where does it say that coaches have to always do things right, never make mistakes, and, above all, never have feelings? Good communication occurs when two human beings talk honestly with each other. Coaches are not perceived by others as "weak" or "incompetent" when they confess to having made a mistake or that they also have feelings about an issue that is important. So, it's okay to say, "I've had difficulty with that, too," or "A similar thing happened to me." Note that this is not a "Oh, you think you got troubles, wait until you hear mine!" kind of response. It is only a sincere effort to connect with the other person, help reduce interpersonal barriers, and improve the flow of communication.

Listening, responding appropriately by acknowledging either the content or the emotion, summarizing throughout, and permitting self-disclosure can help the coach maintain a dialogue with the other person. The idea here is to have a discussion, not a monologue by either the other person or the coach.

If Coaching Is So Great, Why Don't We Do It?

OK, so you now know a bit about coaching by asking questions, and you probably see value in doing it. But sometimes it seems that even though we know better, we still end up telling people what it is they need to do, how they should do it, and when it needs to be done.

The following fable illustrates some of the subtle reasons why coaching can be difficult.

Parchment, Brooms, and a Dragon

Once upon a time, in a land far away, in the Kingdom of Light and Shadow, lived Jenny. She was known throughout the kingdom as a marvelous helper.

Now the Queen of the Kingdom of Light and Shadow was having great difficulty with her court. The parchment work was not getting done and what did get done wasn't done on time. The storerooms were a mess and nobody could find anything when it was needed. The castle rooms were dusty, and guests from other kingdoms usually went home early. There were bugs in the flour, worms in the fruit, and to make matters worse, a dragon in the moat.

The Queen, being busy with queenly things, really didn't have time to deal with these pedestrian problems. So she called for the Wizard and asked what she should do. The Wizard thought for a moment and then wisely informed the Queen that she needed an overseer, someone to manage the court staff and whip things back in shape. The Queen immediately thought of Jenny.

The Queen had heard of Jenny's willingness to help anyone do anything and decided that she should be placed in charge of the royal court. So she summoned Jenny and appointed her the royal boss.

Jenny was thrilled to be so recognized by her Queen but a little frightened about taking over as the new Chief of Staff. She just knew that the staff would resent her and she also knew that they could make her life miserable. As she sat in her dusty room and thought about her new job, a crow flew to her window and cocked one beady eye at her.

"Oh crow," cried Jenny, "whatever shall I do?"

"Be a coach," squawked the crow, "not a boss."

"What does a coach do?" asked Jenny.

"A coach helps people realize their full potential," said the crow as he flew away.

"That I can do," said Jenny to herself.

So she begin to make a long list of the things that needed to be done. First there was the matter of the parchment work. Next were the storerooms and the cleaning staff. Then that pesky dragon, and finally, the worms and bugs.

She set out that very afternoon and first visited the chief scribe. When Jenny asked how she could help the scribing department get caught up, the chief said that he didn't have any idea. Good help was impossible to find, the parchment was just not up to standards, the ink they were using dried too quickly, and the quills wouldn't stay sharp.

"Okay," said Jenny, "let me see if I can get you some good help. Then I'll set up a total quality management system at the parchment company, and I'll contact the ink suppliers about the drying time of their inks. I'm not sure what to do about the quills, but I'll figure something out."

"Oh bless you," said the Chief Scribe. "It is so wonderful to know that my troubles are over."

"No problem," said Jenny, as she left to visit the cleaning staff.

She found the cleaning staff sitting on their buckets, gazing at the sunlight as it streamed through the dusty windows.

"What's wrong?" asked Jenny. "Why are you just watching the dust?"

"The straw in our brooms disintegrates when we try to sweep, the handles break, and our buckets leak," cried the Chief Sweeper.

"Oh dear," said Jenny. "How can I help?"

"Get us some new brooms made with straw that is not rotten, handles of oak instead of pine, and buckets of metal, not leather," said the Chief.

"Let me see what I can do," said Jenny.

"Oh bless you," said the Chief Sweeper. "It is so wonderful to know that our troubles are over."

"No problem," said Jenny, as she left to visit the moat.

"Chief Moat Keeper," said Jenny, "I guess you've heard that I'm your new Chief of Staff. As your new chief, how can I help you do your job better?"

"Take care of that pesky dragon," replied the moat keeper. "It is driving us nuts. It keeps us awake with the noise it makes, it eats the royal fish, and has burned the drawbridge in three places."

"Let me see what I can do," said Jenny.

"Oh bless you," said the Chief Moat Keeper. "It is so wonderful to know that our troubles are over."

"No problem," said Jenny, as she left to find the Dragon.

"Dragon!" shouted Jenny,
"Where are you?"

There was a great churning of the
waters, and with a loud sound
like distant thunder, the Dragon
poked his head out of the water.

"Hey lady, what's all the fuss,
can't you see I'm trying to get a
little shut-eye here?" rumbled the dragon.

"This is the castle moat, not a dragon's bathtub," Jenny replied. "Get your sorry hide out of the moat and hit the road."

"But I'm hungry!" roared the Dragon. "The fish are all gone. How can I hit the road with an empty tummy?"

"Don't worry, you can count on me to be available for you," said Jenny.

"What a wonderful idea," said the Dragon, as he gobbled her up.

———————————————

What do you think is the point of this story? If you were asked to write a snappy one-liner that said, "The moral of this story is . . .," what would you write? Note your answer below.

The crow, flying overhead, was heard to say: *"The moral of this story is . . .*

Don't try to be the answer to everyones problems
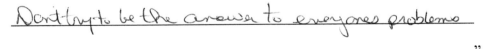
"

One of the best responses I've heard to the question, "What is the moral of this story?" was:

> *"The moral of this story is that coaching others by doing for them can get you eaten alive and you'll never get your work done."*

Over the years, I've talked with others about the difficulty some people have in coaching, and the following are some of the reasons that were given:

- ➢ A number of coaches need to "help" others.
- ➢ Some coaches tend to have dominating personalities.
- ➢ It's often a lot faster to just tell (especially when we think we know the answer) than to ask.
- ➢ It's good for the old ego to be seen as the expert.
- ➢ The other person may think we are incompetent if we ask rather than tell.
- ➢ We feel awkward about doing things differently.
- ➢ Sometimes we don't really know how.

Let's look at each of these in more detail.

"Helpers"

As can be seen in our little story, *it feels good to "help" by telling rather than asking.* There is a bit of the "caretaker" in most of us. Maybe we were nurtured by our parents or other significant figures and learned that it feels good to be nurtured, and in turn, to nurture others. Or, as children, some of us were placed in a caretaker role in our own families and received a lot of psychological payoff in taking on this role.

Some coaches have a skewed view of what it means to be a coach and tend to be caretakers with others. These coaches seem to create dependency in order to feel needed. They are overly helpful, take back work that the other person is having difficulty with, don't want to be the source of the other person's discomfort, and thus have difficulty in creating an awareness of the need for change.

For these coaches, once they realize the need to modify their behavior, changing from a caretaker to a coach is a natural progression in their maturity. When they see and experience the value of coaching, they are able to transform their old behaviors. They will learn that true coaching is doing what is best for others, and that their own psychological rewards are much greater as a result of coaching rather than caretaking.

Dominating Personalities

Coaches are often dominating for a number of reasons. They may have learned that style of relating to others from old bosses or early childhood experiences, they need to control their surroundings because of their own fears, or they really are unusually intelligent or technically competent and believe that they are paid to have all the answers to life's questions.

These coaches, however, can learn that there are more effective ways of relating to others. They can learn that controlling others leads to dependence and dependence leads to resentment. And intelligent and/or technically competent coaches can also learn that coaching allows them to integrate both their experience and the other person's experience in order to create richer ideas and better solutions.

Quicker to Tell

It's often just a lot faster to tell (especially when we think we know the answer) than to ask. It *is* easier to tell than to ask! It takes a lot more time to help others discover their own answers versus just telling them what they need to know. And most coaches today are stressed beyond belief in dealing with life. So where can they find the time to coach? They make time. It's a question of priorities—and investment.

Astute coaches know that what needs to get done will get done. They also know that investing priority time in coaching others can return remarkable dividends. There will be dividends in the form of time saved later because the people who were coached are more self-sufficient, are better performers, and become highly motivated and challenged in what they've been coached to do.

The Ego

It's good for the old ego to be seen as the expert. It does feel good to be perceived as the expert. But it feels even better to conduct an effective coaching session. Wait until you try it! It is truly a wonderful feeling to experience the personal satisfaction that is a result of coaching.

Looking Incompetent

The other person may think we are incompetent if we ask rather than tell. There are some coaches who believe that if they coach people by asking good questions rather than providing the answers themselves, they will be seen as incompetent.

The solution to this problem is easy. These coaches only need to use the coaching strategies and then ask the people they coached how they felt about the experience. Rather than seeing their coaches as incompetent, they in fact see their coaches as being very, very knowledgeable. It's funny, but people who listen and ask good questions are more often than not perceived by others as being very wise, extremely intelligent, and extraordinarily insightful!

New Is Difficult

We feel awkward in doing things differently. Most things that we try for the first time do feel awkward. The first time I rode a bicycle felt awkward. The first time I drove a car felt awkward. And the first time I tried to coach using questions also felt awkward. We aren't born asking questions, we learn how. It takes time and practice to become skilled in something as subtly difficult as using questions to coach. Not only is it possible to become proficient in coaching using this method, but with application and practice it is very likely.

Don't Know How

Sometimes we don't really know how. This is probably the number one reason why coaches are not as effective as they might be in coaching others. In the next section, we'll look at a common-sense model of how we can ask coaching questions.

Coaching Model

By listening actively, we not only communicate to others the fact that we care about them, we also obtain new information. We may discover what works or doesn't work—and why. We can locate problems and elicit suggestions for solving them. If we don't learn the power of listening, we will not get needed information. Remember, it is the listener who asks questions who controls the conversation's outcome, not the speaker.

Dick Leatherman

A coach can use the coaching model discussed below to initiate a discussion with another person, or when the other person initiates the discussion. In some cases, the coach will need to determine where the other person is in the model. For example, if the other person initiates the discussion, he or she may already be "aware" of the opportunity for change. Thus, the coach may choose to start the conversation with Step 2, "Explore Possibilities," rather than Step 1. The key point is that this model is nothing more than a common-sense way of conducting a coaching session. It should not be followed in some sort of lock-step way, rigidly applying the steps whether they "fit" or not. What is important is that the model be used as a guide and used only where appropriate.

What follows is a six-step model that can be used to coach others. In each step, there will be a brief explanation of why the step is necessary, followed by examples of questions that can be asked by the coach.

Six Steps for Effective Coaching

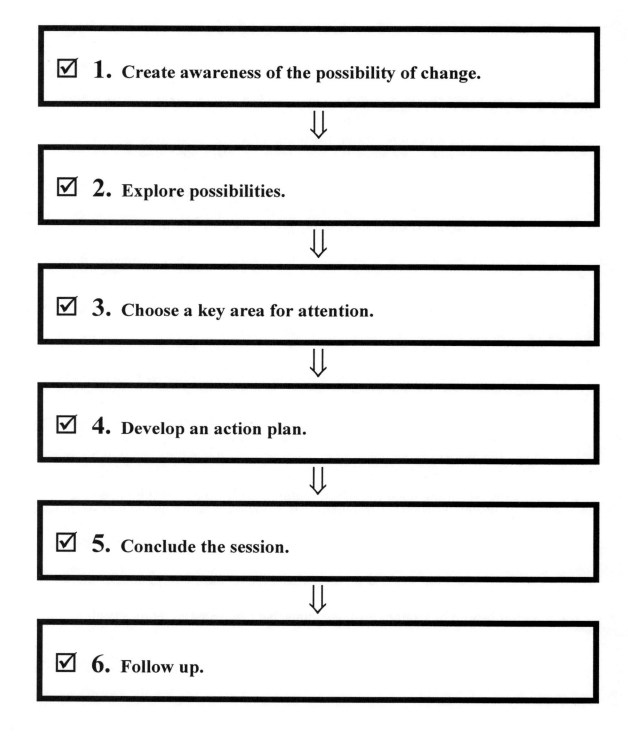

☑ **1.** **Create awareness of the possibility of change.**

⇓

☑ **2.** **Explore possibilities.**

⇓

☑ **3.** **Choose a key area for attention.**

⇓

☑ **4.** **Develop an action plan.**

⇓

☑ **5.** **Conclude the session.**

⇓

☑ **6.** **Follow up.**

☑ **1. Create awareness of the possibility of change.**

It is not a motivating experience for someone to tell me to do my job better if I already think that I'm doing the best that I can. The implication is that whatever I do is never good enough, and that I should have seen opportunities for improvement. And since I didn't, there must be something wrong with me. I'm just not trying. I'm not working hard enough. That's the subtle and not-so-subtle message given by people who say, "You should just try harder."

But it is not simply a matter of asking people to "try harder." The majority of people are conscientious and really want to do the task well. The key to greater productivity is not to focus on how hard people work or to see them as the cause of the "problem," but to ask them what they do and why they do it, analyze how they interact with one another to get the task done, examine and evaluate the processes used, determine if the tools and materials are right for the task, and help them discover better ways to do the task!

That is one reason why a coaching strategy of using questions is so effective. The coach is not pointing out a performance gap. He or she does not call people into the office and counsel them on their "problem." In reality, the coach may not be aware of any specific thing that could be improved. What the coach does know is that life has real, but unknown, possibilities. He or she knows that there is a possibility of further improvement in performance and is willing to spend quality time exploring this possibility with the other person.

The true purpose of using questions to coach others is to create more elastic, yet permeable, boundaries around their existing belief systems. Questions are used to help people see new possibilities in order to achieve higher levels of performance and superior results. Coaching is taking a proactive stance toward future crisis and change by helping others constantly look for ways to be even more effective.

People can proceed from their present status quo to new levels of performance as a result of exploration questions from their coaches. These questions are used to probe the way people feel or think about what they are doing, or the ways they behave while doing the task. To use John Whitmore's example from his book, *Coaching for Performance*, there is a world of difference between exhorting a tennis player to "Keep your eye on the ball!" and asking questions like, "Which way does the ball spin after it strikes the ground?" or "Where exactly on your racket does the ball hit?"

The first does nothing to promote awareness; it only causes frustration. The latter focuses the player's attention on the way he or she is playing because, while thinking about the questions, he or she becomes aware.

Some questions that the coach can use to create awareness in the three areas of feelings, thinking, and behavior are

- Feelings:
  "How do you like doing this?"
  "How do you feel about looking for ways to do this even better?"
  "What concerns do you have about doing this?"
- Thinking:
  "What are the reasons you do it this way?"
  "What reasons might there be to change the way it's done?"
  "On a scale of 1 to 10, how do you rate yourself on it?"
  "What parts of this are most challenging for you?"
  "What do you see as the reasons why this is challenging?"
- Behavior:
  "What do you do as you complete this task?"
  "What are the key steps to completing it?"

It may be, however, that you won't need Step 1 of the model. For example, if the other person initiates the conversation and asks for your help in exploring possibilities for improvement, then you will likely be able to start with the next step, "Explore Possibilities."

 2. Explore possibilities.

Moving from Step 1, "Creating Awareness," to this step is a natural progression. In fact, it is so natural that coaches often find that they have moved into exploring possibilities without a conscious decision. Note here that the emphasis is on encouraging people to develop their own ideas about the possibilities that exist for change and improvement. The coach should *not* jump in and provide suggestions until after the other person has had a chance to thoroughly think about and discuss his or her own ideas. In fact, it may be necessary to give the other person an opportunity to think about the situation and meet at a later time to obtain his or her ideas.

There are several reasons why it's important to ask for others' ideas first.

♦ They might think of a better idea than the coach's, since they often know more than the coach about the details of the task.

♦ They are more likely to be motivated to make needed changes if the idea originates from them.

♦ Coaches communicate by their actions that people are respected and trusted.

♦ Coaches build independent people who are better able to make appropriate decisions when needed.

But asking for another person's ideas is difficult for many coaches. They were probably given the coaching role because they were good at solving problems. Naturally, they often have some strong ideas about what a person should do in order to be more effective. But if the coach offers his or her ideas first, other people are more likely to play the "Yes, but . . ." game. A "Yes, but" game opens by the coach telling someone what he or she should do to improve performance. The other person then replies, "Yes, but . . ." and gives the coach ten reasons why the idea or solution will not work. But few people "Yes, but" their own ideas. That's why if a coach can get the other person to make suggestions, there is a better chance that real changes will occur.

In addition, although one person may be able to suggest several ideas for a specific situation, two people can often devise many more. This is because one person's ideas trigger new thoughts in the other. Thus, when you have two people "bouncing ideas off each other," you greatly increase the chances of creating better quality—and more creative—suggestions. Astute coaches have learned that always to jump in with "the" idea for every problem is, in the long term, a disaster.

If, after careful probing, the person cannot offer any ideas, then the coach should feel free to offer his or her idea. In this initial step, we are looking for "divergent" thinking—that is, ideas that may originate outside of the other person's experience. Therefore, it is appropriate to offer new suggestions that the other person may not have thought of. At this point, the coach can simply ask, "May I make a suggestion?" In most cases, people will respond by saying, "Yes."

Here are typical questions that can be used in this step to Explore Possibilities:

"Which things are the greatest challenge and why?"

"What bottlenecks exist?"

"What changes would you like to see in the way it is done?"

"What other changes could be made?"

"How would you like to be different from the way you are now?"

"What things, if any, prevent you from being more effective?"

"Would you like some time to consider the situation?"

"Would you like me to make a suggestion, or would you prefer to have more time to think of ideas on your own?"

The discussion in this step encourages divergent thinking. Now in the next step, the coach helps the other person think convergently.

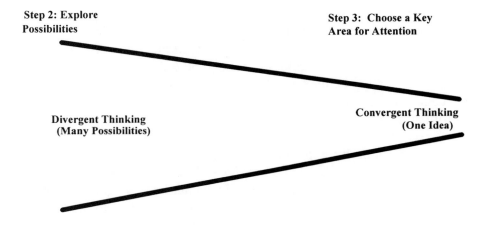

Step 2: Explore Possibilities

Step 3: Choose a Key Area for Attention

Divergent Thinking (Many Possibilities)

Convergent Thinking (One Idea)

☑ **3. Choose a key area for attention.**

During the course of the discussion that occurs in Step 2, the other person may suggest a number of different ideas for analysis. Remember, the discussion in the preceding step encouraged divergent thinking. But in this step, the coach helps others think convergently; that is, the coach assists others in focusing their efforts down to one key area. Attempting to look at many different ideas may result in the failure of them all.

The coach also guides them in considering the constraints that may exist in carrying out the suggestion. For example, there may not be enough money to finance the idea, or maybe there isn't enough time to implement the suggestion.

To conclude this step, the coach helps the other person determine how the results will be measured.

The following are probing questions that the coach can use to accomplish this step:

"Which of these changes should be tackled first?"

"What have you already done about this?"

"What were the results of that action?"

"What are the pluses and minuses of each option?"

"What are the key factors that should be considered (time, money, personnel, supplies, resources, space, skills, personal effort required, chances of success, and so on)?"

"What do think should be the outcome, or goal?"

"Will this get you to your goal?"

"How will you measure the success of your goal?"

But what if the other person selects an area for attention that is not the coach's first choice? Suppose the other person knows something that the coach doesn't, and that would make the coach's choice a poor alternative? Or conversely, maybe the coach knows something that the other person doesn't. Now what?

The coach can still ask questions, depending on the reasons why the coach felt his or her selection was better than the other person's choice. On the following page is a list of reasons and suggested questions.

Typical reasons and corresponding questions are:

The coach thinks his or her own selection will provide greater benefit. (It is possible that the coach will discover—through questions—that the employee's idea actually is better.)	*"What would be the benefits in doing it that way?"* *"What were your reasons for choosing that idea?"* *"Which choice would provide the greatest benefit?"*
The coach has information that the other person doesn't have that affects the other's selected area, or the coach thinks that there is no way that the other person can accomplish the tasks selected for attention.	*"What effect would selecting that area for attention have on . . .?"* *"If you consider . . ., how would that affect your choice?"* *"Given that . . . is a concern, how would that influence your decision to select that area for attention?"*
Although the coach prefers that the other person choose the area for attention that the coach feels is best, the coach suspects that the other person's motivation toward another choice may actually make the other person's selection the best in the long run.	*"How important is this to you?"* *"How do you feel about this area that you selected?"*
The coach feels that the results of the other person's choice will not be worth the effort.	*"Considering the investment of time and effort required to do that, how do you see a return on your investment paying off?"*
The coach knows that the other person's selection will not benefit the organization.	*"How will this help the organization (or department) reach its objectives?"*
The coach believes that the other person's selection will require too much time on the coach's part.	*"How much of my time will you need if you select that area for attention?"* *"Given my present time constraints and the need for my continuous involvement if you select that area for attention, how do you see us making it happen?"*

☑ **4. Develop an action plan.**

After the other person chooses a key area for attention, the coach should then assist him or her in developing steps from which action will be taken. As the steps in the plan are devised, completion dates can be set for each step.

It is also important to consider "Murphy's Law"—what can go wrong, will! Therefore, the coach should anticipate potential problems by asking the other person if he or she can identify any of the steps that are of concern. Potential problem analysis may sound negative. The good news is that if the other person can anticipate potential problems before the plan is carried out, solutions can often be developed that greatly increase the chances that the goal will be achieved.

Finally, by offering assistance, the coach can help reduce the other person's natural anxiety. The coach may need to pave the way for the person who is being coached by talking to others who will be affected by the plan. Or, the coach may want to help the person by interfacing with other departments that may need to be involved. By offering help, coaches demonstrate concern and show that they will do everything possible to ensure that the plans are successful.

It may not be possible for the coach and the other person to develop a complete action plan at the initial meeting. It would then be perfectly appropriate for the coach to ask the other person if he or she needs more time to think through the plan and meet at a later time to review it.

In order to better understand the kinds of questions we need to ask in Step 4, please read the case on the following page and then answer the questions at the end.

The Case of the Careless Coach

Betty Ann was in the middle of what had started out to be a short conversation about Joan's job. Joan had asked Betty Ann if she had a "couple of minutes," but the conversation had dragged on for about an hour. The air conditioning wasn't working the way it should, it was hot and sticky, and the conversation up to this point seemed to have taken forever. Betty Ann had managed to help Joan explore possibilities and Joan had even selected a key area for attention. Betty Ann sighed, surreptitiously looked at her watch, realized that once again she would not be able to eat supper with her kids, and tried to move the conversation along.

1. "Joan," Betty Ann said, "I hate to cut this short, but it is getting late. I think that the area you have selected to work on will give you a good return on your investment of time. Why don't you now consider what steps you will need to take to develop an action plan? To start with, what's the first thing you need to do?"

"Okay, I think the first thing I need to do," replied Joan, as she began to write, "is to get upper management support. That's where I'll need your help."

2. "I agree that the executives need to support what you are doing, but I don't agree that that is the first thing you need to do. For example," asked Betty Ann, "what about the people in this section who have to play a part in making sure that the plan works? Don't you think that you should talk with them first?"

"Oh, I guess that makes sense. I'll talk to Bob, Dick, and Darleen tomorrow, show them what we've done, and ask for their advice."

3. "I think that makes more sense than sending this up the line and then being embarrassed later when the people who have to make it work don't support it," Betty Ann said. "What kind of reaction do you think you'll get from them?"

"My guess is they will be excited," replied Joan. "I know that Bob has been asking for this for a long time, and it is right down Darleen's alley."

4. "Yeah, but maybe that's exactly why you might have a problem."

"What do you mean?"

5. "Since Bob has been asking for it, isn't he going to wonder why you didn't include him in on this conversation? After all, it will affect his performance just as much as it affects yours. I'm curious as to why you didn't consider that before you came to me."

"I just didn't think about it," Joan said. "I know it sounds dumb, but I was so excited that I ran in here to catch you before you went home."

6. As Joan finished talking, Betty Ann glances at her watch.

Joan exclaimed, "Oh, it *is* getting late. I'm sorry that I've kept you so long. Do you want to stop now and pick it up in the morning?"

7. "No," Betty Ann replied, "I've got a nine o'clock meeting with the VP, and then there's the department meeting at eleven. After that is the report that I was supposed to have finished this afternoon. So let's take a few minutes more and wind this up now so you can at least get started."

"OK, if you're sure that's all right."

8. "Sure. Thinking again about your plan, what do you see as the next step?" asked Betty Ann.

"Well . . . I'm not sure. What do you think I should do?"

9. "One thing that occurs to me," responded Betty Ann, "is that you really need to consider the time constraints. That's going to be a critical factor. Let's see, you need to have it finished by the end of this quarter. Say, I've got an idea, why don't you get Bob to help you do it? That'll solve two problems with one solution. Bob will feel more a part of the plan and you'll have the extra help in completing it. What do you think?"

"I guess so," replied Joan reluctantly. "Bob is just such a procrastinator. It's sometimes more work to get him to do something than to just do it myself. But if you really think that that'll help, I suppose I could ask him to help out."

10. "Great! Why don't you talk to him in the morning, review it with him, see if he has any additional ideas, and then ask him if he'd be willing to help?"

"OK, I'll give it a try."

11. "One last thing, Joan. You also need to consider that your present system won't support the amount of memory required for the new program. What do you plan to do about that?"

"I think that my best bet is to get Darleen's compression program and copy it into my hard drive," replied Joan.

12. "Right! And since we don't have a license to copy it, we'll all end up in jail. You know what happened last year. How could you even consider such a thing, Joan?"

"Oh, I thought we had a license. A bunch of people are using it."

13. "No," replied Betty Ann, "we don't have a license. They wouldn't sell us one so we had to buy it each time for each station. What a rip-off!"

"Could you see if you can get another copy, legal that is, for me?" asked Joan.

14. "I'll see what I can do. But for sure not tonight. Looks like we're finished up, so let's call it a night," said Betty Ann. "Why don't you let me know toward the end of the week how you are coming?"

"Okay," replied Joan.

Joan and Betty Ann said goodnight and left.

As Betty Ann helped Joan develop an action plan, what questions did she ask that were appropriate?

looking to dept, ask about each steps forward

What questions did she ask that were inappropriate?

Asking about reactions from department

What questions could she have asked that she didn't?

How can I help -

She made several statements that could have been questions. What were they?

On the following pages are suggested answers for each of the above questions. However, do not read ahead until you have finished writing your own answers.

The following are typical examples of answers to the questions:

What questions did Betty Ann ask that were appropriate?

(Paragraph 1) "To start with, what's the first thing you need to do?"

(Paragraph 3) "What kind of reaction do you think you'll get from them?"

(Paragraph 8) "Thinking again about your plan, what do you see as your next step?"

(Paragraph 11) "What do you plan to do about that?"

What questions did she ask that were inappropriate?

(Paragraph 2) "Don't you think that you should talk with them first?" This question is a typical "loaded question" that asks the other person to agree with the coach's opinion. It puts the other person down because the silent and implied word that the other person hears is "Hey, *dummy*, don't you think that you should talk with them first?"

(Paragraph 5) "I'm curious as to why you didn't consider that before you came to me." This is a difficult query in that it strongly implies that the other person did something wrong and questions her motives.

(Paragraph 12) "How could you even consider such a thing, Joan?" This question is a major put-down!

(Paragraph 14) "Why don't you let me know toward the end of the week how you are coming?" This so-called follow-up action on the part of the coach is not specific. The coach could have helped the other person by setting a specific time when they would get together.

What questions could she have asked that she didn't?

- "What else do you need to consider?"
- "What additional support do you need?"
- "How else can I help?"

She made several statements that could have been questions. What were they?

(Paragraph 2) The statement, "I agree that the executives need to support what you are doing, but I don't agree that that is the first thing you need to do" could have been modified by adding a question to obtain the information from the other person. For example, "I agree that the executives need to support what you are doing. Who else needs to be a part of this action plan, and when should they be contacted?"

(Paragraphs 4 & 5) The statement, "Yeah, but maybe that's exactly why you might have a problem" could have been rephrased as a question. For example, "Since Bob has been asking for this all along, what do you think will be his reaction to being excluded from the planning?"

(Paragraph 9) This entire statement could have been a question. In the preceding paragraph, Joan said, "Well . . . I'm not sure. What do you think I should do?" Betty Ann could have resisted the temptation to be directive and instead asked, "I'm not sure exactly what the next step should be. Would you like to have more time to think this out, and then we could meet at a later time to review your plan?" Instead, Betty Ann moved immediately to analyze the risk and offer her solution instead of again asking Joan.

(Paragraph 12) The statement "Right! And since we don't have a license to copy it, we'll all end up in jail" could have been turned into a question. For example, Betty Ann could have asked, "In light of the fact that this program is copyrighted, how do you plan to obtain it?"

Below are great questions that can be used to coach the other person in the "Create an Action Plan" step:

- *"What is the first thing that needs to be done now?"*
- *"When will it be done?"*
- *"Who else needs to be aware of what you are doing?"*
- *"If you do that, what could go wrong?"*
- *"What is the worst that could happen?"*
- *"Who could 'deep six' your efforts?"*
- *"How could you prevent that problem from occurring?"*

- *"If the problem occurs in the future, what could you do now to reduce its seriousness?"*

- *"What additional steps should be in the plan?"*

- *"What do you think are the chances of pulling this off?"*

- *"What else do you need to consider?"*

- *"What other resources do you need?"*

- *"What support do you need?"*

- *"How do you anticipate obtaining that support?"*

- *"What is the best that can happen?"*

- *"How can I help?"*

 5. Conclude the coaching session.

One good strategy to use in concluding the coaching session is to summarize the high points of the discussion to ensure clear understanding. Misunderstandings result when two people think they clearly understand what was said, when in fact they don't. In addition, if the coach or the other person summarizes the key points each made in the discussion, then both will have a solid feeling of accomplishment. For example, the coach could ask:

> *"Because I don't always hear what was really said, would you mind summarizing what we have discussed?"*

In addition to summarizing the discussion, the coach can ask questions like these:

- *"What else could we consider before we close out this discussion?"*

- *"What other questions do you have?"*

- *"When should we meet to discuss your progress?"*

- *"What will you have accomplished by that time?"*

☑ **6. Follow up.**

Following up does not mean concluding with the familiar statement, "If you have any questions, don't hesitate to call." Following up means the *coach* follows up. The coach is the one who takes the initiative and sees the other person as needed. If the coach spends quality time in coaching and then fails to follow up, the other person will have a legitimate reason to believe that the coach doesn't really care. The coach should not "talk a good game," and then fail to follow through.

But it is important that the coach doesn't over manage the plan that the other person has agreed to carry out. A coach may have trouble keeping his or her hands off once the plan has been implemented. On the other hand, the other person should not be abandoned. There is a great difference between monitoring another's efforts and breathing down his or her neck. A coach can walk this line by letting go of the nitty-gritty details of how the plan should be accomplished, and instead schedule times to review the other person's key activities and final results.

When the coach does follow up, the other person can be given credit for what he or she did that worked as planned; additional coaching can be provided if it didn't. At this review meeting, the coach can ask the other person what he or she learned from completing the plan, and what could be done differently in the future.

If things aren't accomplished as well as expected, the coach should avoid blaming the other person. The coach can help the other person determine ways to accomplish what needs to be done by using the coaching process already presented. The coach needs also to look at his or her role in plans that are not fully successful. If the coach believes that he or she was part of the difficulty experienced by the other person, then the coach should have the courage to say so.

Questions to ask could include some of the following:

- *"How do you feel about your progress in carrying out your plan?"*

- *"What did you learn from this experience?"*

- *"In hindsight, what would you do differently if you had to do it all over again?"*

- *"How else could I have helped you?"*

- *"Now that you have completed your original plan, what is the next thing you would like to work on?"*

Using the question technique of coaching will enable you to assist the other person to

- Create better ideas

- Become more independent

- Take responsibility for future action

- Build his or her self-esteem

- Feel challenged by what he or she does

And if you coach by asking questions, you don't have to be an expert on what the other person is doing.

To paraphrase Dennis Kinlaw, coaching today is not an option. It is a part of living! Successful people do it well. And the good news is that coaching is a set of skills that can be learned, and then applied to help the other person become more than he or she ever imagined.

The following pages show an outline of the six key steps and a list of all the preceding questions.

Coaching Questions

 1. Create awareness of the possibility of change.

- Feelings:
    - *"How do you like doing this?"*
    - *"How do you feel about looking for ways to do this even better?"*
    - *"What concerns do you have about doing this?"*
- Thinking:
    - *"What are the reasons you do it this way?"*
    - *"What reasons might there be to change the way it's done?"*
    - *"On a scale of 1 to 10, how do you rate yourself on it?"*
    - *"What parts of this are most challenging for you?"*
    - *"What do you see as the reasons why this is challenging?"*
- Behavior:
    - *"What do you do as you complete this task?"*
    - *"What are the key steps to completing it?"*

 2. Explore possibilities.

- *"Which things are the greatest challenge and why?"*
- *"What bottlenecks exist?"*
- *"What changes would you like to see in the way it is done?"*
- *"What other changes could be made?"*
- *"How would you like to be different from the way you are now?"*
- *"What things, if any, prevent you from being more effective?"*
- *"Would you like more time to consider the situation?"*
- *"Would you like me to make a suggestion, or would you prefer to have more time to think of ideas on your own?"*

3. Choose a key area for attention.

- *"Which of these changes should be tackled first?"*
- *"What have you already done about this?"*
- *"What were the results of that action?"*
- *"What are the pluses and minuses of each option?"*
- *"What are the key factors that should be considered (time, money, personnel, supplies, resources, space, skills, personal effort required, chances of success, and so on)?"*
- *"What do you think should be the outcome, or goal?"*
- *"Will this get you to your goal?"*
- *"How will you measure the success of your goal?"*

 4. Develop an action plan.

- *"What is the first thing that needs to be done now?"*
- *"When will it be done?"*
- *"Who else needs to be aware of what you are doing?"*
- *"If you do that, what could go wrong?"*
- *"What is the worst that could happen?"*
- *"Who could 'deep six' your efforts?"*
- *"How could you prevent that problem from occurring?"*
- *"If the problem occurs in the future, what could you do now to reduce its seriousness?"*
- *"What additional steps should be in the plan?"*
- *"What do you think are the chances of pulling this off?"*
- *"What else do you need to consider?"*
- *"What other resources do you need?"*
- *"What support do you need?"*
- *"How do you anticipate obtaining that support?"*
- *"What is the best that can happen?"*
- *"How can I help?"*

5. Conclude the coaching session.

-   *"What else should we consider before we close out this discussion?"*
-   *"What other questions do you have?"*
-   *"When should we meet to discuss your progress?"*
-   *"What will you have accomplished by that time?"*

 6. Follow up.

-   *"How do you feel about your progress in carrying out your plan?"*
-   *"What did you learn from this experience?"*
-   *"In hindsight, what would you do differently if you had to do it all over again?"*
-   *"How else could I have helped you?"*
-   *"Now that you have completed your original plan, what is the next thing you would like to work on?"*

Preparation for Coaching Worksheet

Write below the questions that you would use to coach a real person. Also consider how the other person might answer your questions.

1. Create awareness of the possibility of change.

_____

_____

_____

_____

2. Explore possibilities.

_____

_____

_____

_____

3. Choose a key area for attention.

_____

_____

_____

_____

4. Develop an action plan.

_____

_____

_____

_____

5. Conclude the coaching session.

_____

_____

_____

_____

6. Follow up.

_____

_____

_____

7

Leadership
Improving Employee Performance Through Counseling

When Yen Ho was about to take up his duties as tutor to the Duke of Wei, he went to Ch'u Po Yu for advice.

"I have to deal," he said, "with a man of depraved and murderous disposition. How is one to deal with a man of this sort?"

"I'm glad," said Ch'u, "that you asked this question. The first thing you must do is not to improve him, but to improve yourself."

Taoist story of ancient China

Employees who are constantly late for work, keep cluttered work areas, and take too much time for breaks and lunch are a "pain in the neck" for their leaders. The employee usually knows better—so the problem isn't normally ignorance of your policies or regulations.

The cause of most poor performance often lies elsewhere. You may have said, "He is just lazy," or "She really ought to wanna stop doing that." But somehow these feelings—especially when expressed to the employee—don't bring about much change. We end up giving formal warnings, and even suspensions. And still little permanent change may take place. Why? Possibly it has something to do with us—the leaders!

Have you ever seen a leader who had a special knack for handling his or her employees' problems? A super leader who could take marginal workers and turn them around? Very likely you have. There are many effective leaders who consistently take performance problems and solve them so that they stay solved.

When we look closely at such leaders we see certain things they all do—common sense ways that they handle their "people problems." Somehow they have an ability to tell the employee what is expected, to get the employee involved to discover a solution, and to develop with the employee a plan of action that really seems to work.

This is how they do it.

Preparation

In order to conduct an effective counseling interview with an employee, we must prepare. Counseling is too important to the organization, to leaders, and to the employee to just "wing it"! As you will see, effective counseling is a complex process and requires solid preparation. Let's look now at the four key steps that should be followed to prepare for a counseling session with an employee.

 1. Describing the performance concern

The first thing we should do to prepare for the counseling interview is to describe the employee's behavior in *specific* and *behavioral* terms. We avoid general statements like "Jane is not performing satisfactorily," "Bill is not motivated," or "He or she has a poor attitude." Statements like these do not describe behaviors nor are they specific. In addition, we avoid "absolute" statements that are probably untrue, like: "Tom *never* completes his work on time," or "Joe is *always* late."

The key question is, "What is the employee doing or saying that needs improvement?" Then, we write the answers to this question using numbers and/or examples to illustrate the situation. It usually takes more than one statement to adequately describe the employee's behavior. For example, we might make comments like:

1. *"Her work is not completed in a satisfactory manner."*
2. *"He has a poor attitude."*
3. *"She talks excessively and consistently interrupts others."*

. . . and rewrite them in specific, behavioral terms as follows:

1. *"She is 50% deficient in meeting work quotas, and 20% of her work contains errors (which resulted in 8 to 10 complaints per week)."*
2. *"He was tardy 8 days out of 10, absent 4 days in the past 2 months, laid his head on the desk during his training, and made 10 errors this week."*
3. *"She interrupts her coworkers at least once every 30 minutes. Does 50% of work during a full work day."*

☑ 2. Stating what we expect

The second step in preparing to conduct an employee-counseling interview is to write out what we expect of this individual. For every statement written about what is going on, there should be a corresponding statement about what it is that we expect.

The key questions to ask ourselves are "What do I expect of this employee?" "What specific things do I want this employee to do differently?" "What are the requirements for this employee?" and "Specifically, what is 'good' performance?" Again, we need to be specific and use numbers and/or examples to describe exactly what job performance is required. For example, if we had written a problem statement such as *"The employee is tardy an average of 1 day per work week and has been absent 2 days during the past month,"* we could write a corresponding standard of performance like *"The employee needs to arrive on or before 8:30 each morning, 19 out of 20 times, during any 4-week period for the next 6 months."*

Note that our written standard of performance should be realistic. In other words, we should not be setting up the employee for failure. Our job is to create realistic standards in order to help the employee achieve success.

☑ 3. Exploring probable causes

The third step to complete before conducting a counseling interview is to explore probable causes. The operational word here is *probable*. The realities of the work world are that, in many cases, the leader may not know the real cause of the employee's difficulty in advance of the actual interview. Therefore, it is important that we identify what we think might be the cause of the situation and not lock ourselves in on a specific cause.

This is not to say that we shouldn't carefully analyze the possible causes—only that we need to keep an open mind about what the cause actually is until we talk with the employee.

To gain a better understanding of the variety of causes we should investigate, please read the following case:

The Case of the Enigmatic Employee

Betty Anne is 26 years old, married, two children, and has been with us for six years. She was, at one time, one of the best employees in the section. But recently, I have had nothing but problems.

She just seems to have a bad attitude. She will do what's required, but not a whole lot more. Some of the other employees are grumbling a little because she's not doing any extra work when things pile up. As a result, she doesn't seem to be getting along with them like she used to.

Several months ago, I was asked to take on the leadership job of our section. Betty Anne had been here about six months longer than I, but she had let everybody know that she didn't want to be a leader. I am almost certain that Betty Anne was asked if she wanted my new job, but I don't know for sure, as I haven't talked about it with my boss.

It has also been a problem for her to get to work since the organization moved from downtown to the West End. I suspect that childcare has been a problem for her.

Somebody must have said something about the situation to my boss, and now my boss wants me to appraise Betty Anne's performance and submit a plan of action. I'll bet her problem has something to do with arranging transportation for her children.

Write below what you think is the *one* most probable cause of Betty Anne's performance problem: Be very specific in your answer.

Circumstances outside the work place. Children + getting to work, both are influencing her work

Now consider that there are three basic categories of causes: 1) managerial and organizational shortcomings, 2) employee's personal factors, and 3) outside influences. For example, we could have identified any of the following as legitimate causes of Betty Anne's performance problem:

1. Managerial and Organizational Shortcomings:

> *"The new leader and/or management did not communicate appropriately with Betty Anne when the section's promotion was announced."*

2. Employee's Personal Factors:

> *"Betty Anne is not doing any extra work, which results in poor peer relationships."*

> *"Betty Anne really wanted the leader's job but chose not to be 'up front' about her needs."*

3. Outside Influences:

> *"The downtown move has resulted in child care/transportation problems for Betty Anne."*

In looking back at the most probable cause you identified in "The Case of the Enigmatic Employee," which cause did you select—and in which category does it fall? If you selected the *employee* as the primary cause of the problem, then you are not alone! At least 1000 leaders have read this case and 95% of them suggest causes—and resultant solutions—where the employee is the major cause of the problem, and the employee needs to change in some way. But this case was carefully crafted so that any of the three causes could be selected equally. Why is it then that the vast majority of leaders identify causes that are related to the employee?

Could it be that, when looking at employee problems, we tend to focus on the employee rather than on the organization or ourselves? Probably true! But if we don't look at *all* the possible causes objectively as possible, then we may do what Peter Drucker says is "taking the right action on the wrong problem—which is always a disaster."

On the following page is a list of causes, arranged by category, which was compiled by Lawrence L. Steinmetz. This list clearly shows the large number of possible causes of employee problems.

The Lawrence L. Steinmetz Probable Cause List

1. Managerial and Organizational Shortcomings

- Lack of Motivational Environment
  - No opportunities for advancement
  - No challenge in present job
  - Lack of knowledge of advancement possibilities
  - Not recognizing employee's changing needs
- Personality Problems
  - Personal clashes between the employee and his or her leader and/or coworker
  - Personal clashes with the "personality" of the organization itself
- Inappropriate Job Assignments
  - Employee doesn't know how to do the job
  - Employee feels it is necessary to take an undesirable job to avoid limiting his or her future chances
- Improper Leadership
  - Leader doesn't know how to lead
  - Leader knows how to lead, but doesn't
  - Leader doesn't have time to lead
- Lack of Training
- Failure to Establish Duties
  - Job tasks not communicated
  - Goals are not set with the employee
  - There are minimal performance expectations

2. Employee's Personal Factors

- Lack of Motivation in the Right Direction
- Limited Goals
- Problem Personality
- Dissatisfaction with Job Assignment
- Failure to Understand Duties
  - Didn't listen, didn't understand, or forgot
- Chronic Absenteeism
  - Alcoholism or other drug-related problems
  - Chronic illness (mental or physical)

3. Outside Influences:

- Family Problems
  - Sickness (physical and/or mental)
  - Death of family member
  - Separation and/or divorce
  - Children "acting out"
  - Spouse lost his or her job
- Social Morals (Conflicts: social values/organization values)
- Conditions of Labor Market

Consider that leading human resources theorists clearly state that the leader and/or the organization is often—note the word is *often*, not *sometimes* or *occasionally*—the cause of employee problems. For example, Douglas McGregor proposes that the leader's attitude drastically affects the employee's performance; Abraham Maslow believes that the leader is primarily responsible for creating an environment where the employee's higher-level needs can be met; and Frederick Herzberg points out that a leader's positive affirmation, or the lack thereof, highly affects an employee's morale and motivation.

The quality of the solution implemented to "fix" the employee's problem is directly dependent on the accuracy of the identified cause. Therefore, it is critical that we spend time thinking through probable causes, both in preparing for the counseling interview and in conducting the interview.

We explore probable causes by thinking through the situation in detail before meeting with the employee. We need to determine what facts we have, and what facts we need. We need to be clear about the specific questions we should ask during our discussion with the employee.

Look at past records. Is there an observable pattern? Has the problem always existed—or is it recent? Do we have enough information? Do we need to talk with others? What is the employee's record compared with others in our section? In the department? In the organization?

Questions like these may not always tell us with certainty what is causing the performance problem. But they will often give clues to the important questions to be asked during the meeting.

It is remarkable how often we think the cause of a performance problem is one thing and then find out during a counseling meeting that it is something else. The "problem" hasn't changed. We have! This is because new information from the employee can greatly alter our understanding of the problem.

Few things are more frustrating to an employee than to be told to "work harder" when the cause of a problem is something he or she can't control. We can learn much about what the real difficulty is by taking the time to explore the cause. Any solution that's going to work must be based on a sound grasp of this cause. Therefore, before the meeting we need to think through possible causes by asking ourselves the following questions:

- Is the employee aware of his or her below-standard performance?
- Does he or she know what is expected?
- Are there any factors this employee cannot control?
- Does he or she lack ability or knowledge?
- Is there a lack of motivation?

Thinking through probable causes before the meeting will give us a chance to get additional information if needed. But again, remember that these probable causes are only tentative—because our information is incomplete until we talk with the employee.

☑ **4. Developing tentative solutions**

The last step in our preparation is to develop a tentative "real world" solution for each of the most likely causes identified. To do this, we can seek out ideas from other respected leaders and brainstorm a list of solutions for each major cause. Then, when we evaluate the quality of the solutions, we discuss their positive values before we destroy them with sixty-nine reasons why they won't work. Finally, we need to select specific and practical *tentative* solutions for the key causes that we can implement or help implement.

Note here again, the solutions selected are *tentative*! We really don't know for sure what *the* best solution should be until we have had an opportunity to talk with the employee. On the other hand, we don't use the principle of employee involvement, i.e., asking the employee for his or her analysis of cause and suggested solutions, to abdicate our responsibility to think through possible causes and solutions. Both the leader *and* the employee need to spend time thinking about what should be done to improve the employee's performance in order to improve the quality of the final action taken.

In the next section, we will examine how we use the information gained from careful planning to conduct the counseling session with the employee.

Conducting the Counseling Interview

☑ **1. Describe the performance concern.**

An employee must be aware of what he or she is presently doing incorrectly before being expected to improve. In a few cases, of course, the employee may be unaware that his or her performance is poor. Chewing out an employee who honestly doesn't know a rule, regulation, or what is required doesn't make much sense. It would be more appropriate to chew ourselves out for doing a poor job of communicating or training in the first place.

When we discuss a situation with the employee, we describe performance—not the employee's personality. We need to stay away from statements like "You don't work fast enough" or "You have a bad attitude." "Fast enough" is not really specific, and "bad attitude" attacks the employee, rather than giving needed information about the performance.

Therefore, it is better to first say, "I'm very concerned about this situation," rather than "You have a problem." After all, if you are the leader, it's your problem too!

Then, we talk about performance, and in specific terms. For example, "I am concerned because the number of errors has increased 6% during the past month." Or "Today was the third time this week you were over five minutes late coming back from break."

Often this is not as easy as it sounds. We may know what is wrong, but find it difficult to express the "wrongness" in words. It's usually easier to make a general statement about "poor attitude" or "poor performance" than to be specific.

We need to stop and ask ourselves questions such as "Why do I think this employee has a bad attitude? What has he or she said or done that makes me feel this way?"

Questions like these lead to understanding employee behavior. Behavior is what an employee says or does. If we can define the behavior specifically, we have gone a long way toward solving the performance problem. But this means we must do our homework by giving the performance problem sufficient thought before meeting with the employee.

2. State the expected standard of performance.

In Step 1, we describe specifically the actual performance. Then, by telling the employee exactly what we expect in Step 2, we have clearly defined the *performance gap*.

Here, as before, being specific is the goal. We should avoid statements like "I expect better performance," "You really need to work harder," and "You ought to change your attitude."

"I expect better performance," for instance, is a wishy-washy expression that avoids the "How much is better?" question. "Work harder" and "change your attitude" are not only nonspecific statements, they are also solutions that ignore possible causes.

"What do I expect from this employee?" is the question that needs to be considered carefully before the meeting. Examples of clear performance expectations are:

> *"Under standard operating conditions, the maximum error rate allowed is zero."*
>
> *"Breaks are ten minutes long."*
>
> *"Horseplay of any kind is not allowed."*
>
> *"All employees are due at work before 8:00 a.m."*

3. Explain why the standard is important.

"Because it's organization policy" is not a very good justification for a performance standard, at least not from the employee's point of view. It's all right to indicate that something is organizational policy; but then we go on to give the rationale behind the policy. Most policies exist for good reasons. (If we don't know the reasons, we need to find out before the meeting!)

So consider the regulation or policy from the employee's perspective. Why should the employee arrive at work on time? Why should he or she want to keep the work area clean? Why is it important for the employee to get back on time from breaks? Why is it critical that employees earn a return on the organization's investment in salary and benefits?

Chances are that our reasons for concern about the employee's performance (increased production, looking good to my boss, a better raise for me in the future, etc.) are not the same as the employee's. His or her motivation might be concern about losing a job and/or wages; pressure from fellow workers; disciplinary action; or lack of recognition from you, the boss.

Our objective is to foster an internal desire within the employee to improve his or her performance. We can, of course, impose external force to require him or her to change (tell him or her that he or she *will* change). In some cases this may be necessary. But far better results come when the employee decides to improve his or her performance because of a clearly perceived reason.

☑ 4. Express our concern.

Next, we need to express our expectation that the employee's performance will change. It is important that we tell employees that we, personally, are greatly concerned about their poor performance. After all, we are their leaders. If employees feel that substandard performance is "no big deal" to management, they probably won't take the situation very seriously.

In the press of our duties as leaders, we often don't take the time to spell out how we feel. Thus, the employee may not really perceive our concern.

But poor performance is serious, and in this step we should say so clearly. For example, we could say, "I'm deeply concerned about performance. It's important to the organization, it's important to me, and it's important to you!"

☑ 5. Determine the cause of the situation.

A basic law of troubleshooting is "Don't do anything until you have identified the probable cause of the problem!" This is also sound advice for performance problems.

Remember that our goal is to help the employee discover the cause of the problem during the interview. We can greatly help the employee understand the problem by asking questions to explore possible causes.

During the meeting, we try to ask *open* questions. Open questions begin with the key words "Who," "What," "Where," "When," "How," and "Why." Open questions draw out more information than "closed" questions do. Closed questions begin with "Do you . . .?" "Have you . . .?" and "Did you . . .?" and are usually answered with a "Yes" or "No." For example, the question, "What relationship do you see between absenteeism and performance?" is likely to obtain much more information than "Do you see any relationship between absenteeism and your performance?" Though they seem to be the same question, the first one will tend to elicit the desired information, while the second will probably get only a less helpful "yes" or "no" response. We need information to determine causes—and open questions are best for getting it!

To help the employee look at all sides of a problem, we can also ask, "What other things might be causing this situation?" Solutions (the next step) only work if they're aimed at the right cause. That's why we need to spend some quality time on this step. The cause of the problem must be accurately identified before we will have any chance of really correcting the performance problem.

☑ 6. Ask for solutions.

There are several reasons why it's important to ask for the employee's solution to the problem.

- The employee might think of a solution that we have not considered that's even better than ours.

- The employee is more likely to change behavior when the solution comes from him or her.

- The employee will see that we are really concerned about him or her. This will result in greater trust and better future relations.

Asking for the employee's solution is difficult for many leaders. We were probably promoted to leadership because we were good at solving problems. Naturally, we often have some strong ideas about what an employee should do in order to improve. But we nonetheless need to hold onto our solution while we first ask the employee for his or hers.

Note also that if we begin by stating our solution, we are likely to initiate the "Yes, but . . ." game! A "Yes, but" game opens with the leader telling an employee what he or she should do to improve performance. The employee then replies, "Yes, but . . ."—and gives the leader a number of reasons why the solution will not work. But few people "Yes, but" their own ideas. That's why if we can get the employee to suggest a solution to the problem, we stand a better chance of seeing real change.

Furthermore, although one person may be able to develop several solutions to a problem, two people can often come up with many more. This is because one person's ideas trigger new thoughts in the other. Thus, when we have two people "bouncing ideas off each other," we greatly increase the chances of reaching a good solution.

We need to remember that what is important is not so much what the employee says at the meeting, but what he or she does after the meeting to improve performance. The employee who suggests the solution or is a part of the solution plan is more likely to view the idea as workable and accept the responsibility to make sure that the solution is implemented on the job. So we ask questions in the meeting such as "What do you think we should do about this situation?" or "What other things could we do?"

A final suggestion: It's sometimes easier to change the environment around a problem than it is to change the employee. For example, if the employee has a "trashy" work area, it may be better to fix the problem by putting a trash can closer to the employee's area!

 7. Discuss each solution and offer assistance.

If the employee offers general solutions like "I guess I'll just have to try harder," request that he or she be more specific. Ask "How are you going to do that?" or "What are you going to do to improve your performance?" Instead of accepting "I'll try to improve my performance," inquire "How much can you improve?" The more specific the improvement target or goal, the better the employee's chances of producing real results.

Now is the time to offer our ideas if appropriate. This can be done two ways. We might make suggestions to improve the quality of his or her solution. Or even better, we can ask "How to" questions to help enhance the employee's solution—like, "What would that accomplish?" "How do you see this being done?" or "What can you do to help make that happen?" Such questions will lead the employee to improve the quality of his or her solution. Our job in this step is to help the employee develop a specific solution by asking key questions and then offering our assistance.

Few employee ideas are perfect. On the other hand, completely useless solutions are also rare. Most ideas and solutions fall somewhere between perfection and "zero."

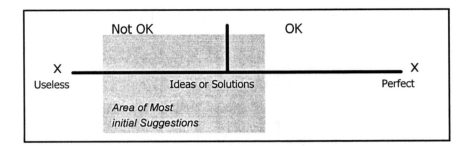

An effective leader recognizes the above situation and focuses the discussion upon the positive value of the employee's suggestion and refrains from immediately emphasizing what's wrong with a solution. First, the leader asks questions and discusses the positive points about the employee's idea. Then, the leader can make suggestions that might improve the employee's solution.

☑ **8. Agree on specific action for follow-up.**

Action summaries at the conclusion of the meeting will help produce commitment and will reduce the possibility of later misunderstanding. An action summary makes clear the leader's future expectations by communicating to the employee the specific action that is to be taken. It's called "ensuring follow up"!

Some leaders make notes on their calendar—in the presence of the employee—showing a follow-up date and the improvement expected. Other leaders have the employee write out a short summary of what he or she will accomplish during the improvement period, with both parties keeping a copy. Whatever method we use, we do need to make a summary—and follow-up!

⌘ ⌘ ⌘ ⌘ ⌘ ⌘ ⌘ ⌘ ⌘ ⌘ ⌘ ⌘ ⌘ ⌘ ⌘ ⌘ ⌘ ⌘ ⌘ ⌘

On the following pages is a "Leader's Checklist" that will help you plan and conduct your next employee performance counseling interview.

Performance Counseling Interview
Leader's Checklist

In reviewing the following checklist, plan what you will say at each step. The examples given are only those—illustrative examples!

☑ 1. Describe the performance concern.

- Do your homework; get the facts.
- Use the "We" technique.
  "We have a situation that concerns me."
- Be specific. Ask yourself, "What has the employee done or not done, said or not said, that makes me believe he or she is performing poorly?" For example:
  "Today was the third time this week that you were over five minutes late coming back from lunch."
- Describe the poor performance; do not attack the employee. Examples:

  - *"The number of errors has increased 6% during the past month."*

  - *"The records show there have been ten days of absenteeism during the past three months."*

  - *"The area around your work station has material spilled on the floor."*

☑ 2. State the expected standard of performance.

- Tell the employee exactly what is expected. For example:

  - *"Under standard operating conditions, the maximum allowed error rate is 1 error per 1000."*

  - *"Breaks are ten minutes."*

  - *"Material should not be on the floor."*

  - *"Horseplay of any kind is not allowed."*

☑ **3. Explain why the standard is important.**

- Provide the reasons behind a policy, regulation, or performance standard.
- Provide "employee" reasons, if possible. Identify reasons that relate to the employee's personal interest. For example:

  - *"This much absenteeism causes a real hardship for the rest of the people in your section."*

  - *"The policy of 'no horseplay' is for your protection. It could prevent you from having an accident that might cripple you for the rest of your life."*

  - *"We must meet performance standards so that the organization will continue to stay in business, and you will continue to have a job."*

☑ **4. Express your concern.**

Examples:
  - *"I am—and always will be—deeply concerned about performance. It's important to the organization, it's important to me, and it's important to you."*

  - *"To me, excellence is a way of life. The organization believes in it; and my employees must not only believe in excellence, but practice it!"*

☑ **5. Determine the cause of the situation.**

- Before and during the meeting, ask yourself:
  - *"How does this employee's record compare with the records of others in the section or department?"*

  - *"Are there any observable patterns in this employee's poor performance?"* (For example, Mondays or Fridays? Holidays? A particular time of year?)

  - *"How long has this problem existed?"*

  - *"When did it start?"*

  - *"Where is the problem occurring?"*

  - *"When and where doesn't this employee have the problem?"*

  - *"Have any changes occurred that might have caused the problem?"*

  - *"Are there any other symptoms of this problem?"*

- Ask the employee:

    - *"What do you feel is causing this situation?"*

    - *"What other major reasons do you see?"*

    - *"What are the things that interfere with your performance?"*

☑ 6. Ask for solutions.

Examples:

- *"What are your ideas about this situation?"*

- *"What suggestions do you have for increasing your performance?"*

- *"What can you do to resolve this situation?"*

- *"What else could you do?"*

☑ 7. Discuss each solution, and offer assistance.

- Focus on specific solutions, not general ones.

    - *"What would that accomplish?"*

    - *"How do you see this being done?"*

    - *"What can you do to help make that happen?"*

    - *"What can be done to make this work?"*

    - *"Do you see any problems that might occur in carrying that out?"*

- Offer your assistance.

    - *"How can I help?"*

☑ 8. Agree on specific action for follow-up.

For example:

> *"This has been a good discussion. I appreciate your ideas and solutions. We have agreed that you will . . . and I will . . . (summarize the solution). Is that correct? Good. We'll get together in 2 weeks* (making a note of the date and time on your calendar) *and discuss your progress. I feel good about your commitment to improve and I know you can do it."*

Counseling Planning Sheet
ON-THE-JOB APPLICATION

Use this worksheet to write out what you will say when you need to conduct a counseling interview on the job.

☑ 1. **Describe the performance concern.**

_____
_____
_____
_____

☑ 2. **State the expected standard of performance.**

_____
_____
_____

☑ 3. **Explain why the standard is important.**

_____
_____

☑ 4. **Express your concern.**

_____
_____

☑ 5. **Determine the cause of the situation.**

_____
_____

☑ 6. **Ask for solutions.**

_____
_____

☑ 7. **Discuss each solution and offer assistance.**

_____
_____
_____

☑ 8. **Agree on specific action for follow-up.**

_____
_____
_____

Counseling Follow Up

ON-THE-JOB APPLICATION
Page 1 of 2

Immediately after the employee leaves your office area, fill out this form. Then meet with your leader and discuss the results.

☑ 1. Describe the performance concern.

How well did I describe the employee's situation?

_____

_____

Did the employee get defensive? _____   If yes, why?

_____

_____

☑ 2. State the expected standard of performance.

How well was I able to describe the expected standard of performance?

_____

_____

☑ 3. Explain why the standard is important.

What reasons did I give?

_____

_____

Were these employee reasons or my reasons?

_____

What, if anything, could I have done or said that would have been more effective?

_____

_____

☑ 4. Express your concern.

What did I say?

_____

_____

☑ 5. Determine the cause of the situation.

What questions did I ask?

_____

_____

Did I get to the root cause of the situation? _____
If not, what do I think is the real cause?

_____

_____

Counseling Follow Up

ON-THE-JOB APPLICATION
Page 2 of 2

☑ 6. Ask for solutions.

What solutions did he or she suggest?

_____

_____

How successful was I in getting the employee to do most of the talking?

_____

_____

☑ 7. Discuss each solution and offer assistance.

How specific did we get in the final solution?

_____

_____

What assistance did I offer?

_____

_____

☑ 8. Agree on specific action for follow-up.

What was my action summary?

_____

_____

General Discussion Questions

A. How do I feel about the interview?

_____

_____

B. How do I think the employee feels as a result of the interview?

_____

_____

C. What do I think are the chances for success?

_____

_____

D. What else can I do?

_____

_____

_____

Leadership
Handling Employee Complaints

It's no accident that your maker created you with two ears—and only one mouth!

Unknown

When an employee storms into our office or area furious about something we did, it is hard to remain calm. And when an employee is upset, unhappy, or angry about something, it is easy for him or her to use language normally considered inappropriate. At this point, some leaders assert their authority and chew out the employee for being "disrespectful." But look at the cost of this approach.

An employee who leaves a confrontation with a chip on his or her shoulder can create ill will among other employees, negatively affect morale and efficiency–and may be a potential safety problem "looking for a place to happen"!

The best way to handle this kind of situation is to deal immediately with the employee's feelings. Before taking action on the situation he or she is upset about, take action that considers his or her emotions. Take the right kind of action–action that produces positive results.

Here is a method that works:

 1. Listen! Listen! Listen!

Real listening is hard work! If someone else is angry, it's difficult to keep from taking it personally and becoming angry ourselves. We may think we already know what the employee should do. And this makes it doubly difficult to keep from jumping in, cutting him or her off, and telling the employee what we think or feel.

But if we hold our tongues and listen, without interrupting, we can

- A. Learn more about the situation
- B. Demonstrate to the employee that we really care about him or her
- C. Give ourselves more time to think about how the situation can best be handled
- D. Give the employee an opportunity to express his or her feelings, thus reducing the emotional level

As we listen, we need to stop doing whatever it was we were doing, make good eye contact, nod our head appropriately, and respond with, "I see" or "Uh-huh." Encourage the employee to continue to talk as long as is necessary to "ventilate" his or her feelings.

2. Summarize what we think we heard.

In this step, we repeat to the employee, in our own words, what we think we heard and then ask whether what we heard was correct. This accomplishes three things:

A. Ensures that what we thought we heard was what was really said
B. Shows the employee that we do care about him or her
C. Lets the employee know we really do understand what he or she is upset about

For example, if an employee bursts into my office and starts shouting about a new job assignment, I need to listen first. Then, when the employee has finished talking, I simply repeat what I think I heard—in my own words. For example, I might say, "Let me see if I understand. You're upset because you were assigned to another location when you were prepared to go to your regular workplace. Is that correct?"

But this is not as easy as it might seem. It's sometimes hard to listen to even one or two minutes of emotional statements without interrupting. It's even harder to remember all that was said. But this practice forces us to listen, because we know that we will have to sum up and repeat what we just heard. And when we summarize, we show the employee that we listened, that we understood, and—most important—that we do care about him or her!

 3. Acknowledge the employee's feelings.

Acknowledging the employee's feelings by saying "I understand how you feel," lets the employee know that we care about the way he or she feels. It is not agreement, but understanding. We're not saying, "Yes, you should be mad," but rather that we respect his or her right to have such feelings.

Now before moving on to the next step, please read the following case, and then write your answer to the question that appears after the case.

The Case of the Wrathful Worker

Jodi, the section's supervisor, leaned back in her chair, looked out the window, and thought about her day. It had not been good. It seemed like everyone wanted a piece of her time. "Jodi, would you be willing to help me design this report?" "Jodi, I can't get my computer to save this document. What do I do?" Jodi do this, Jodi do that. She sighed as she considered all of her own work she had yet to do because she had spent time helping others.

Suddenly, she became aware of an angry tone of voice in the hallway. As she looked up, one of her employees, Bill, stormed into her office. She knew that her day was not going to get any better!

"Somebody opened a personal letter that was addressed to me!" shouted Bill as he waved a letter at her. "Nobody, but nobody has the right to open and read my personal mail! If a letter is addressed to me, then I am the only one who has the right to open it."

"Well," Jodi replied, "I can see that you're really angry that your private mail was read. I would be angry too if someone had read my personal mail. But in this case, it was probably just opened by mistake in the mail room."

"Then somebody needs to raise hell with those jerks in the mailroom," Bill replied angrily.

"I'll tell you what," Jodi said, "I will make a point to talk to the mailroom supervisor and ask her about it." Jodi reached for her notepad and asked, "Who was the letter from?"

Bill looked embarrassed as he said, "Well, uh, it's a final late notice from the finance company about my car payment. I don't know why they sent it to me at work, but in any case, it should have never been opened."

"You're right," Jodi said, "It should *not* have been opened! I'll talk to the mailroom supervisor and make sure that it doesn't happen again."

"Thanks, Jodi," Bill replied. "It's downright embarrassing for this to be read by others. Let me know what you find out."

"OK, Bill," she said. "I will make sure that it doesn't happen again."

As Bill left, Jodi could hear him muttering about those incompetent, brain-dead people in the mailroom.

Please answer the following question:

What action should Jodi take now?

<u>To talk to the mailroom Supervisor.</u>

After you have written the action Jodi should take, please read the "rest of the story" on the next page.

The Case of the Wrathful Worker
Part II

Jodi sighed as Bill left her office. "Oh well," she thought, "what's one more thing in an otherwise lousy day?" She left her office, took the elevator down to the mailroom, walked in, and asked for Betty, the supervisor. "She's on break," one of the clerks said.

Jodi took the elevator back up to the third floor and looked in the break room. Spotting Betty at one of the tables with a group of other supervisors, Jodi walked over and asked, "Betty, can I see you for a minute?"

"Sure," Betty replied as she got up from the table, "I'm finished."

The two women walked over to the corner of the room where Jodi told her about what had happened with Bill.

"I remember that letter," Betty exclaimed. "It was *not* actually addressed to him. It was supposed to go to the accounts payable department. They sent it back to me after they opened it, and I sent it on to Bill."

"I'm confused," replied Jodi, "Who was it addressed to?"

Betty rubbed her chin, "Well, if I remember correctly, it was a little confusing. I *do* know that it was addressed to the accounts payable department, but referenced Bill's name on the envelope. Evidently they opened it, saw that it was actually supposed to go to him, and sent it back through interoffice mail. But we definitely don't open anyone's personal mail! It irritates me that someone would think we did!"

Jodi looked at her watch. "OK, sorry to have bothered you about it. Let me go back and talk to Bill and find out what happened."

Jodi took the elevator back up to her area, walked over to Bill's desk, and asked, "Bill, can I see the envelope of that letter?"

"Sure," he replied. He opened one of his desk drawers and handed her the letter.

She looked at the address. It stated:

Reference: Mr. Bill Williams
Accounts Payable
The Sorata Organization
Box 299012
Richmond, VA 23235-9012

"Bill," Jodi exclaimed, "I've wasted almost forty-five minutes complaining to the mailroom about a letter that was obviously addressed incorrectly. Look at this address," she said exasperatedly, "It was sent to you at your work address and was supposed to say 'Mr. Bill Williams, Reference Accounts Payable.'"

"Oh," replied Bill sheepishly. "Sorry I put you to so much trouble."

What should Jodi have done before she went to the mailroom?

The purpose of this exercise was to allow you to experience for yourself the need to determine the *cause* of a particular problem before jumping to some sort of action.

☑ 4. Ask diagnostic questions.

An effective leader is also a good troubleshooter. And good troubleshooters ask questions to diagnose the cause of a problem.

In some cases we may already know the full details of the situation. In other cases, the employee may not know that we know. Thus asking questions at this point may not only provide us with some additional information, but the employee will also know that we really do understand the situation.

When we ask the employee for additional information, we should ask *open* questions that begin with the words, "Who," "What," "Where," "When," "How," and "Why."

Open questions can give us more information for diagnosing the situation. And asking open questions not only gives us additional facts and communicates to the employee that we really do understand the situation, they also help the employee to better understand the problem.

☑ 5. Ask for the employee's suggestions.

By this time, we probably feel we have a good idea of what should be done to remedy the employee's situation. And that's what makes this step so difficult! It is hard not to jump in with our solution! But it is a great deal better, in the long run, if we can get the employee to tell us what should be done. Employees are usually more open to their own ideas than to ours. And if the employee's solution is in line with ours, why not let him or her suggest it? In fact, leaders who use this technique say that many times the employee's idea or solution turns out to be better than their own.

☑ **6. Present our position.**

If we agree with the employee's idea or solution to the problem, we need to say so. If we don't, we should clearly state our position, and give the reason(s) why. But, we need to stay away from the "It's organizational policy" kind of answer. Most policies exist for a reason. Employees respond better if we give common-sense reasons for our position.

☑ **7. Decide on specific follow-up action.**

At this point, the leader should summarize the discussion, and agree on the action that will be taken. This helps to prevent later misunderstandings by making sure the leader and the employee agree on what will happen after the discussion.

☑ **8. Thank the employee.**

Thank the employee? Thank an employee who barged into our office and raised his or her voice? Yes!

For it's far better that the employee talked to us than not. Angry or upset employees are poor workers. They can cause reduced production and create lower morale. Thanking the employee for coming to see us helps to

A. Ensure that he or she feels free to see us again
B. Improve our image as a leader who cares about our employees
C. End the meeting on a positive, morale-building note

This eight-step method for handling complaints comes from the experience of leaders who care about their employees—leaders whose main responsibility is to get the job done through others. It's from leaders who know that organizations don't run by themselves—they need employees. Using this method will help you be a better leader, not just a "boss."

Handling Complaints
Leader's Checklist

☑ **1. Listen! Listen! Listen!**
- Focus attention on the employee.
- Nod your head to show understanding.
- Say *"Yes," "I see,"* or *"Uh-huh"* as the employee talks.

☑ **2. Summarize what we think we heard.**
"Let me see if I understand. You are upset because . . . ."
Repeat in your own words what you heard. Then ask, *"Is that correct?"*

☑ **3. Acknowledge the employee's feelings.**
"I understand how you feel."
"I can appreciate your concern."

☑ **4. Ask diagnostic questions.**
"Who is—and isn't—involved?"
"What has occurred?"
"Where is the problem occurring?"
"Where is the problem not occurring?"
"When did it start?"
"When was everything OK?"
"Why do you think it happened?"

☑ **5. Ask for the employee's suggestions.**
"What do you think we should do about the situation?"
"What other suggestions do you have?"

☑ **6. Present our position.**
If the employee's suggestion in Step 5 is acceptable, say,
"That sounds like a good idea." If the suggestion does not seem appropriate,
present your position. *"I'm sorry; I really wish we could do that. But we
can't, because . . ..*
What I suggest we do is . . .."

☑ **7. Decide on specific follow up.**
"Now let's see. I will . . .. And you will . . .. Do we agree?"

☑ **8. Thank the employee.**
*"I really appreciate your coming to me with your concerns. And if you have
any other questions about this, please feel free to talk with me about them."*

ON-THE-JOB APPLICATION

☑ **1. Listen! Listen! Listen!**
How well did I listen to the employee?

_____

☑ **2. Summarize what we think we heard.**
A. What was the employee's original complaint?

_____

B. How accurate was my summary?

_____

☑ **3. Acknowledge feelings.**
What did I say to show empathy for the employee's feelings?

_____

_____

☑ **4. Ask diagnostic questions.**
What (if any) questions did I ask?

_____

_____

☑ **5. Ask for his or her suggestions.**
What ideas did he or she have?

_____

_____

☑ **6. Present your position.**
A. If the employee's suggestion was OK, what did I say?

_____

B. If the employee's suggestion was not OK, how did I handle it?

_____

_____

☑ **7. Decide on specific follow-up action.**
What follow-up action was agreed to?

_____

_____

☑ **8. Thank employee.**
What did I say?

_____

_____

The Processes of Leadership

9

Leadership Delegation

Moreover, thou shalt provide out of all the people able men, such as fear god, men of trust, hating covetousness; and place such over them, to be rulers of thousands, and rulers of hundreds, rulers of fifties, and rulers of tens: And let them judge the people at all seasons: and it shall be, that every great matter they shall bring unto thee, but every small matter they shall judge; so shall it be easier for thyself, and they shall bear the burden with thee. If thou shalt do this thing, and God command thee so, then thou shalt be able to endure.

Exodus 18: 21 – 23
King James Version

OK, it's quiz time! See how many of the following questions you answer with a "yes." Do you . . .

1. Take work home at least once a week?

2. Often feel overworked and overstressed because you have too much to do?

3. Keep missing your important deadlines?

4. Have to deal with constant, recurring crises?

5. Find you don't have time for important issues such as long-range planning?

6. Spend significant time putting Band-Aids® on symptoms of problems, rather than fixing the problems themselves?

7. Think that if you don't do it, it won't get done?

8. Enjoy doing things for others, especially your employees?

If you answered "yes" to one or more of these questions, you may have a problem, possibly a very serious problem. A problem that could kill you—figuratively and literally!

Not being able to delegate is a killer. The stress from it can stop your heart! And even if you survive the stress, it can kill your chances of ever being considered suitable for more responsibility.

It's an organizational reality that the more responsibility we are given as we move up the promotional ladder, the more we must delegate. In fact, a promotion is a formalized, ritualistic way that organizations take all of our work and delegate it to someone else. So if we can't delegate, our chances of being promoted are slim.

Of course there are some tasks that can't be delegated. For example, it's tough to delegate a task that can't be taught, or leadership aspects of our jobs that only we can do, or a task that has an unacceptable risk of failure. But in most cases, we not only can delegate—we *should* delegate.

Reasons for Not Delegating

Unfortunately, there are lots of reasons why leaders don't delegate. Some are good reasons, and some are not good. When we group them, there are personal reasons, task reasons, staff reasons, and organizational reasons. So let's examine some of the common reasons why leaders who ought to know better don't delegate when they should.

Personal Reasons for Not Delegating

"I can do it better myself." No doubt! If we have always done the task, then obviously we are probably able to do it better than an employee who has never done it. So what do we do? Keep taking on more work as we become evermore experienced on the job, or as our boss delegates more and more to us? Somewhere along the line, we will *have* to delegate—we will have no choice. At this point, we must assign some of our work to others and teach them how to do it—or collapse.

"I don't trust my people." If this is our reason, we had better back up and ask "Why?" Why don't we trust them? If the answer points to a psychological problem—like an inability to trust anybody—then we should seek professional help. But if the answer is simply that our people are new or inexperienced, then the solution is clear—and with time the problem will resolve itself. Employees grow with experience. So we can best help them grow by providing them with ongoing training. We can delegate small tasks to them and then offer appropriate training and follow-up. We can reward them for good performance—and then give them slightly larger tasks to do. It's called "developing subordinates." And it is a big part of our job as a leader.

"I like doing it." Now here's an honest reason! When I was a kid growing up in the mountains of Virginia, I never got any mail. So as an adult there is still this little mail-deprived kid inside of me that wants to get mail. And guess who opened all of the mail that came into my old office? You're right—me! We had extremely competent employees who could be opening and routing the mail. In fact, some of them could likely do it better than I did. But I liked opening the mail. It was the highlight of my day. So I sacrificed about thirty valuable minutes daily because I was unwilling to delegate this job to the people who should have been doing it.

If you are laughing at my stupidity, think about the things in your job that you do just because you like doing them. What are those tasks that you like to perform so that you can have the satisfaction of scratching them off your "to-do" list? These are the little things that feel good to do, but eat up our time. When you have identified some of them, figure out the cost of not delegating them to others.

"My subordinate might take over my job." This reason for not delegating is frequently listed in books on delegation—though it is difficult for me to imagine that leaders actually worry about losing their jobs to subordinates because they delegated work. If delegation is a necessary part of leadership, we are really failing in our job if we *do not* develop your employees by delegating appropriate tasks. Also, how are we ever going to get promoted if we 1) can't delegate, and 2) don't train our replacements? It is the leader who doesn't delegate that should worry about a subordinate taking over his or her job!

"I won't get credit for doing the job." I used to produce all the videotapes for my old organization. You know, I was the big-time producer. I wrote the scripts, hired the actors, and directed the productions. Real exciting. Action! Take One! And when the videotape is played, it reads, "Directed by Dick Leatherman." Nice. Good for the old ego! If you've already read the "Motivation" chapter, you know that I like recognition for my accomplishments.

But as the organization grew, new things needed to be done, such as long-range planning, and managing a team of employees. So I gave up the excitement of being the producer. My name was no longer on the videotapes. I felt some loss over not being recognized. But my staff's videos were better. And the quality of my work became better, because I had more time to devote to the tasks that really mattered for our organization.

"If I delegate to others, I give up my power." We need to recognize that this reason is mostly "bunk." In forty years in the business world, I have never seen a leader lose power because he or she delegated properly. (I have seen some so-called leaders that actually lost power, or were demoted or even fired, because they *didn't* delegate.) You may know of a leader, somewhere, who lost power because he or she delegated tasks to a subordinate. But ninety-nine percent of the time, when we delegate, we don't lose power—we gain it. The more we appropriately delegate, the more work can and will be done by our section or department, and the more time we will have to devote to other, more important tasks. And the more quality work that gets done the more real power we have. In fact, we will be well on our way to becoming irreplaceable to the organization—and promotable!

"I'll lose control if I delegate. When I'm in control, I feel safer." This reason for not delegating is true—but only when the leader mishandles the delegation process through ignorance of how to do it. That's why I've used the term "appropriate delegation" so far in this chapter. Presently, you'll see a step-by-step process that will help you delegate tasks effectively without losing control.

"I'm a perfectionist and I know that my employees can never do it to my satisfaction." If this is the real reason for not delegating, we need help that this chapter can't give us. Leaders who are perfectionists to the point of not being able to delegate are doomed to a lifetime of miserable, mediocre leadership. If in fact we don't delegate because we can't stand to see our employees make mistakes as they learn, we are back again to the need for professional help. Perfectionist tendencies will not only drive others crazy, they can also destroy us.

When I see a perfectionist, I see a frightened person desperately trying to maintain security by keeping tight control of everything—and ultimately failing. But with help, a perfectionist can figure out why he or she is so afraid, what or who caused the fear, and begin to move to a new paradigm for living. It's not easy. But it can be done. And when this happens, life becomes a lot easier for everyone, especially for the leader.

Task Reasons for Not Delegating

Task reasons for not delegating have to do with the assignment itself. Let's look at some of them.

"It takes too long to train someone else to do it." Sure, it does take time to train employees to do delegated tasks. But look at it as a return-on-investment decision. If the benefits we gain by delegating a specific task exceed the cost of delegating—then delegate.

Certainly we will need to weigh the factors that affect our decision to delegate. For example, how long will it take us to train this particular employee to do this task? Is this the right employee to do the task? Will taking on this responsibility enhance the employee's morale? And of course, how much time will it save us that can be devoted to more important tasks?

"I really don't have the time to delegate." If this is true, and it might be, we are probably in this situation because we didn't delegate as we should have in the past. But it is almost never too late to start. We can look at our job. We can select a task to delegate that won't take huge amounts of our time in employee training. Then, we can take the time to delegate the task. Next, with the time we have saved through delegating this task, we select another task to delegate—one that has a greater payoff for us, even though it will take time initially to train the employee. And we can enjoy the payoff! Busy, "pressed and stressed" leaders will never experience the great benefits of delegation until they make it happen.

"The task cannot be delegated." There are tasks that can't be delegated. Tasks concerning our leadership responsibilities are usually ones that we will have to do ourselves. For instance, we will probably not be able to delegate the task of conducting a counseling session with an employee who has an attendance

problem. Also, it's part of our job to provide positive feedback to our employees on an ongoing basis.

On the other hand, you might be surprised at some of the things we can delegate. For example, in some organizations today, new employees are hired by a team of other employees rather than by the leader. Other organizations are having their employees' performance appraisals conducted by a group of peers instead of the leader. At the least, we can share the performance appraisal responsibility with the employee by asking him or her to fill out the appraisal form in advance, and to come prepared to do most of the talking in the interview. Or if we are hiring someone for the section or the department, it makes good sense to include in the interview and selection process some of the key people who will be working with this individual.

Generally speaking, there is not much that we can't delegate. Many of our interactions with our boss, or our boss's boss, can be delegated to our subordinates for their growth, development, and increased motivation. Special reports, budgets, trips, visits to clients, and professional shows can appropriately be delegated. In fact, we would be hard-pressed to identify any task in which part of it can't be delegated. And at the least, someone else could look at the task to see how it might be delegated either entirely or in part. We sometimes have trouble seeing the "parts and pieces" of our jobs in terms of tasks that could easily be delegated. And we tend not to because we don't *want* to!

Staff Reasons for Not Delegating

Another reason we don't delegate has to do with our perception of the people to whom we would be delegating. I call them "staff reasons." Let's look at some of the important ones.

"My people are too inexperienced." In some cases, this is a legitimate reason. There may well be situations where our staff really is too inexperienced to be given additional responsibility at that moment. The solution here is obvious—train, and then delegate.

"My employees lack confidence in themselves." Uh, oh! This statement tells more about us as leaders than it does about our employees. I would not want to give this reason to my upper management, they will wonder how I 1) got my job and 2) kept my job! If I said, "I've got an employee who lacks confidence," then the cause of the problem might not be me. But if I believe that all of my people are lacking confidence, I do have a severe problem—and that problem is me!

There are a couple of ways to look at this situation. If we think that our people don't have adequate confidence, then we will tend not to delegate additional responsibilities. And guess what? They will not develop confidence in themselves. Or if we have trouble delegating and then tolerating less than perfect results, we may have a tendency to jump in and save the day by doing the delegated task ourselves. About the second time we do this, we will be convinced that 1) the employee can't do the job, and 2) we may as well not delegate anymore tasks to him or her. Both of these problems—not delegating when we should and performing delegated tasks when we shouldn't—are symptoms of lack of trust in our employees, a key problem already mentioned.

"No one reports to me, so it's kind of hard to delegate." This is another one of those reasons that sounds legitimate but isn't. For even if we don't have direct reports, we can still delegate a great deal. Think about the people you work with in your section or department, and the ways in which your job and its tasks overlap their jobs and tasks. Next, imagine who would perform your work if you were no longer employed in your organization, and weren't replaced? This exercise suggests that there are people around you who can do at least some of what you do, and also what tasks might be delegated first. So if you are overwhelmed with work, the chances are good that you can ask for help from your coworkers—and get it.

We can even practice "reverse delegation" if absolutely necessary. That's when we ask our leader to give us a hand with a specific job task. Leaders are usually happy to help out on a temporary basis (sometimes only too glad, for the reasons already mentioned!)

"I don't have anyone else who can do it." If the meaning of this statement is that everyone truly is that overworked, then there may be validity to it (but see the next paragraph). Or if the task is such that no one is actually capable of doing it, and that would be a very unusual task, then we would be justified for the time being in not delegating. But if this statement actually means that we don't *think* we have anyone capable of doing the task, we need to read again what has been said concerning the leader's trust, and employee lack of confidence.

"My people are already overworked and don't have time to do additional work." As just indicated, if this is true, it is a genuine problem, and one that we are going to have to resolve creatively. So, we need to think about how our people got to be overworked. Did a budget crunch cause the organization not to replace those that were promoted, quit, retired, or died? Has our organization grown faster than the number of employees available to handle the work? Has the work changed so as to require more people? Are other departments or sections dumping more work on our employees? Are our people using antiquated methods of doing their jobs? Could they be more effective? Could the work be reorganized so that they would be less overworked?

Have we spent time analyzing the causes of the overload and creating solutions to resolve them? To handle this kind of situation we must spend *quality* time doing some heavy-duty thinking about the problem. We need to generate a list of possible causes of the "overwork," and then create specific solutions for the most probable causes.

One thing is certain, the problem is not going to go away. It is only going to get worse! And the problem will probably not be entirely fixed simply by hiring more people, even if we have the money to do so. But fortunately, a full analysis of the causes of the problem will normally suggest workable solutions.

The bottom line is twofold, we *can* do something to resolve problems of overwork, and then begin to delegate. And whatever needs to happen won't occur until we take the initiative and make it happen!

"If I give my employees more responsibility, they'll ask for more money. And more money isn't available." This reasoning is, to speak plainly, hogwash—and as you can see, I don't have much patience when I hear it! If a leader believes this idea, then he or she needs to reexamine his or her personal values, as well as his or her perception of others. Let's take an example. Think of the people who have joined the Peace Corps. As a rule, these individuals have made little or no money, toiling in places that we probably wouldn't want to go, under marginal living conditions, and likely working a lot more hours than we work. Do they ask for more money? And what about teachers, priests, ministers, and rabbis? Why do they stay in jobs in which many are typically underpaid and overworked? Because they like what they do.

Now consider our employees. If we enrich their jobs by delegating more responsibility, they will find more joy in their work. And when their work is stimulating, they normally will not go around grumbling and complaining about money. Not that we all don't need money to pay the bills. But when employees earn a fair income, more money is as much as anything a form of recognition. Delegation is equally a form of recognition. When we delegate, in effect we are telling our employees that we trust them, that we see them as being competent, and that we care about their continued growth on the job.

If our organization has enough money in its budget to reward employees who have become more valuable through our delegation of responsibility, then naturally we need to recognize their new worth monetarily. But if we really don't have the money in our budget, we will find that most employees understand this fact of life, especially if they like what they are doing and we make their jobs more meaningful and productive through delegation.

Organizational Reasons for Not Delegating

"My boss doesn't delegate and doesn't want me to either." Granted, this is a difficult situation to deal with—but not impossible. It *isn't* easy to work for a boss who doesn't delegate. But at some point, "the buck stops here." We simply

will have to find the old-fashioned guts to do what needs to be done for our employees in spite of the fact that our boss doesn't see the need to delegate to us. So, we can do it quietly. We delegate aspects of our job that aren't highly visible, and encourage our people to do it with their subordinates.

Or do it noisily! We can stand up to our boss. (Note that I'm not using the word "leader" here. Bosses that don't delegate are not leaders.) We can tell him or her to "get a grip," "get with the program," or, at least, get out of the way and let us do what needs to be done with our employees. And we can give him or her this book to read with this chapter marked. I don't mean to sound flippant—for I couldn't be more serious. Somewhere along the line, a real leader has to take a stand. If my boss wouldn't delegate to me, I would take that stand. We really don't have much choice—not only so that we can "look at ourselves in the mirror" each day, but also so we can look at our employees in good conscience.

"A strong union prohibits delegation." (I.e., "It's not in my job description!") This reason used to have some validity. Today, however, tremendous changes are occurring everywhere. And organizations are flattening, downsizing, putting quality first, and giving responsibility for quality to all employees.

Total Quality Performance. Total Quality Management. Continuous Quality Improvement. Statistical Process Control. Quality Circles. Leaderless Work Teams. Employee Empowerment Programs. Everywhere we look we find overwhelming evidence that times indeed are changing. Today we see world markets, not regional ones. We see the very survival of organizations threatened by foreign competition. And as a result, we see front-line employees, and their unions, working hand-in-hand with management to keep their organization competitive and in business.

So if our employees belong to a union, we can still delegate. Sure, we'll have to take it a little slower, and play by the rules. But we need to stick with it. The results achieved in unionized organizations through delegation of major responsibilities to employees have been remarkable. It's worth the extra effort!

Reasons for Delegating

As we've seen in answering a variety of objections to delegation, there are many important reasons to delegate work to our subordinates. They fall under two different kinds of reasons: theirs and ours. Let's look at them from both viewpoints.

Leader Reasons for Delegating Work

- We need to develop our subordinates.

- We are so overworked that we have no choice but to delegate.

- We're ambitious, and know that the higher up we move in our organization, the more we will have to delegate.

- We need to free ourselves to do more critical and important tasks.

- We don't want to do a task. In fact, we can't stand doing it!

It's the last reason for delegating that gets us in trouble. There may be something we do that we hate doing, but that one of our employees would love to do. If so, there is no problem—delegate. But sometimes a leader has what medical students call "skut work," a routine task that the leader hates to do, is tired of doing, or is just too proud to do, and nobody else wants to do it, either. If part of our job is to take out the garbage, than delegating that particular task to an employee will not be enriching to him or her either.

There were a couple of tasks like this in my shop. Changing the empty water cooler bottle was one—no fun! Since our organization was not big enough to have the services of a water bottle changer, we had to do it ourselves. So we carried forty-five pounds of bottled water up two flights of steps, and tried to pour the water into the cooler without spilling it all over the floor. And since nobody looked forward to having the full-time responsibility of carrying water up two flights of steps, we took turns. So here was the CEO of the organization— namely, me—carrying the water bottle up the stairs. Of course, I could have delegated this responsibility, but I needed the exercise. And my people needed a boss who was willing to share the "skut work."

Employee Reasons for Delegating

- It makes more sense to delegate the task to the employee because of the relationship of the task to the employee's job.

- The employee may be better suited to do the job than we are.

- The task may provide the employee opportunities for recognition.

- Delegation usually increases the motivation of our employees in that their jobs become more challenging.

- The task is specialized, and someone else has skills to do it that we don't have.

It is possible, of course, for negative results to come from delegation. But, as indicated, this is most often due to improper delegation. Suppose that our employee messes up a delegated task, and we are blamed for using bad judgment in asking him or her to do it. The real solution to this problem is to ensure that it doesn't happen in the first place by 1) selecting the right employee to do the task, 2) properly training the employee to do it, and 3) following up after the task is delegated. All these things will greatly increase the chances that our employee will succeed. And that is exactly our goal when we delegate, to set up our employee for success!

So let's look at how we can delegate effectively, with a high probability of success.

How to Delegate

The following information on how to delegate for success is not new. In fact, most of the ideas described below have been around a long time. But they are presented in a logical, step-by-step order that will make it easy for new leaders to learn how to delegate and will help those old bosses who don't understand delegation learn how to be true leaders.

 1. Prepare to delegate.

The first step in delegation is to answer some questions about our job. We need to determine:

- The key tasks in our job

- Our authority level for each task

As an example, let's look at how I would analyze one of the jobs in my old organization to determine what could be delegated, using a *Delegation Planning Worksheet* (found at the end of this chapter). Suppose I am the Director of Program Development. The first thing to do is to list all of the major tasks in my job on a *Job Analysis Worksheet.*

Job Analysis Worksheet

1. **Task List**

    - Write proposals and reply to proposal requests
    - Make presentations to key potential clients
    - Attend annual training shows (two per year)
    - Attend professional meetings (monthly)
    - Research content for training modules
    - Observe pilot programs conducted by others
    - Read books and professional journals
    - Negotiate with authors who write for us
    - Edit work contracted by us
    - Write training modules
    - Provide one-on-one coaching and counseling as needed for staff
    - Meet with key clients
    - Conduct informational meetings with staff
    - Drive to the post office to pick up the mail

If we regularly use a planning calendar, or keep a daily "to-do" list, it is easy to go back over the notes we wrote for each day to see the actual tasks on which we spent our time.

The next step is to determine our "authority level" for each of these tasks. In that I was the real-life CEO of my organization, I didn't have a boss to whom I reported. But since I am here playing the role of Program Development Director in my old organization, I will imagine that I had a kind, lovable, wonderful boss named Dick Leatherman, who was terrific at delegating. So as Dick's employee, I reviewed my task list to decide which of the following authority levels I had concerning each task:

Level 1 = I have total authority to do the task. It is a routine part of my job.

Level 2 = I can do the task, but *after* it is done I need to let Dick know that I did it.

Level 3 = I need to check with Dick *before* I do the task.

Next, I carefully evaluate each task to determine 1) if it's a task that I can delegate, and 2) whether I want to delegate it. It may be that even though I can delegate the task, I choose not to for one reason or another.

At this point my *Job Analysis Worksheet* looks as follows:

Job Analysis Worksheet

1. Task List

	Authority Level			Delegate?			To Whom?	Notes
	1	2	3	No	Maybe	Yes		
Write proposals, and reply to proposal requests		x			x			
Make presentations to key potential clients		x			x			
Attend annual training shows (two per year)	x					x	Matt	
Attend professional meetings (monthly)	x			x				
Research content for training modules	x					x	Mary	
Observe pilot programs conducted by others	x			x				
Read books and professional journals	x			x				
Negotiate with authors who write for us			x		x			
Edit work contracted	x					x	Mary	
Write training modules	x					x	Mary	But not yet, need to get someone to do parts of her job.
Provide one-on-one coaching and counseling for staff as needed	x			x				
Meet with key clients		x			x		Matt	Start taking him with me
Conduct informational meetings with staff	x				x		All	Rotate meeting leadership
Drive to the post office to pick up the mail	x					x	Gayla	Start tomorrow

Notice that I have delegated many of the tasks I rated "1" for authority level (i.e., I have total authority to do the task). However, some I did not. The personal improvement tasks, "Read books and professional journals" and "Attend professional meetings," are not ones that can normally be delegated. Similarly, tasks that relate to the leadership aspects of my job, such as "Provide one-on-one coaching and counseling for staff as needed," would not usually be delegated.

Other tasks, such as "Make presentations to key potential clients" or "Write training modules," are ones that I might be able to delegate, but probably only portions of them. On the other hand, the task "Drive to the post office to pick up the mail" is, of course, one that should have been delegated ten years ago! And I should delegate several other tasks at the point when I have the time to invest in training, and the employees who can take on the responsibility.

After completing a *Job Analysis Worksheet* to determine which parts of our job to delegate, we need to spend time thinking about how these tasks should be delegated, and to whom (already indicated in my example *Worksheet)*. We can ask ourselves these questions:

- Which tasks can be done better at a lower level? What is the lowest level that can handle the task?

- Which tasks are leadership tasks that cannot be delegated (for example, taking disciplinary action, handling confidential issues, or giving rewards and recognition to others as the leader)?

- Are there any problems that stand in the way of delegating a task?
    - Is there time to delegate the task?
    - Does my boss have a problem with my delegating this task?
    - What is the risk if the employee fails in the delegated task? Is the risk acceptable?
    - What is the complexity of the task, i.e., can the task be taught in a reasonable amount of time?

- Who is best suited to take on the task?
    - Is there someone who can do it better than I can?
    - Will the individual be overloaded if he or she takes on this additional responsibility? If so, are there aspects of his or her work that could be delegated to others?
    - Does this individual want this additional responsibility?
    - Will performing this task help the individual grow and develop?

- Is it better to split up the task into several subtasks and assign each part to a different employee (lightening the load, and giving each one a chance to show what he or she can do)?

- What should the employee's authority level be for the delegated task?

- What is a successful performance of the task, i.e., how will I, and the employee, know that the delegated task has been done well?

- What will a specific training plan look like for this employee on this task?

- Who else should be informed that this task is going to be delegated?

At the end of this chapter you will find a *Delegation Planning Worksheet* that you can copy and use as a guide in thinking through these questions. And as you make decisions about tasks to be delegated, you can note this information on your *Job Analysis Worksheet* as I did in my example.

In addition, you may need to complete training plans for more complex tasks before meeting with your employees. Here is an example of a plan that I, as the hypothetical Director of Program Development, could use to train one of my employees:

Task to be delegated: Attend annual training shows (two per year)

Employee Training Plan

	Date to be completed:
Activities:	
1. Order booklet: "Working the Show"	Today
2. Review and list our show objectives	1 June
3. Design a check sheet for the show	3 June
4. Schedule a meeting with Matt	4 June
5. Meet with Matt to	6 June

- Discuss show objectives
- List items to be taken (books, video-player and monitor, training modules, catalogs, business cards, etc.)
- Review list of workshops to attend
- Review list of distributors' booths to visit
- Discuss face-to-face client contact procedure
- Set follow-up meeting to review Matt's progress

6. Follow-up meeting with Matt	1 July

☑ **2. Describe the task to the employee.**

After we have prepared to delegate by identifying what we will delegate and to whom, and have designed a training plan, we need to set up meetings with these employees to discuss the tasks that will be assigned. In this step we will need to tell them

- What needs to be done

- Why it needs to be done

- How the delegated task fits the overall objectives of the section or department

- *Suggestions* as to how the task could be completed

- Whom he or she needs to contact to complete the task

- Expected results

- Priority of this task relative to other tasks in the employee's job

- When to start on the task, and by what date it should be finished

- Any other needed information—especially things that we know but are not in writing

☑ **3. Offer training if necessary.**

Step 2 assumes that the employee already knows how to do the task, and needs only general instructions on how to carry it out. But if the employee does not know how to perform the task, we may need to provide additional training. Information on how to train is presented in the chapter on one-on-one training skills—an especially important chapter! The thing to note here is that we first need to spend time planning out our employees' training using the *Delegation Planning Worksheet,* as discussed in Step 1. Then, we meet with these employees individually and tell them how to do the task. Next, we *show* them how to do it. Finally, we let them *do* the task while we observe them doing it, showing respect for their efforts throughout.

☑ **4. Offer help.**

Good leaders recognize that employees are apt to feel a little anxious about taking on a new responsibility. By offering our assistance, we help to reduce their natural anxiety. We may need to pave the way for an employee by talking to his or her coworkers who will be affected by the delegation of this task. Or we may want to help the employee by delegating part of his or her task to someone else. By offering our help, we demonstrate that we care about the employee and will do everything possible to ensure his or her success in the new task.

☑ **5. Determine required interaction points.**

This step is designed to avoid trouble. If we have decided how the employee should accomplish the task, we also know when we need to meet with him or her to make sure that everything is going all right. But if we have delegated to the employee the responsibility for how the task will be accomplished, we may need to ask him or her to develop a plan describing how the new task will be done. In such a plan, the leader will be able to spot the "mileposts," when the leader and the employee need to touch base to determine how things are going.

It is important, however, that we don't overmanage a delegated task. And it may not be easy for us to "keep our hands off." After all, we're the expert. We may even feel that we performed the task the best that it has ever been done. But it is far better for the employee that we allow him or her to manage the new assignment. I didn't say "abandon" the employee! But there is a great difference between monitoring an employee's efforts, and breathing down his or her neck. We can walk this line by letting go of the nitty-gritty details of how the task should be done, and scheduling times when the two of us can get together to review the employee's key activities and final results. Managing the delegated task in this fashion will significantly increase the employee's self-confidence. We may even be surprised to find in the end that the employee has figured out a way to do the task better than we did!

Dennis LaMountain, organizational consultant, has an interesting way of looking at this issue. He believes that most people have delegation style tendencies that affect the way in which they help others. If we know our "natural" delegation style tendency, we are better able to make decisions about when it is appropriate to use it—and when it is not. Dennis has created four short cases and a process that is remarkably valid in determining delegation style (used here with permission of the author). Read each of the situations on the following pages that represent typical cases that could be encountered on the job.

In each of the cases, there are four possible ways of handling the situation. While none of the ways may be exactly the one you would choose, select one of the four statements below (or following each case) *that most nearly describes the way you would handle each situation.* Place a "4" in the space opposite this statement. Do the same for the statement you would *next most likely use,* placing a "3" opposite it. Continue ranking the remaining statements in a similar manner (next with a "2," and, finally, placing a "1" beside the response you would be least apt to use). Do this for each of the four situations.

SITUATION #1: "No One Else Available!"

There is a monthly statistical report you have been preparing for several years. You finally decide that one of your employees could do it, freeing up your time for other things. It would be an important learning experience for someone. But for whom? The only person who has time available and knows something about statistics hasn't been on board very long. But you decide to try him. After explaining the task to him, however, he says:

"Well . . ., yes. It sounds like a challenge. But I'll have to tell you that I haven't done anything quite like this before, and it sounds pretty important to get it right. Are you sure you want me to do it?"

———————————————

Assume that you would begin by telling him you have confidence that he could do the report. Then, you would most likely (give your first choice a "4," second choice a "3," third choice a "2," and last choice a "1"):

__1__ A. Show him step-by-step how you have been preparing the report and the way you want it to look.

__3__ B. Say that although you are available if absolutely necessary, you would prefer that he take the initiative of preparing a first draft of the report on his own.

__4__ C. Show him samples of previous reports, and ask him questions to get him to think through the process for himself.

__2__ D. Get him started doing it while you watch, making suggestions or correcting him as necessary.

SITUATION #2: "The Missing Shipment!"

You have just finished reading a note from Jane, one of your more experienced and reliable employees. The note says that the BMI shipment has not arrived at its destination yet, and that she is having trouble tracking it down. Both of you know that this shipment will provide the basis for a key demonstration at 8:00 tomorrow morning. You still have the note in your hand when Jane appears at your door, out of breath and looking a little panicky. She exclaims:

"Good! I'm glad you saw my note and I caught you in! I'm afraid we won't find the shipment in time! That meeting tomorrow is very important! Maybe you should take over."

_____

Assume that you would first obtain more information on the problem from Jane. Then, you would most likely:

_3_ A. Remind her that it is her responsibility and you are confident that she can handle it.

_2_ B. Ask her what she planned to do to correct the situation, and help her think through the resolution of the problem.

_1_ C. Tell her exactly what needs to be done to correct the situation in time for the demonstration.

_4_ D. Leave her in charge, but explain how she should handle the more critical aspects of the problem.

SITUATION #3: "The Great Idea!"

One week ago you interviewed and hired a new employee. It was clear to you at the time that she had all the necessary skills and capabilities for the job, and that she had all kinds of ideas about the way that things should be done. Although you liked her enthusiasm, you did not agree with all of her ideas. Just now, she called to say she wanted to see you about a great idea! You invited her into your office, and she said:

"I have a great idea for reformatting the monthly report—really give it eye appeal, and make it easier to understand the numbers. I'm sure I know how to use the computer graphics program well enough to generate some really snazzy charts and graphs before our Tuesday deadline. What do you say?"

You would most likely:

4 A. Tell her that you have had some similar thoughts and that you would like to work with her on the graphs. Coach her on the best appearance and rule out any unworkable ideas.

1 B. Commend her for having a good idea, tell her you will give it some thought, and later show her how you would like the graphs and new format to look.

3 C. Ask her some general questions to see how well she has thought this idea through. If she is on the right track, then give her a "go-ahead," but ask to see the final draft.

2 D. Commend her for her idea and tell her to go ahead with the project. Then tell her you are available if she needs any help, and ask to see the final draft Monday afternoon.

SITUATION #4: "Sloppy Documentation"

Pat is one of your more experienced and trusted employees. He came to you recently saying he has some time on his hands and wondered if you have any special projects that he could handle. For some time, you have been thinking that documentation in the department is far too haphazard, and inconsistent in quality. You call Pat in, explain your concern to him, and tell him that you would like to see the department prepare—and stick to—one format for documentation. You ask him if he would be interested in that kind of a project. He responds:

"Yeah, I would. Should have suggested that myself. I agree with you about our documentation; and I've seen a lot better formats! Sounds like an interesting project!"

You would most likely:

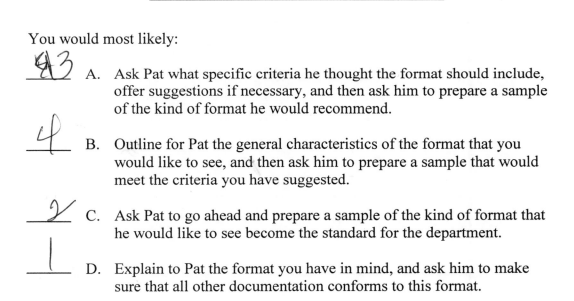

_____ A. Ask Pat what specific criteria he thought the format should include, offer suggestions if necessary, and then ask him to prepare a sample of the kind of format he would recommend.

_____ B. Outline for Pat the general characteristics of the format that you would like to see, and then ask him to prepare a sample that would meet the criteria you have suggested.

_____ C. Ask Pat to go ahead and prepare a sample of the kind of format that he would like to see become the standard for the department.

_____ D. Explain to Pat the format you have in mind, and ask him to make sure that all other documentation conforms to this format.

Delegation Style Tally Sheet

1. In order to determine your personal style, transfer your answers from Situations 1 - 4 to the corresponding boxes below. For example, for Situation #1, if you had a "1" opposite alternative "A," you would put a "1" in the un-shaded area under Style 1 below. If you had a "4" for Alternative "B" for Situation #1, you would place a "4" in the un-shaded area under Style 4 below—and so on.

2. After you have entered all the numbers for each Situation's Alternatives, total the four columns (Style 1 - Style 4) and record the result in the bottom row of the table.

3. If the numbers were entered and the columns added correctly, the total of all the numbers in the bottom row should equal to 40.

Situation	Alternative	Style 1	Style 2	Style 3	Style 4
1.	A.	1			
	B.			3	3
	C.		4		
	D.			2	
2.	A.				3
	B.			2	
	C.	1			
	D.		4		
3.	A.		4		
	B.	1			
	C.			3	
	D.				2
4.	A.			3	
	B.		4		
	C.				2
	D.	1			
Totals		4	16	10	10	= 40
		Style 1	Style 2	Style 3	Style 4

After you have totaled your rankings correctly, turn to the next page for further instructions.

Delegation Style Profile

4. Transfer and record the totals from the bottom of the previous page here.

Totals from previous page

Totals	4	16	10	10	= 40
	Style 1	Style 2	Style 3	Style 4	

5. Plot the points for each of these totals in the corresponding column of the graph below

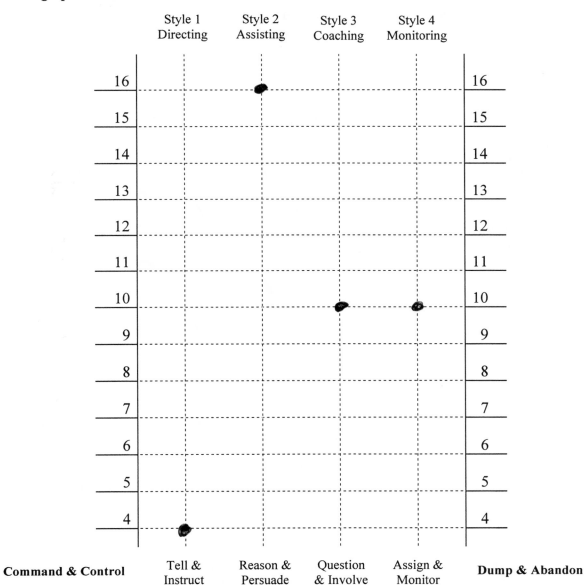

Note: The highest point or bar on the profile represents the style you used most often in the four situations.

One of the major considerations in effective delegation is the leader's selection of the most effective level of involvement in the delegated assignment. In each of the situations you just faced, we asked you to experience these kinds of decisions, forcing you to choose between four different levels of personal involvement in the delegated assignment. These levels of involvement are often referred to as delegation styles.

Notice that the points you plotted represent your level of involvement in the delegated assignments. Leaders who "command and control" have total personal involvement and essentially keep the responsibility for the project. At the other end of the chart are leaders who have total lack of involvement in the project. Of course these are two extremes and it is unusual for any leader to actually delegate in this way.

If we examine what underlies these two extremes, we find that the leader's willingness to accept risk, or uncertainty, determines his or her delegation style. If I am willing to accept a high degree of risk, then I am more apt to be less involved with my employee. Conversely, if risk is scary to me, then I am apt to be more controlling.

This relationship is illustrated in the following graph showing the impact of various delegation styles as a result of the leader's need to avoid risk and his or her involvement in the delegated task.

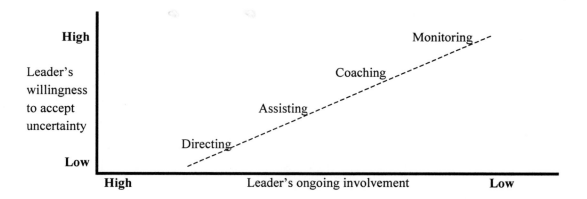

At the four points along the graph's diagonal line, we have indicated delegation style. Note that these labels do not imply that the leader has a fixed style that does not change. On the contrary, effective leadership involves moving up and down along this diagonal line in order to use the approach or style that best suits the individual who is assigned the delegated task and the specific task that is assigned.

The four styles are as follows:

> ***Directing.*** Here, the leader delegates the assignment but tells and instructs the delegatee exactly how the assignment is to be done. This style of delegation is especially appropriate for new employees or when we assign a new task to a less-experienced employee.

> ***Assisting.*** The leader assumes that the delegatee is capable of handling some of the assignment without specific instructions. The leader, however, thoroughly explains the more difficult or risky aspects of the task.

> ***Coaching.*** The leader defines the expected end result, and then asks a few questions to see if the employee has a good idea about the way that the assignment could be completed.

> ***Monitoring.*** The leader defines the expected end result, and then allows the employee to reach that end in his or her own way.

Dennis LaMountain theorizes that most of us have a natural delegation style that we feel the most comfortable using. He believes that knowing which style we tend to use most often and most effectively has a positive impact on our leadership performance. Even though each of us tends to have one delegation style we use most comfortably and naturally, we are capable of learning to use other styles effectively when needed.

 6. Follow up.

Finally, we need to follow up on delegated tasks. When we do, we can provide feedback on employees' performance, both good and not so good. We can let our employees know specifically what they did that we liked and what we didn't like. We can suggest concrete ways in which their performance could be improved, or how a satisfactory performance could be made even better. And we can ask them what they learned from the experience and what they will do differently in the future.

Remember, also, that more often than not, we bear some of the responsibility for the employee's performance if things aren't accomplished as well as expected. Therefore, when providing feedback to our employees, we need to be sure to let them know when we see ourselves as part of a particular problem. And we avoid blaming an employee for what goes wrong. Instead, we simply make sure that the employee knows how to do it properly the next time.

Summary

We need to delegate every day in little ways! When an employee asks, "What should I do?" we can respond by asking, "What do you feel you should do? What do you think is the best thing to do?"

And we can stop rubber-stamping! Are we signing documents just because we're the *boss*? Do we make our employees come to us for our approval because we are the boss? Do we make all the contacts with people outside the organization because we're the boss? Do we make all the presentations to others in the organization because we are the boss? Do we always talk to other bosses because we're a boss? If this is you, then you are a *boss*, not a leader! And you need to begin delegating.

At the end of this chapter you will find three forms. The first is a *Delegation: Job Analysis Worksheet* that you can use to evaluate your job and determine what tasks can be delegated. Next is a *Delegation Planning Worksheet* that you can use to plan exactly how a specific task should be delegated. Finally, there is a *Delegation Evaluation Worksheet* that you can use as a guide in evaluating your performance on a delegated task. Using this worksheet, you can ask your employees, if you have the courage, how you can improve your delegation skills. This form asks thoughtful questions such as, What could I have done that would have made it easier for them to do the tasks that I delegated? Should I have provided more training? Met with them more often? Less often? Did I provide them with the authority to do the task? Did I let them do it? Did I take over, or take back, the job? These and other key questions are listed in an employee's *Delegation Evaluation Worksheet* at the end of this chapter. Give this *Worksheet* to your employee to use to provide you feedback—both on what you did well in delegating, and how you could improve the next time.

Delegation: Job Analysis Worksheet

Name of leader whose job you have listed below: _____

Task List	Authority Level			Delegate?			To Whom?	Notes
	1	2	3	No	Maybe	Yes		

Delegation Planning Worksheet

Task to be delegated: _____

Task assigned to: _____

| Date task assigned: _____ | Date task to be started: _____ | Date task to be completed: _____ |

1. Is this person best suited to take on this new responsibility?

- How well can the individual do the task? _____
  _____
  _____

- How willing is the individual to take on the additional responsibility? _____
  _____
  _____

- How will doing this task help the individual grow and develop? _____
  _____
  _____

- How does this task play to the employee's strengths? _____
  _____
  _____

- What problems might this employee have in completing this task? _____
  _____
  _____

- How overloaded will the individual be if he or she takes on this additional responsibility? _____
  _____

  If so, can any of his or her present responsibilities be delegated to others? If so, what work should be delegated, and to whom? _____
  _____
  _____
  _____
  _____
  _____

Would it be better to split up this task into several subtasks and assign each part to a different employee (lightening the load, and giving several people a chance to show what they can do)? If so, what are my plans to accomplish this?

_____

_____

_____

- Is there someone else who could perform this task better?
  If so, who?

  _____

  State the reasons why the task is assigned to the above-named person.

  _____

  _____

2. **What problems stand in the way of delegating this task?**

- How much time (training and follow up) is required to delegate this task?

  _____

- Is there time to delegate this task? _____

  If not, how will I be able to find the time? _____

  _____

  _____

  _____

- Does my boss have a problem with my delegating this task? _____

- What is the risk if the employee fails in this delegated task? _____

  _____

  _____

  _____

  How acceptable is the risk? _____

  _____

  _____

  How could the risk(s) be reduced? _____

  _____

  _____

  _____

  _____

- What is the complexity of this task, i.e., can the task be taught in a reasonable amount of time? _____

_____

_____

- What should be the employee's authority level for the delegated task?

_____

3. What is a successful performance of this task?

- How will you and the employee know that the delegated task has been performed well?

_____

_____

_____

- What things should not happen in doing this task?

_____

_____

_____

4. Who else should be informed that this task is going to be delegated?

_____

_____

_____

5. Employee training plan (if needed)

Activities: Date
                                               completed:

_____ _____

_____ _____

_____ _____

_____ _____

_____ _____

_____ _____

_____ _____

_____ _____

_____ _____

_____ _____

Delegation Evaluation Worksheet

To be filled out by the *leader* on his or her employee

Employee: _____

Date form
completed: _____

Person completing this form: _____

Delegated task: _____
_____
_____

What was the quality of the completed task?
_____
_____
_____
_____

What did this employee do well in completing this task?
_____
_____
_____
_____

What could have been done more effectively? How?
_____
_____

Was the task accomplished within the allotted time? _____
    If not, why not?
_____
_____

How was the employee's other work affected by the delegation of this task?
_____
_____

Was this the right person to do this job? _____
If not, why not?
_____
_____

Delegation Evaluation Worksheet

To be filled out by the *employee* on his or her leader

To: _____   From: _____

Re: Feedback on my delegation of the following task: _____

_____

Date: _____

Please provide me with feedback on my delegation skills by honestly answering the following questions. When you have completed this check sheet, please return it to me. After I have reviewed it, we will meet together to discuss your comments.

1. What did you like about the way I delegated this task to you?

_____
_____
_____
_____
_____

2. How could I have improved? Consider such things as:

- Were you the appropriate person to do this job? Should I have selected someone else?
- Did I tell you whom to see, and who else needed to be contacted?
- Did you know the results that were expected before you started?
- Should I have provided more training? Less training?
- Should I have met with you more often? Less often?
- Did you feel I was available to answer your questions as they came up?
- Did I provide you with the authority to do the task?
- Did I let you do it? Did I take over, or take back, the job in any way?
- Did I provide you with positive and/or corrective feedback when you finished the task?
- Did you encounter any problems that I should have foreseen?

Please list below how I might delegate better in the future. Be specific. Note examples where possible.

_____
_____
_____
_____
_____

Leadership
Problem Solving

Making the right decision on the wrong problem is usually a disaster. Making the wrong decision on the right problem one can usually fix!

P. Drucker

Some people seem to have a knack for coming up with the best solution to a problem. Others—with the same intelligence and experience—seem to come up with solutions before they are even sure what the problems are! We've all seen examples of disasters that occurred when the cause of the problem wasn't analyzed before expensive action was taken: decisions that resulted in wasted time, materials, and money; plans that looked perfect on paper, but failed in real life.

I remember a meeting I once attended where one person asked five times during a one-hour meeting (that had been scheduled for thirty minutes), "Yes, but what is causing the problem?" Another person kept saying, "Let's *do* something! Anything! We need to take action now!" Someone else continued to push his solution to the problem, and I wasn't sure why I had been invited to the meeting. The guy next to me wanted to have sidebar conversations with me about a fishing trip he had taken, and another attendee kept suggesting the group should explore different alternatives to obtain a better solution. The big boss showed up ten minutes late for the meeting and left after fifteen minutes. The key person who had most of the data was paged twice and had to leave the meeting. Nobody took minutes of the meeting, and no one used the easel to obtain group focus. And, I ended up with a headache!

Typical? You bet. Effective? No! Part of the problem was that they lacked knowledge of the basic principles of problem solving. Therefore, a great deal of time was spent running off in all directions. Besides correcting the obvious problem of meeting interruptions and late arrivals, there are some very simple things they could have done to make their problem solving more effective.

This chapter will help you develop skills in problem solving. It will show you logical—and simple—ways to make your problem-solving more effective.

A key step emphasized in this chapter is *writing out the problem!* It is amazing what a simple thing like writing down information can do to increase our success with problem solving. We don't always have a clipboard in our hand. But whenever we have a problem, we can begin by taking a minute to make the problem "visible" in writing.

Visibility does several things:

- If a problem-solving process is taking place only in our minds, no one can help us! Others are kept from pointing out oversights, errors, or faulty assumptions.

- If we don't make our thinking visible, we don't have a reliable way to review how we attempted to solve a problem—and therefore to learn from our mistakes.

- Writing down the problem will help us see the whole problem rather than just some parts and pieces of it.

- Part of our job as a leader is to help our people develop. We may be outstanding problem solvers. But if we can't make what we think visible, how can we teach?

- In a team meeting, visibility will help keep our group on track and focused on the problem at hand.

In this chapter, you will see two common-sense tools for solving problems: first, a tool called Situation Analysis, and second, Diagnosing Causes.

Open the Door to New Opportunities...

*with
Dana University
Business School's*

*Certified Dana
Supervisor Award*

DANA

Dana University Mission Statement

Reinforce the Dana Style,

philosophy, policy, identity,

and strategic direction through

the development and delivery

of our education, training, and

communication services.

DANA UNIVERSITY

P.O. Box 1000
Toledo, Ohio 43697

Situation Analysis

Situation Analysis (SA) is a problem-solving tool that will help us break a large—even messy—situation down into manageable pieces. These pieces become the problems, decisions, plans, and even new problem situations ("messes") to be analyzed.

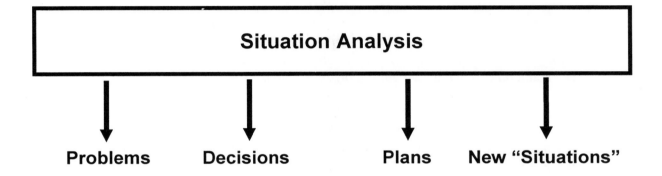

So when we have a problem that is big, complex, bulky, and has lots of parts and pieces, it is probably the time for SA. Issues such as high turnover, low morale, dirty facilities, or high cost are often called problems. Technically they are not problems at all, but statements about symptoms of problems. And for concerns like these, a good tool to reach for is Situation Analysis.

Let's take a messy situation and examine how SA can be used to break it down.

"I just don't understand those leaders," thought Old Jake, a senior manager with I.T.A. "Back when I was a foreman, excuse me, I mean foreperson, an employee took a lot of pride in the fact that he or she was a leader at the best organization this side of the Mississippi. But now if morale were any worse, I'd have to jack my people up with a hydraulic lift. They are grumbling and complaining worse than a bunch of workers who just got an across-the-board pay cut.

"Now, because I've been here longer than anyone else, the boss wants me to come up with some bright ideas to solve the morale problem. I don't even know where to start on this one. It's a real mess because so many things are causing the situation. Maybe it's because every time there is a dispute between a team leader and a worker, the team leaders get shot down by personnel.

205

"Of course, it could be that the team leaders just aren't as tough as they used to be in my time. I mean, after all, we used to be called 'foreman.' We had respect! And it seems like the workers can sense when a foreman, I mean a 'team leader,' is weak. And then they needle him or her constantly until something blows.

"The low morale might also be a result of some team leaders not being able to make that big transition from being a worker to being a leader. I've seen several like that. Tom is a good example. He's the most miserable human being I've ever seen. He loved doing what he was doing, and was good at it. Then he was promoted to leader, and now he can't keep his hands off the equipment.

"Another problem is that there's so much pressure to get high production. A team leader who achieves high production gets a lot of recognition from everybody. But sometimes things happen outside a leader's control that hurt his or her production. Then we've got a morale problem.

"I don't know," thought Old Jake. "Maybe the problem of low morale is caused by the new 'work team' program. Delegating authority and responsibility to workers is fine—I'm all for it. But it seems to me like the workers really weren't ready for all that authority and responsibility. Now the team leaders are having fits trying to get their people to work together as a team, to take charge of their own goals and objectives, and at the same time keep up production. They're having meetings about having meetings! Why couldn't the organization spend some of its dollars on giving the workers some training before dumping a new way of operating on them? It's crazy!

"What a mess!" sighed Old Jake. "I'm usually an optimistic kind of person. But things aren't going well. Something needs to change."

 **Step 1. Write down the problem.**

The first step in using Situation Analysis is to make the problem statement visible. Write it down!

Low Team
Leader Morale

 **Step 2. Separate the problem into its related parts.**

Next, separating the pieces of a problem allows us to focus our energy on those areas that most affect the initial problem—and at the same time lets us see the problem as a whole. At this point, we don't have to analyze or conclude anything. We just jot down as many parts and pieces of the problem as we can think of. In the example, Old Jake would ask himself this question: "What are the things that make me think, 'We've got low team leader morale'?"

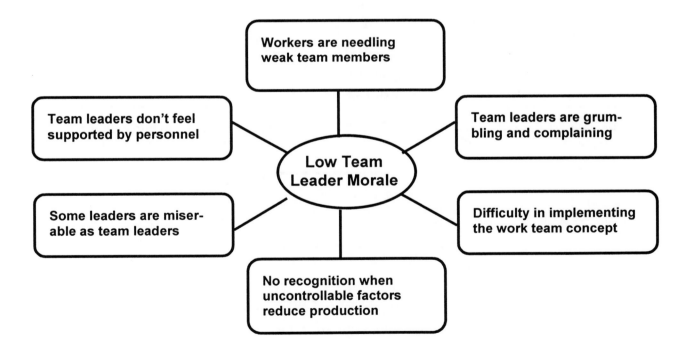

☑ **Step 3. Determine which parts of the problem are probable causes and which are probable results.**

In Step 3, we decide which of the separate pieces are causes, and which are results of causes. To fix a mess, we must attack the causes, not the results. When four people who work for you suddenly quit their jobs, you do have to replace the people. But you don't stop there! In order to fix the cause of the problem, you must find out why they quit. You haven't solved the real problem just by replacing the employees. So when we analyze a messy situation, we need to determine the probable causes—and first take action on them, not on the results.

We can indicate a probable cause by drawing an arrow pointing toward the problem situation and a probable result with an arrow pointing away from the problem. Then we cross out the "results," and focus our energies on the causes. Here's an example:

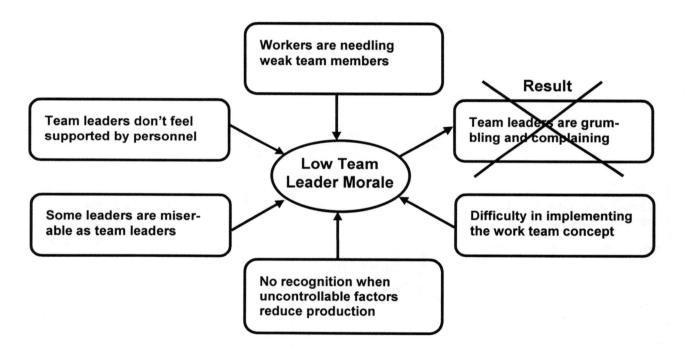

The team leaders' grumbling and complaining is probably a result of low team leader morale and should be "X'ed" out. If a piece of the situation seems to be both a probable cause and a probable result, treat it as a probable cause.

☑ **Step 4. Set priorities.**

Many problems have a number of related causes, some major and some minor. To be effective, we need to devote our time to the major causes that can be changed. With today's tight schedules, we simply don't have time to do everything. Therefore, we fix the things that matter most by making them visible components, determining causes and results—and then, in Step 4, assigning priorities only to the causes, not to the results.

A simple way to assign priorities is to use the categories of "Seriousness," "Urgency," and "Growth." Rate each suspected cause as having a high (H), medium (M), or low (L) degree of 1) seriousness, 2) urgency, and 3) growth.

Seriousness:

- How serious is this cause in relation to the other causes?
- How big is it?
- How bad is it?
- How frequently is it occurring?
- Dollarwise, how important is this part of the problem?

Urgency:

- Do I have to drop everything else and take care of this today?
- Can I do it just as well next week?
- Can this part of the problem wait until next month?

Growth:

- If I don't take care of this cause now, will it get worse?
- Will it soon spread out of control?
- Does it have a growing financial impact?

Old Jake finds that he can now analyze his problem fairly easily by using the "Seriousness / Urgency / Growth" (S.U.G.) system to rate each cause. It seems to work best to rate the "Seriousness" of each cause first, then the "Urgency," and finally the rate of "Growth."

Here is what his chart looks like now.

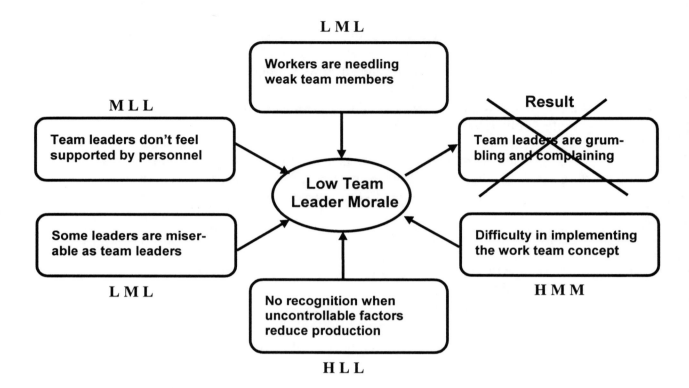

L M L

Workers are needling weak team members

M L L

Team leaders don't feel supported by personnel

Some leaders are miserable as team leaders

L M L

Low Team Leader Morale

Result

Team leaders are grumbling and complaining

Difficulty in implementing the work team concept

H M M

No recognition when uncontrollable factors reduce production

H L L

At this point, note that Old Jake rated two parts of his problem as "high" in seriousness: "No recognition when uncontrollable factors reduce production," and "Difficulty in implementing the work team concept." But his urgency rating for these two causes was not "high," but "low" and "medium," respectively. You may feel that if the seriousness of a problem is high, then the urgency must be high, and thus the growth factor will also be high. But we need to be careful not to allow a high seriousness rating influence our ratings of urgency and growth. In Old Jake's case, "Difficulty in implementing work team concept" was serious to him. But he also felt that the urgency of this cause was only medium, and that the growth factor was also only medium.

Likewise, even though he rated "No recognition when uncontrollable factors reduce production" as high in seriousness, he rated it low in urgency. Jake's management needs to do something about this part of the problem. But realistically, it is not something that must be handled today—or even this week. In fact, it might be better to give this cause some time and solid thought before talking to management about it. Jake wisely rated this piece of the problem as low in growth. Yes, the problem is bad. But, no, the problem is not likely to get any worse. It is probably as bad as it is ever going to be. Therefore, it has low growth potential.

☑ **Step 5. Decide which of the situation's causes are problems, decisions, plans, or new situations to be analyzed.**

The final step in Situation Analysis is to analyze each of the major causes of the problem situation as follows:

Problems to be diagnosed. For example, "Difficulty in implementing the work team concept" may be a problem to Old Jake because he doesn't really know what the cause is. He thinks it might be lack of worker training. But that is only an assumption at this point. He needs to discover why the teams are not working out. Only when he determines why this is occurring is he ready to take some kind of action to address the problem.

Decisions that must be made. Jake knows why there is no recognition when uncontrollable factors reduce production. And since he knows the cause of this situation, his next step is to make some decisions about fixing it.

Plans to be implemented. Jake also knows why some leaders are miserable as team leaders. He even knows what needs to be done about it. But he feels that determining how to do what needs to be done will require some planning.

New problem situations that must be further broken down. For instance, team leaders not feeling supported by the personnel department may be a new situation to be analyzed, with its own set of causes and results.

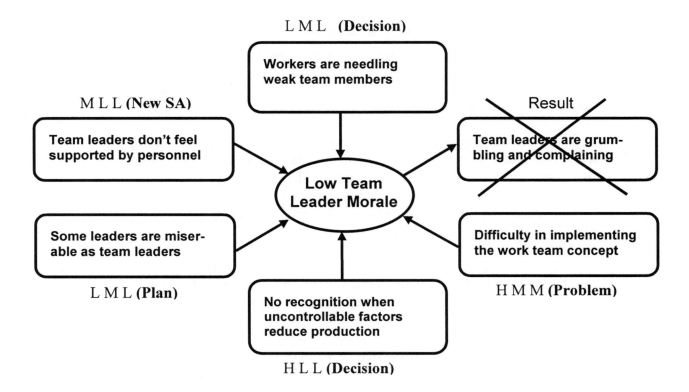

L M L **(Decision)**

Workers are needling weak team members

M L L **(New SA)**

Team leaders don't feel supported by personnel

Result

~~**Team leaders are grumbling and complaining**~~

Low Team Leader Morale

Some leaders are miserable as team leaders

Difficulty in implementing the work team concept

L M L **(Plan)**

H M M **(Problem)**

No recognition when uncontrollable factors reduce production

H L L **(Decision)**

After we have analyzed our problem using Situation Analysis, we are ready to devote our time to the high-priority causes. The SA tool will not hand us a predetermined solution to our problem. But it does help us with the key task of making the various parts of our problem visible, evaluating each part in a meaningful way, and deciding where to focus our energy.

Each priority part of a Situation Analysis can be regarded as an opportunity—an opportunity to do something differently and better.

On the following page is a *Situation Analysis Worksheet* that you may duplicate and use in analyzing your problem situations.

Situation Analysis Worksheet

1. Write down the problem.
2. Separate the problem into its related parts.
3. Determine which pieces are probable causes and which are results. Draw arrows into the center for "cause," out for "results."
4. Assign S.U.G. priorities for each cause.
   (H = High, M = Medium, L = Low).
   Seriousness: How bad? How big? How much money?
   Urgency: Must it be taken care of today?
                Will next week be just as good?
   Growth: Is the cause getting worse?
                Or is it already as bad as it is going to get?
5. Label the major causes: "Problem," "Decision," "Plan," or "New Situation Analysis."

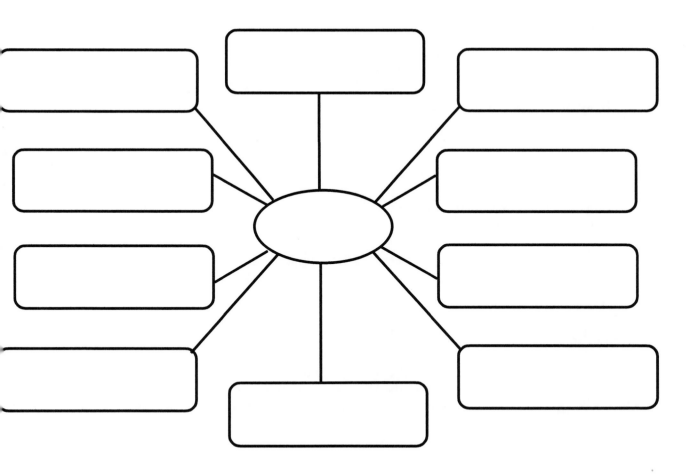

Diagnosing Cause

When trying to remedy a problem, many people jump into action without thinking. They just can't seem to help it: they want to be "doing" something—anything! In fact, taking action without thinking, no matter how unproductive, can become a way of life. Before, repeat, before we take action to solve a problem, we need to look for causes. When we find the probable cause, we should fix the cause that is most clearly connected to the problem.

When we problem-solve, we are finding the cause of a problem, not analyzing a situation, making a decision, or implementing a plan. We are problem solving when

A) We have a deviation from the standard.

Something should be happening, but it isn't. It was supposed to happen, but it didn't. It wasn't supposed to happen, but it did. All these are deviations from the standard.

B) We are uncertain about the cause of the problem.

If we already know the cause, then our next step is to make a decision by selecting the best way to fix the problem.

C) We are concerned about the problem.

If we see a deviation from the standard and we don't know for sure why it happened, but we are not really concerned about it, we have no problem.

We can find the cause of a problem by following these seven steps:

 Step 1. Develop a specific written problem statement.

In writing out our problem statement, we need to make it specific and in the negative. We write "Poor Morale in the Data Processing Section," not just "Poor Morale." This not only helps pinpoint the problem, but also highlights what the real issue is.

Step 2. Ask "What, Where, and When" the problem is occurring, and "What, Where, and When" the problem is not occurring.

At times causes can be located more quickly if we clarify what is not the problem, as well as what is. The better we define the boundaries of a problem by specifying where the problem isn't occurring, the easier it is to determine the most probable causes.

Also, in Step 2 ask, "What is the extent of the problem?" That is, how bad or serious is the problem? This information can keep us from developing a $500 solution to fix a $3.00 problem.

These "what, where, when and extent" questions help us locate and isolate the problem area, and thus show us where to look for causes. An electronics technician calls it "troubleshooting"; a doctor calls it "diagnosing." We might say it's "working smarter, not harder."

For example, suppose I have a bad pain. Now what kinds of questions would my doctor ask before he or she says, "Take two aspirin and call me in the morning?" He or she might ask, " Where does it hurt? When does it bother you? When did you first notice it?" and "How much does it hurt?"

But good doctors don't stop there. They also ask questions about what the problem is not. For example, my doctor might ask, "Have you been experiencing pain anywhere else?" "Have you ever had this pain before?" and "When don't you notice the pain?"

From asking such questions, the doctor might discover that my problem is only in my right elbow, and not any other part of my body. It hurts all day, not just at certain times of the day. The pain first started six weeks ago. And I didn't have it before then, except when I was in high school.

 Step 3. Closely examine the differences between where and when the problem is occurring, and where and when it isn't.

If a problem exists in one area and not in another, the differences between the two areas can produce clues to help locate the cause. So we ask, "What peculiar differences exist between where the problem is occurring, and where it is not occurring?" or "What is different about when the problem occurs and when it doesn't?"

In the example of the pain problem in Step 2 above, by specifying what, where, when, and to what extent the problem is and is not occurring, my doctor is able to identify the particular differences. For example, the doctor might discover that I'm right-handed, and that I was a softball pitcher in high school. Then, by determining the peculiar differences between what, where, and when the problem is and is not, he or she is then able to look for changes in and around the differences.

☑ **Step 4. Look carefully for changes that have occurred in and around the environment of the problem.**

Changes can cause problems. In fact, problems by definition are always caused by changes. Remember that problems where no change has occurred are not truly problems. They are decisions that must be made or plans that should be implemented. For example, guess what my doctor discovered I was doing with my child every night after supper for the past six weeks? Right! My child joined the local little league baseball team and needed practice in catching.

☑ **Step 5. Develop "Probable Cause Statements" concerning the changes discovered in Step 4 by linking each change to the problem.**

Every change will produce its own unique probable cause statement. In the example of elbow pain above, a probable cause statement could be:

> *"Pitching softball with my child each night after supper has resulted in tendinitis in my elbow."*

☑ **Step 6. Test each probable cause statement against all of the IS and IS NOT facts, in order to determine the most probable cause.**

For example, my doctor might ask:

> *"If it is tendinitis, would that account for the fact that the pain is in the right elbow and not the left?"* YES.

> *"Would it account for the fact that it hurts constantly, and not just certain times in the day?"* YES.

"That the pain first started six weeks ago and you never had it before except when you were a pitcher in high school?" YES.

Since tendinitis checks out against the known set of facts, my doctor would then move to the next step—verifying that this really is the cause.

☑ **Step 7. Verify the most probable cause to make sure it is the real cause.**

In this final step, the doctor can verify the cause of my pain by gently probing my elbow, or by taking X-rays.

Note that these seven steps of Problem Solving are usually inexpensive. They involve only paper and pencil mental analysis and sometime phone calls to gather confirming information. Taking action to remedy the problem, of course, may involve financial commitment and many lost dollars if we fail to follow the problem-solving process above.

Yet, many people start their problem solving efforts by throwing money into an ill-conceived solution before thinking through the problem. They jump in with both feet to take action. Any action! They often end up spending much unnecessary time and money—and the problem still isn't solved.

Diagnosing Cause Example

The following is an example of the seven-step process:

1. Problem statement: _____

_____

2.	IS	IS NOT	3. DIFFERENCE	4. CHANGE
What?				
- Defect?				
- Object?				
Where?				
When?				
Extent?				

5. **Write probable cause statements.**
      1. _____
      2. _____
      3. _____

6. **Test the probable causes statements against the initial set of is and is not facts.**

7. **Verify the most probable cause.**

Now let's illustrate the seven-step problem-solving technique with a real-life example:

The Case of the Rejected Promotion

Tom Swift, Director of Marketing, shook his head in amazement. Jean Williams, one of his best telephone salespersons, had just turned down a promotion to outside salesperson. Of course, it would have meant a move outside the close-knit telemarketing group, but the possibility of a substantial increase in salary should have been tempting. It wouldn't have been so bad except that this was the second person to turn down the position. Tom had asked Sue Atkinson first, and, after thinking it over, she said, "No."

Tom had asked both of them why they turned down the promotion. Jean and Sue both had similar responses. Jean said that she was happy where she was and didn't want the stress of taking on new responsibilities. "And besides," she said, "I really enjoy the relationships that I have established over the years with my customers." Sue similarly said that she enjoyed her work and the people she worked with, and, like Jean, said that she had made many friends among her customers and didn't want to give them up.

A couple of years ago, Tom would have had to beat off outside sales applicants with a stick! Now, even though the opening had been posted for three weeks, not a single person had applied for it. Since there was a strong policy of promoting from within, it would be difficult to get approval to look outside the organization for a salesperson. Other departments in the organization had no problem finding applicants wishing promotions to other jobs.

"I don't know," thought Tom. "Maybe it's Betty." Betty had been Tom's outside sales manager for about three years, and had a reputation for being the toughest taskmaster in the organization. "Firm but fair" was her motto. And was she firm! Betty set high goals, and saw to it that her salespeople met them year after year. "Maybe that's the reason I can't get anybody to take this job," Tom thought. "Betty is just too hard to work for. She's not like Bill, the old manager who retired. He was a great leader and his people really liked him."

"Of course," Tom reflected, "it might be the telemarketers are afraid to make sales calls in person. Making sales calls face-to-face is a whole lot different than talking on the telephone. In some ways it's actually easier. You can see the customer's non-verbals and respond to them. As a result, our outside salespeople's call-to-sales ratio is better than the telemarketers' are.

"But in other ways it's harder to make calls in person. I think the salesperson feels rejection more keenly in a face-to-face situation than on the phone. Since neither Jean nor Sue has ever done this, they may just be afraid to face rejection in person.

"Also, an outside salesperson usually works alone. The telemarketers do work alone on the phone, but they have lots of opportunities to talk with each other during the day."

"The other big difference between in-person and telemarketing sales is the amount of time required on the job," mused Tom. "Sure, the outside people make more sales, and as a result make more money. But it's definitely not a nine-to-five job like telemarketing. The outside people spend more evening and weekend time preparing for their calls. And they leave home earlier, and usually get back later.

"But neither Jean nor Sue has a family, so the extra time shouldn't have been that much of a problem—considering how much better the money is. Besides, Sue said she would like to be considered for the telemarketing leader's job if it ever opens up, and that's definitely not a nine-to-five job!

"I just don't know what the problem is," thought Tom. "I do know that the telemarketers feel really good about working together. Ever since last year when we did those three team-building training workshops with the telemarketers as a pilot program, they have gotten along so much better. They're such good friends. And it's great to see the way they support each other."

Tom knew that his boss was going to ask him at the afternoon managers' meeting how he was doing filling the outside sales job. At this point, Tom didn't know what to say. "I don't want to jump to conclusions or do anything until I really know what's causing this problem," Tom thought. "But I bet it's Betty. Maybe I should think about what I can do to help her become a more congenial supervisor to work for."

As we examine the above example, we can see many possible reasons why the two telemarketers turned down this promotional opportunity: a tough supervisor, more responsibility, working alone without a support group, extra time required in an outside sales job, and fear of face-to-face rejection. As with most actual cases, there are a number of possible causes and each cause requires a different solution. If action is taken on the wrong cause, not only will the problem not be solved, but also there is a chance that the problem will get worse.

So Tom's first job is to get paper and pencil and write out a problem statement. He writes:

1. **"Two telemarketers have turned down a promotion to outside salesperson."**

Next, in Step 2, he lists what the problem is, followed by where, when and to what extent it is occurring, as follows:

2. THE PROBLEM IS			
WHAT: - *Telemarketers refusing promotion* - *Promotion to outside salesperson*			
WHERE: - *Telemarketing department*			
WHEN: - *Now*			
EXTENT: - *Serious—two people rejected promotion* - *No applicants*			

After Tom has written down what the problem is and where, when, and to what extent the problem *is* occurring, he next describes what, where, when, and the extent to which the problem *isn't* occurring.

1. "Two telemarketers have turned down a promotion to outside salesperson."

2. THE PROBLEM IS	THE PROBLEM IS NOT		
WHAT: - *Telemarketers refusing promotion*	- ***Telemarketers' job***		
- *Promotion to outside salesperson*	- ***Promotion within telemarketing department***		
WHERE: - *Telemarketing department*	- ***Other departments***		
WHEN: - *Now*	- ***Prior to two years ago***		
EXTENT: - *Serious—two people rejected promotion* - *No applicants*	- ***OK (the two telemarketers' acceptance of a promotion)*** - ***A number of applicants***		

In Step 3, Tom determines the difference between the situation in which the problem is occurring, and where it does not exist. That is, what factors are connected with the problem situation that are not present where there is not this problem? Thus Tom notes the factors in the "Difference" column:

1. "Two telemarketers have turned down a promotion to outside salesperson."

2. THE PROBLEM IS	THE PROBLEM IS NOT	3. DIFFERENCE	
WHAT: - *Telemarketers refusing promotion*	- *Telemarketers' job*	- ***Responsibility*** - ***Hours***	
- *Promotion to outside salesperson*	- *Promotion within telemarketing department*	- ***Established customer relationships*** - ***Betty, the boss***	
WHERE: - *Telemarketing department*	- *Other departments*	- ***Team-building training***	
WHEN: - *Now*	- *Prior to two years ago*		
EXTENT: - *Serious—two people rejected promotion* - *No applicants*	- *OK (the two telemarketers' acceptance of a promotion)* - *A number of applicants*		

Note that the "Difference" column may, and often will, be left blank in some of the rows (the EXTENT rows in this example). Also note that in solving real problems, there may be many differences between what the problem is and what it is not. Only list those factors (differences) that have a direct bearing on the problem. For example, a key difference between the "Telemarketers refusing promotions" and the "Telemarketers' (present) job" is that the promotion involves an increase in salary. But it doesn't make sense that someone would turn down a promotion to a new job because it pays more. Thus, even though "money" is a major difference between these two positions, it is not listed in the "Difference" column because it is not likely to be a cause of the telemarketers' refusing a promotion to outside sales.

In addition, note that the difference, "Betty, the boss," could have been written twice, once as shown adjacent to the set of is and is not facts, "Promotion to outside salesperson" and "Promotion within telemarketing department"; and once as the first set of "What" is and is not facts, "Telemarketers refusing promotion" and "Employees in other departments refusing promotions." Once we have "captured" a major difference on the grid, it is not necessary to rewrite it in other rows.

Tom's next step, #4, is to look carefully for changes that have taken place or would take place that might affect the thinking of the telemarketers concerning the promotion. So Tom wrote in the changes in column four.

1. "Two telemarketers have turned down a promotion to outside salesperson."

2. THE PROBLEM IS	THE PROBLEM IS NOT	3. DIFFERENCE:	4. CHANGES:
WHAT: - *Telemarketers refusing promotion*	- *Telemarketers' job*	- *Responsibility* - *Hours*	- ***Greater responsibility*** - ***Longer hours***
- *Promotion to outside salesperson*	- *Promotion within telemarketing department*	- *Established customer relationships* - *Betty, the boss*	- ***Loss of valued customers*** - ***Tougher supervision***
WHERE: - *Telemarketing department*	- *Other departments*	- *Team-building training*	- ***Closer relationships with peers***
WHEN: - *Now*	- *Prior to two years ago*		
EXTENT: - *Serious—two people rejected promotion* - *No applicants*	- *OK (the two telemarketers' acceptance of a promotion)* - *A number of applicants*		

After Tom identifies situational differences and critical changes, he is now ready for Step 5, *to create probable causes of the problem* (called "probable cause statements") related to each of the change factors. For example, in the illustration above, "Longer hours" is one of the changes involved in the promotion. Thus Tom would write a probable cause statement that relates this new change factor to his initial problem statement, as follows:

> *"Because a promotion to outside salesperson entails longer hours, two telemarketers turned down the promotion."*

Note here that Tom cannot say with certainty at this point, "Eureka, I've found the cause!" What he has identified is a probable cause—not a verified one. In fact, Tom finally identified five probable causes of the problem (one statement for each of the changes). He then constructs a chart in which he

1. Writes down each of the selected change factors.
2. Relates each change to the problem (rejected promotion) using a common sense link.

Thus he writes,

5. Write probable cause statements.

Change ➞ **Link** ➞ **Problem**

Longer hours	*may require telemarketers to give up too much personal time, thus resulting in*	*their rejection of the promotion*
Greater responsibility	*could be a hassle, thus causing*	*their rejection of the promotion*
Loss of established customers	*might be too upsetting, leading to*	*their rejection of the promotion*
Tougher supervisor	*could be very difficult to work for, therefore causing*	*their rejection of the promotion*
Closer relationships with peers	*as a result of the team training program may be the reason for*	*their rejection of the promotion*

In Step 6, Tom numbers his six pairs of "is/is not" facts concerning the what, where, when, and extent of the problem, and prepares to test his probable cause statements against these known sets of facts.

1. "Two telemarketers have turned down a promotion to outside salesperson."

2. THE PROBLEM IS	THE PROBLEM IS NOT	3. DIFFERENCE:	4. CHANGES:
WHAT: *(1) - Telemarketers refusing promotion*	*- Telemarketers' job*	*- Responsibility* *- Hours* *- Established customer relationships*	*- Greater responsibility* *- Longer hours* *- Loss of valued customers*
(2) - Promotion to outside salesperson	*- Promotion within telemarketing department*	*- Betty, the boss*	*- Tougher supervision*
WHERE: *(3) - Telemarketing department*	*- Other departments*	*- Team-building training*	*- Closer relationships with peers*
WHEN: *(4) - Now*	*- Prior to two years ago*		
EXTENT: *(5) - Serious—two people rejected promotion* *(6) - No applicants*	*- OK (the two telemarketers' acceptance of a promotion)* *- A number of applicants*		

Then on the right-hand side of his Probable Cause Statements chart, he adds six narrow columns corresponding to the six sets of "is/is not" facts. This makes a grid on which he can test each probable cause against the known facts, by answering the question:

"Does this probable cause statement account for the 'is/is not' facts concerning the WHAT/WHERE/WHEN and EXTENT of the problem?"

5. Probable cause statements.

6. Test cause statements

Change ——→ Link ——→ Problem

Set of facts #'s:

Change	Link	Problem	(1)	(2)	(3)	(4)	(5)	(6)
Greater responsibility	*could be a hassle, thus causing*	*their rejection of the promotion*	✓	A	A	A	✓	✓
Longer hours	*may require telemarketers to give up too much personal time, thus resulting in*	*their rejection of the promotion*	✓	A	A	A	✓	✓
Loss of established customers	*might be too upsetting, leading to*	*their rejection of the promotion*	✓	✓	✓	A	✓	✓
Tougher supervisor	*could be very difficult to work for, therefore causing*	*their rejection of the promotion*	✓	✓	✓	A	✓	✓
Closer relationships with peers	*as a result of the team training program may be the reason for*	*their rejection of the promotion*	✓	✓	✓	✓	✓	✓

Tom takes the first probable cause statement and asks, "If greater responsibility could be a hassle, thus causing their rejection of the promotion, does this explain why the telemarketers are refusing promotions ('is' fact), and there is no problem that is apparent with the telemarketers' job ('is not' fact)?" If Tom considers *only* this first set of facts, then his answer must be "Yes." So he puts a "✓" mark in the first box under "#1," as shown on the chart.

Using this same probable cause statement, Tom tests it against each of the other five sets of "is/is not" facts, and records his answers in column #1 of the chart. Because this probable cause statement makes sense and therefore is answered "Yes" in all six sets of facts, he records a "✓" in each of the boxes in column #1.

If a specific probable cause statement doesn't check out against a specific set of facts, he records an "A"—which stands for "Assumption." In other words, he assumes that something else must account for that set of "is/is not" facts. For instance, the second probable cause statement (longer hours) does not check out with set of facts #2. For Sue had said she would like a promotion to head up the telemarketing group. In other words, it does not make sense that people are refusing promotion to outside salesperson and not a promotion within the telemarketing department because both would require working extra hours. Likewise, in set of facts #3, promotions would usually require longer hours throughout the organization, not just in the telemarketing department. Nor does this probable cause check out with set of facts #4 —the problem is occurring now, but was not present prior to two years ago—because outside sales have always involved longer hours than telemarketing.

Tom checks out each probable cause against each set of "is/is not" facts, recording "✓'s" when the cause statement checks out, and an "A" when it doesn't. (If we don't have enough information to know whether one of our statements accounts for a set of facts, we can use a "?" to indicate this.)

After Tom checked all of his cause statements against all six of his sets of "is/is not" facts, only one cause appeared to account for every set of facts concerning the problem: "Closer relationships with peers as a result of the team training programs."

Tom's last step, #7, is verification of the most probable cause statement. Until he verifies that closer relationships resulting from the telemarketers' team training is the key reason for their rejection of the promotion offer, he cannot say that "closer relationships" is *the* cause, only the most probable cause.

Tom's probable cause grid analysis has not yet eliminated any causes, but rather tells him which cause to try to verify first, that is, "Closer relationships due to team training." If he cannot verify this as being the cause of the problem, he will then attempt to verify the next most probable cause or causes; in this case, "Loss of established customers" and "Tougher supervisor."

This problem solving approach is based on recognizing that a problem situation involves effects that, upon analysis, indicate a most probable cause. The effects point to a very particular kind of cause—one that would produce just the unique effects (problem) that have been observed.

As we have seen, the cause of any problem leaves a telltale imprint of clues (effects) that can be investigated along four lines. The first is *identity*. In "The Case of the Rejected Promotion," the problem's "identity" was the telemarketers' refusal of a promotion to an outside sales position. The second clue is *location*. The problem occurred in the telemarketing department, and not in other departments. The third clue is *timing*. The problem occurring now was not present prior to two years ago. And the fourth line of investigation is the *extent* of the problem—its size and severity. In the case above, with two people rejecting promotion to outside sales and no other applicants for the job, the problem is serious and needs attention. But because this problem was carefully analyzed, probable causes were identified for verification and any action will be directed to a verified cause.

Try using the seven-step problem-solving grid on the last page of this chapter to solve a problem you have. Note that when you complete this grid on a real problem, you may have some blank spaces in the grid. And since many people are task-oriented and want to solve a problem immediately these blanks can cause frustration. This is not only a normal reaction, it is often a positive one, since it gives you clear direction on where to go and whom to ask for the missing information. In other words, the grid process protects us from jumping to conclusions and taking the right action on the wrong cause!

One final point—problems that fit the criteria of a real problem (there must be a deviation from the standard, the cause is unknown, and we are concerned about the problem) don't stay problems for long. We will normally be motivated to find the cause and fix the problem. But, when we identify a list of existing problems, we will often find that our list includes a number of old problems. And these old problems frequently have known causes but haven't been solved simply because we have not made decisions about them. These are not true "problems" at all. They are situations requiring decisions (covered in the next chapter), not problem solving.

Skill Development

The following case will assist you in developing skills in actually using the Diagnosing Cause process.

The Case of the Unhappy Employee

Betty, office manager for the Department of Operations, was discouraged. She had just finished talking with her boss about Laurie, and the boss wanted to know what was causing Laurie to be such a problem. Betty didn't know. It was downright embarrassing. She had met with him to get some ideas on how to motivate Laurie and he had ended up lecturing her! "You don't do anything until you find out the cause of the problem," he said.

"Everything was great up until six months ago," thought Betty. "She was one of my best employees and then, almost overnight, she became one of my worst. I've got thirteen people in the department and they are a great bunch—except for Laurie. She is moody, unhappy, and has a poor attitude. She also comes in late, and I know that she even took sick leave when she wasn't really sick. It's like she just doesn't care anymore. A couple of times I asked her what was wrong, and she said, 'Nothing,' but she sure didn't look like nothing was wrong. I guess the main problem is she is just plain unhappy.

"Maybe she is still upset over the desk situation," thought Betty. "When we got ready to move, they told me I could set up the seating arrangement any way I wanted to, so that's what I told my people. Because Laurie has seniority in the department, she got first pick of the desks. But when we moved in, she had to take another desk because of the way the phones were arranged.

"Laurie is also a non-stop talker. It wasn't so bad in the old office six months ago when we were off to ourselves. Now there is a lot of traffic through the department and she grabs everybody that comes by. When she takes time to talk, it not only cuts down on the amount of work she does but also affects the production of the others. I really could put up with the talking if she were as good a worker as she used to be. The extra traffic doesn't seem to bother the other employees like it does Laurie.

"I also wish she would spend less time on the phone. A year ago she was elected president of her college alumni association, and now she spends time doing alumni business on organizational time. She calls the school alumni office, types memos, and seems to be thinking more about the alumni association than she does about her job.

"I just don't know what is causing Laurie's problem. Maybe it's the fact she doesn't get along with Joan. I've had to put her with Joan a number of times over the past two months. She hates Joan's work and doesn't like Joan either. A couple of years ago they were best friends. Now they can't stand each other. I guess if I had to work with someone I couldn't stand, I'd be unhappy too. I think that must be the real cause of Laurie's low morale.

"I think I'll tell the boss that the cause of Laurie's problem is the fact I've had to put her with Joan. So, what I could do is train one of the other employees to help Joan out and leave Laurie alone. This should take care of the problem," thought Betty with a sigh of relief. "I guess the boss is right: figuring out the cause of the problem is the first step."

Before you start analyzing this case using the grid found at the end of this chapter, here are some hints that may make it easier.

1. Normally, fill in the "Is" and "Is Not" columns first. Next, look for peculiar and pertinent differences between what the problem "Is" and what the problem "Is Not." Then, determine which of the differences involve changes.

2. In "The Case of the Unhappy Employee," differences and changes in the "Defect" (first block) and "Extent" (last block) do not normally occur. Therefore, in this case, we have crossed them out for you.

3. If there are numbers available in the "Extent" columns, use them, as they can tell us how serious the problem is. In other words, we can tell if the problem warrants spending the amount of time or money it may take to fix the problem. We don't wish to be guilty of later developing a $50,000 solution to fix a $3.00 problem.

4. In this case, there are three different "Is" and "Is Not" sets of facts that define the object. We have already listed one set ("Is Laurie" and "Is not the twelve other employees.") In all three sets, "Laurie" is the object, but the "Is Not" facts are different.

5. There are also two sets of "Is" and "Is Not" facts in the "Where" section of the grid. One of these has already been written for you. See if you can determine the other set.

6. The probable cause statements (possible diagnoses) are derived directly from the change column. Each change should have a specific probable cause statement.

7. Probable cause statements are written best by connecting the specific change being explained to the end result by a common sense link. Take each change, one at a time, from the change column and connect it to the end result ("Laurie is unhappy"). For example, the change "Works with Joan" could be written as follows:

Change	Link	End Result
Works with Joan . . .	*whom Laurie dislikes which results in . . .*	*Laurie's unhappiness.*

Or, it could be written as:

"Laurie doesn't like working with Joan which makes her unhappy."

8. The sixth step in the process is to test each probable cause statement against the original sets of facts. We do this by saying,

"If this statement is true, does it clearly explain why it IS this and IS NOT that (for each set of "Is" and "Is Not" facts)*?"*

To test out the first statement against each set of facts, we simply put a "✓" if the statement makes sense, a "?" if we honestly lack data, and an "A" if it doesn't check out at all. The "A" stands for "assumption." In other words, we would have to assume that something else must be true in order for the statement to check out in that specific set of "Is" and "Is Not" facts.

See if you can solve the Case of the Unhappy Employee by using the problem-solving grid on the next page. Then, when you are finished, turn to the next page and check your work.

A problem exists when (1) a deviation from an expected standard has occurred, (2) the cause of that deviation is uncertain, and (3) the deviation concerns you.

1. Problem Statement: _Laurie is unhappy_

STEPS IN DIAGNOSING CAUSE		2. Problem IS	Problem IS NOT	#	3. Difference (between IS / IS NOT)	4. Changes (concerning Difference)
1. Write a specific, negative problem statement.	What is the Defect?			1		
2. Describe the problem by writing what, where, when, and to what extent the problem IS and IS NOT occurring.	What is the Object? (who/what failed)	_Laurie_		2		
		Laurie		3		
3. Determine any peculiar, pertinent differences between what the problem IS and what the problem IS NOT.		_Laurie_	_12 other employees_	4	_Relationship with Joan_	_Works with Joan_
					Non-stop talker	_No Change_
4. Look carefully for changes that have occurred in and around the differences.	What?			5		
5. Write a probable cause statement for each change discovered in Step 4 above.		_Job_	_PTA_	6		
6. Test each probable cause statement against each specific set of IS and IS NOT facts, and identify the most probable cause.	When?			7		
7. Verify the most probable cause statement, take appropriate action, and monitor results.	Extent? (seriousness)			8		

6. Test each probable cause statement against each set of "IS/IS NOT" facts.

Probable cause does explain facts = ✓ Does not explain facts = A Needs more info. = ?

	(1)	(2)	(3)	(4)	(5)	(6)	(7)	(8)
				✓		✓		

5. Probable Cause Statements

(One for each change from column 4)

Change	Link (to problem)	Problem
Works with Joan	_whom she hates_	_making her unhappy_
		making her unhappy
		making her unhappy
		making her unhappy

7. Most Probable Cause Statement: _____

- What can be done to verify that this is the cause? _____
- Given this cause is verified, what actions can be taken to correct the initial problem? _____

A problem exists when (1) a deviation from an expected standard has occurred, (2) the cause of that deviation is uncertain, and (3) the deviation concerns you.

1. Problem Statement: _____ **Laurie is unhappy**

STEPS IN DIAGNOSING CAUSE		2. Problem IS	Problem IS NOT	#	3. Difference (between IS / IS NOT)	4. Changes (concerning Difference)
1. Write a specific, negative problem statement.	What is the Defect?	Poor Attitude / Moody / Sick Leave / Unhappy	Complaining / Happy	1	✕	✕
2. Describe the problem by writing what, where, when, and to what extent the problem IS and IS NOT occurring.	What is the Object? (who/what failed)	Laurie	Supervisor	2	Job Responsibility	No Change
3. Determine any peculiar, pertinent differences between what the problem IS and what the problem IS NOT.		Laurie	Joan	3	Laurie hates Joan's work	No Change
4. Look carefully for changes that have occurred in and around the differences.		Laurie	12 other employees	4	Relationship with Joan / Non-stop talker	Works with Joan / No Change
5. Write a probable cause statement for each change discovered in Step 4 above.	What?	New office	Old office	5	Desk / Desk Location / V.P. of PTA	New Desk / Traffic flow increased / V.P. one year ago
6. Test each probable cause against each specific set of IS and IS NOT facts, and identify the most probable cause.		Job	PTA	6	Supervisor	Increased traffic flow
7. Verify the most probable cause statement, take appropriate action, and monitor results.	When?	6 months ago	Not prior to that time	7	(Ditto: New office/old office)	(Ditto: New office/old office) / New desk location
	Extent? (seriousness)	Serious	OK	8	Moved / Traffic flow	Increased traffic flow

6. Test each probable cause statement against each set of "IS/IS NOT" facts.

Probable cause does explain facts = ✓   Needs more info. = "?"
Does not explain facts = "A"

	(1)	(2)	(3)	(4)	(5)	(6)	(7)	(8)
	✓	✓	A	✓	✓	✓	A	✓
	✓	✓	✓	✓	✓	✓	✓	✓
	A	A	A	A	✓	A	✓	A
	A	✓	✓	✓	A	A	A	✓

5. Probable Cause Statements (One for each change from column 4)

Change	Link (to problem)	Problem
Works with Joan	whom she hates	making her unhappy
New desk	is undesirable	making her unhappy
Increased traffic flow	distracts Laurie	making her unhappy
New PTA responsibilities	take time	making her unhappy

7. Most Probable Cause Statement: _____ **Laurie's new desk is undesirable making her unhappy.**

- What can be done to verify that this is the cause? _Go talk to Laurie and ask specific questions about the desk._
- Given this cause is verified, what actions can be taken to correct the initial problem? _1. Express understanding and empathy._ **_2. Make any needed changes, if possible._**

Diagnosing Cause Summary

In this chapter, we have seen the

- Importance of thinking through a problem before attempting to solve it
- Need to make the problem visible in writing
- Benefit of using a problem-solving process
- Importance of not jumping to conclusions and taking premature, costly action

The problem-solving technique we have reviewed is as useful in the hands of a group as it is for the individual problem solver. As a participative leader, you can use this process with your employees in group meetings or with your coworkers in team meetings by asking the following oral questions:

☑ 1. Problem statement

"What is wrong?"

☑ 2. Problem description

What Defect?

"What symptoms do we have?"
"What symptoms don't we have that we might expect?"

What Object?

"What/who has failed?"
"What/who has not failed?"

Where?

"Where do we have the problem?"
"Where don't we have the problem?"

When?

"When did it start?"
"When was everything OK?"

Extent?

"How serious is it?"
"How big is it?"
"What is normal?"

☑ **3. Differences**

> *"What is different/unusual/peculiar about this problem?"*
> *"Why is it doing this, and not that?"*
> *"Why did this fail, and not that?"*
> *"Why did it happen here, and not there?"*
> *"Why did it start then, and not before?"*
> *"Why is it this much bigger or more serious than normal?"*

☑ **4. Changes**

> *"What has changed?"*
> *"How has it changed?"*
> *"When did it change?"*

☑ **5. Probable causes**

> *"How could this change cause the problem?"*

☑ **6. Mentally testing**

> *"If this is the cause, does it explain all the facts of our problem-description?"*

☑ **7. Verification**

> *"Who else can we talk to, what records can we check, and what evidence can we find to determine that this is the real cause of our problem?"*

By using this seven-step diagnostic process, we can resolve problems quicker, correct causes, not just effects, solve problems so they stay solved, and prevent new problems by taking the right action.

On the following page is a problem-solving grid you may duplicate to use as a guide in solving your own problems.

PROBLEM-SOLVING WORKSHEET

A problem exists when (1) a deviation from an expected standard has occurred, (2) the cause of that deviation is uncertain, and (3) the deviation concerns you.

1. Problem Statement: _____

STEPS IN DIAGNOSING CAUSE		2. Problem IS	Problem IS NOT	3. Difference (between IS / IS NOT)	4. Changes (concerning Difference)
1. Write a specific, negative problem statement.	What is the Defect?				
2. Describe the problem by writing what, where, when, and to what extent the problem IS and IS NOT occurring.	What is the Object? (who/what failed)				
3. Determine any peculiar, pertinent differences between what the problem IS and what the problem IS NOT.	What?				
4. Look carefully for changes that have occurred in and around the differences.	When?				
5. Write a probable cause statement for each change discovered in Step 4 above.	Extent? (seriousness)				
6. Test each probable cause against each specific set of IS and IS NOT facts, and identify the most probable cause.					
7. Verify the most probable cause statement, take appropriate action, and monitor results.					

5. Probable Cause Statements (One for each change from column 4)

Change	Link (to problem)	Problem

6. Test each probable cause statement against each set of "IS/IS NOT" facts.

Probable cause does explain facts = ✓
Does not explain facts = A

	(1)	(2)	(3)	(4)	(5)	(6)	(7)	(8)	(9)

7. Most Probable Cause Statement:
- What can be done to verify that this is the cause? _____
- Given this cause is verified, what actions can be taken to correct the initial problem? _____

240

11

Leadership
Decision Making

The decision to which there is only one alternative is always a bad decision.

P. Drucker

With the elimination of layers of management, organizations today are delegating downward ever more responsibility for making decisions. All employees, from non-exempts to department heads, are making decisions that have greater impact on their working environments. Not only have decisions been transferred to the employees who actually do the work, but these decisions often have greater impact. This is because problems drive decisions, and the severity of problems has increased in our world. In other words, problems require solutions, and serious problems require major decisions. To compound the situation, decisions also require action and action requires a plan.

Making poor decisions, however, can have costly consequences. Selecting the wrong new employee, promoting the wrong person, or deciding on the wrong procedure can, in the long run, cost hundreds of thousands of dollars. Not only is money wasted, time is also lost and morale suffers.

Unfortunately, most schools don't teach effective decision making. Simplistic processes like Force Field Analysis and PERT charts abound. But proven, step-by-step decision-making processes are not normally seen in our educational institutions. Happily for us, two individuals, Charles Kepner and Benjamin Tregoe, conducted extensive research and wrote a now classic book called *The Rational Manager*. In this book, they detailed a process for effective decision making and planning. The ideas that are presented here result from their earlier work and continued application by many other writers.

In the following two chapters, you will see two processes: 1) Selecting the Best Alternative, and 2) Planning. Selecting the best alternative (solution) is only one half of effective decision-making; the other half is implementing that decision with a plan and then protecting that plan from potential problems. Both phases are crucial in successful decision making. A decision without a protective plan is as likely to fail as a plan based on a poor decision.

Like many effective on-the-job tools, they work not only in occupations, but they also work at home. Because it is often easier to relate to a generic home example, some of the examples given in this chapter are life decisions that have little to do with the job. What are taught are processes! Processes can be learned in one setting and then easily applied to another.

In this chapter, you will learn how to 1) write open decision statements, 2) determine the underlying objectives in making decisions and the difference between *must* and *want* objectives, 3) create alternatives, and 4) evaluate the risks involved before making a final decision. You will see a logical, step-by-step method that will help you make even more effective decisions. We'll begin with some important ideas on how to write a decision statement.

☑ **Step 1. Write an open decision statement.**

The first step in effective decision making is to take the time to write an open decision statement. This forces us to think through the decision before it is made, makes it easier to get help from others, keeps us from making snap decisions, puts our false assumptions on the table, and allows us to learn from our past written decisions.

In addition to making decision statements visible by writing them out, we also need to examine the way we write the statement. The word binary, commonly used in computer departments, is used to describe something that has two parts. Binary decisions are statements such as "Accept or reject that proposal," "Go to San Francisco or not," "Vote 'yes' or 'no' on gun control," or "Quit my job or not." These statements may force us to make a premature comparison of only two alternatives.

To make more effective decisions, we keep decision statements open for more than two alternatives. For example, we could take the binary decision statement, "Accept or reject that proposal," and rewrite it to give us other alternatives. If we start decision statements with the words "Select the best . . .," we can almost guarantee an *open* decision statement. Thus, the first binary statement above can be written, "Select the best proposal." The second binary decision statement, "Go to San Francisco or not," becomes "Select the best city to visit." Now we are free to choose to go to San Francisco, New York, or even New Orleans.

How would we turn "Vote 'yes' or 'no' on gun control" into an open decision statement? (I'm not advocating for or against gun control, but it does make a good example.) Sometimes it helps to ask the question, "Why would someone want gun control?" Note that gun control is one possible solution to at least two different problems—reducing crime and preventing gun accidents. As Peter Drucker said, "Trying to solve two problems with one solution very seldom works." In this case, identifying the underlying reasons for gun control allows us to examine two entirely different problems: 1) reduce crime, and 2) prevent gun accidents.

Rather than limiting our decision statement to only one solution, it seems far better to determine the primary problems involved and put each problem in a decision statement. This will allow us to develop a whole list of different alternative solutions for each decision statement. For example, the "reduce crime" and "prevent gun accidents" problems could generate a whole list of solutions as follows:

Problems:	High Crime Rate	Gun Accidents
Decision Statements:	Select best way to reduce crime.	Select best way to reduce gun accidents.
Alternatives:	1. Gun control 2. Stiffer penalties 3. More police 4. Better security	1. Gun Control 2. Education 3. "Safety" ammunition 4. Childproof guns

Note that making the decision statements *open* now makes many different alternatives available. We can still implement gun control if we wish. But by transforming the initial gun control statement into two pertinent open statements, there now are a variety of possible choices.

 Step 2. Develop objectives.

The next step in decision making is to decide what we want to do—our goals, objectives, desired results—before creating alternative solutions. Developing objectives before alternatives counteracts the tendency to choose only those objectives that fit our pre-selected solutions.

Objectives come from questions such as:

"What factors should I consider?"

  Examples:

- Time
- Location
- Approvals

"What results do I want?"

Examples:

- Efficiency
- Productivity
- Safety
- Recognition

- Saving money
- Satisfaction
- High morale

"What resources are available?"

Examples:

- People
- Equipment
- Skills

- Budget
- Materials
- Knowledge

"What restrictions are required?"

Examples:

- Law
- Standards
- Ethics

- Policy
- Values

We need to get help from others in writing out our list of objectives. Include all-important items that are considerations in making the decision. The more sound data we have here, the better our final decision will be.

Take a look at the following example. Read the case study, noting what you feel are the important objectives in this situation.

The Case of the Difficult Dwelling Decision

Matt and his wife, Cathleen, sat at the kitchen table talking about their plan to purchase a home. Their lease would expire in four months, and Matt knew that Cathleen was looking forward to leaving the cramped three-bedroom rancher. With four children—two girls ages 16 and 5, and two boys 15 and 9—it had been difficult for everyone. It was hard on their teenage daughter who had to share her room with her little sister. It was also hard on the boys. They fought constantly, each blaming the other for messing up the room, and neither would accept responsibility for the mess that the other one had made. Fortunately, the house they had rented had a large yard for the dogs.

Matt hoped that they could find a 90% mortgage; they could just manage to put $20,000 toward a down payment and closing costs. It would wipe out their savings, and with no way of borrowing extra money for emergencies it would be risky, but it would be well worth it.

Matt hoped that they could get a garage for the boat, as he hated having to leave it out in the rain. Cathleen said they needed at least two baths. In fact, she said if a house didn't have two full baths, she wouldn't consider it. She was sick of "Grand Central Station" as she called their single bathroom. Their house must have public sewage, water, and gas, because all their appliances were gas, and Matt had sworn never to have a septic system again. It would be nice to be located within one mile of a shopping area. That was the one redeeming factor about their present home—it was only two blocks from a small shopping center.

Fortunately, schools were no problem; the school system in the area was excellent no matter where you lived.

To get the size house they needed for the money they had to spend, Matt and Cathleen knew they would have to buy a considerable distance from town. They didn't mind the drive, as long as the house wasn't more than 20 miles from work by the expressway and they didn't have to drive with the sun in their eyes in the morning and evening.

What are the objectives in this case? Write them in the space provided below.

1. _____
2. _____
3. _____
4. _____
5. _____
6. _____
7. _____
8. _____
9. _____
10. _____

When we finish writing down our objectives, the next step is to decide which of them are required ("must" objectives), and which are desired ("want" objectives). Then when we develop alternative solutions, each solution must meet the required must objectives or it is not acceptable. This will save time later by preventing us from considering alternatives that don't meet the required objectives.

Establish must objectives by looking at basic needs such as budget, time, policy, rules, or law. For example, must objectives might be statements such as "The fourth-quarter budget clearly restricts us to a maximum of $24,000 for that project" or "The plan must absolutely be implemented by January the 5th of next year." By definition, a must is 1) important to the individual writing the objective and 2) quantifiable to everyone. In other words, everyone would agree on whether or not the must objective is a measurable statement.

Although the budget is not to exceed $24,000, it would be great to bring the project in under budget and in less time. Or, even though it must be completed by January 5th, it would be nice to have it in less time. These are "want" objectives. Want objectives are often comparisons, such as low cost, least time, largest, nicest, best, biggest, etc. An objective may be extremely important, but if it can't be measured, then it would still be a want.

Now, considering the objectives in the "Case of the Difficult Dwelling Decision," which of the following do you think are "must" objectives and which are only "wants"?

		Must	**Want**
1.	Available in 4 months		
2.	Minimum of 4 bedrooms		
3.	Large Yard (approx. 1/4 acre min.)		
4.	Maximum of $20,000 out of pocket		
5.	Garage for the boat		
6.	Two baths		
7.	Public Utilities (sewage, water, gas)		
8.	Near shopping area (within 1 mile)		
9.	Not more than 20 miles from work		
10.	Not west of town		

Note that must objectives are not desirable unless they are absolutely necessary. There is a human tendency to put in lots of must objectives, but they do restrict alternatives. The more must objectives, the fewer options are available.

In the Case of the Difficult Dwelling Decision, your must and want objectives probably would be different from Matt and Cathleen's if you were making this judgment for yourself. In their case, however, they felt that the objectives "available in 4 months, minimum of 4 bedrooms, maximum down payment and closing costs of $20,000, two baths, and public utilities" were musts.

Three alternatives are listed below. Which, if any, of these alternatives don't meet the objectives that Matt and Cathleen established in the decision to purchase a home?

1. A new tri-level home with a tiny yard, 4 bedrooms, 2-1/2 baths, and available for only $200,000. It was approximately 15 miles from work with no shopping area nearby. Public gas, water, and sewage were available. They could get a 90% mortgage with immediate possession, and the builder, who was quite anxious to sell, would pay all the closing costs.

2. A new house that Matt really liked had 4 bedrooms and a single-car garage. In addition, it had 2 baths and a shopping area that was only 4 blocks away. The yard was very small, but it did have public utilities including gas. It was only 10 miles from work and would be available in 3 months. It was listed at $180,000, a 90% mortgage was available, and the builder would pay 1% of the 2% closing costs.

3. This house was Cathleen's choice. The house was about 6 years old and in a beautiful neighborhood. The huge yard had many trees and a chain link fence for the dogs. Matt liked the fully developed yard, the fact that it was only 6 miles from work, and the large single-car garage with extra room for a workshop. Because it was a "resale" and not a new home, an 80% mortgage was the best that could be obtained. However, the owner had agreed to pay all closing costs. There was a shopping area only three blocks away and the elementary school was only four blocks from the house. Gas and public sewage were available, and the house had 4 bedrooms and 2 baths. The older couple who had kept the house spotless was moving out in 2 months, and at only $190,000, it was a bargain.

After reviewing the alternatives in the Case of the Difficult Dwelling Decision, it is obvious that Matt and Cathleen just don't have the funds for the third alternative. In real life, they looked at this house three times before they regretfully determined there was no way they could purchase it. They wasted their time, the owner's time, and the real-estate broker's time, all because they didn't take the time in the beginning to establish their objectives and specify which were wants and which were musts.

In order to develop additional skills in determining the difference between a must and want objective, read the following list of objectives. Determine if each statement is 1) important to the writer, and 2) measurable to everyone who reads the statement. Place a check in the first column if the statement is very important to the writer and in the second column if the statement is measurable. Then indicate which statements received both checks and therefore qualify as a must objective. When you have finished, turn the page and check your answers.

Is It a Must?

Objectives:	Important to the writer	Measurable to everyone	Must or Want
1. I'll only hire someone who's really easy to get along with.			
2. My new home must be all brick.			
3. It would be nice to have the meeting in building 220, but we could go elsewhere.			
4. I'd like to work in an office with a good view, but I really don't care too much.			
5. The only car I will consider is a van that seats a minimum of 6 people.			
6. It's imperative that we find a hotel that's comfortable.			
7. According to our estimate, we shouldn't pay more than $50 for a new wombat, but actually we can go over that if we have to.			
8. If the restaurant doesn't have a private dining room that accommodates 35 people, we can't consider it.			
9. For us to accept that new product, it must be feasible.			
10. I *must* be able to get along with the person I report to.			

The correct answers to the *Is It a Must* exercise are as follows:

Objectives:	Important to the writer	Measurable to everyone	Must or Want
1. I'll only hire someone who's really easy to get along with.	✓		**W**
2. My new home must be all brick.	✓	✓	**M**
3. It would be nice to have the meeting in building 220, but we could go elsewhere.		✓	**W**
4. I'd like to work in an office with a good view, but I really don't care too much.			**W**
5. The only car I will consider is a van that seats a minimum of 6 people.	✓	✓	**M**
6. It's imperative that we find a hotel that's comfortable.	✓		**W**
7. According to our estimate, we shouldn't pay more than $50 for a new wombat, but actually we can go over that if we have to.		✓	**W**
8. If the restaurant doesn't have a private dining room that accommodates 35 people, we can't consider it.	✓	✓	**M**
9. For us to accept that new product, it must be feasible.	✓		**W**
10. I *must* be able to get along with the person I report to.	✓		**W**

The key learning points from these must and want exercises are that 1) we don't want to have must objectives unless we really need them, 2) the writer of the objectives determines how important the objective is, and 3) everyone should agree on the measurability of the objective.

Before proceeding to the last two steps, creating alternatives and analyzing risk, let's look at another example that will help tie the process together. Read the following case study, noting what you feel are the important objectives in this situation.

The Case of the Complex Choice

Bill, maintenance team leader for the Wonder Wombat organization located in Craigsville, Virginia, needed to hire a new employee for his section.

1. Write an open decision statement.

He called a meeting of his team, and as they watched expectantly, wrote out a decision statement on a flip chart as follows:

"Select best entry-level employee for our maintenance team"

As he wrote, Bill said, "You know that we have been authorized a new entry-level maintenance person. This is the first time we have been given the authority to select our own team member. So, let's do it right."

2. Develop objectives.

"The first thing we need to do," Bill continued, "is to generate a list of the things we want in the new employee. In other words, what knowledge, skills, or abilities does the new person need to do the job? What ideas do you have?"

After a moment's silence, Joan, the electronics technician, said, "It would be good if he or she already had a fundamental understanding of basic electricity. You know, if he or she could do things like change a lamp fixture, replace a florescent ballast, install a socket or switch, and most important, read an electronic schematic."

Tom, the pipe specialist, said, "Yes, it would help if he could read a schematic, but how about using simple tools? He should be able to solder using a gun or torch, use basic hand tools, know a voltmeter from a pressure gauge, and be willing to take on the nasty jobs that sometimes have to be done. I don't want a prima donna who's too good to unstop a commode!"

"Yeah," said Rick, another member of the team, "handling tools is important. But we can teach him what he doesn't know. It seems to me that what's more important is that whoever we hire has a good attitude. You know, gets along well with people."

"And with a good attitude," responded Tom, "is the need for good work habits. We need somebody that we don't have to pick up after, gets to work on time, and doesn't hold up the rest of us. In other words, let's get somebody who's a hard worker and doesn't goof off!"

"Say," suggested Joe, a technician, "what about my brother? You all met him at the picnic last month. He's a hard worker and a great guy! I know he is tired of driving a beer truck. He'd fit right in with the rest of us."

Bill, who had been writing objectives on the flip chart with a magic marker, paused and said, "Hiring your brother is a good idea, Joe. But personnel won't let us because he is your brother. So let's hold off considering alternatives until we've had a chance to finish the objectives. OK? So what other factors should we consider in hiring a new employee for our section?"

"How about reading and writing?" asked Rick. "I know it sounds stupid, but there are people in the job market who can't read and write. Any maintenance person we hire must be able to read!"

"Good point," said Bill. "I'll add that to the list. What else? How about you, Chuck? Any other ideas?"

Chuck, who hadn't said anything up to this point, thought for a minute and said, "I don't know. The only thing I can think of is that whoever takes this job has to be willing to work for the money we pay."

Bill, writing, said, "OK, good suggestion. 'Accepts salary limitations.' Anything else?"

Bill waits for a moment, and then says, "I've got one. We need to hire someone who is available now, or at least within the next few weeks."

"Hey, I've got another," exclaimed Chuck. "You know that we are getting more and more requests for hardwiring computer networks. Joyce, you can do it, but you don't have time. Getting that outside contractor in here is a pain. It would be great if the guy we hired knew something about computer networks!"

At this point, the team had developed the following objectives to use to make its decision:

- *Understands basic electricity*
- *Knows how to use hand tools*
- *Willing to do any type of task*
- *Gets along with others*
- *Has good work habits*
- *Able to read and write*
- *Meets salary requirements*
- *Is available to work in 3 weeks*
- *Can hardwire computer networks*

Bill then explained must and want objectives to his team. They felt that "Available to work within 3 weeks," "Meets salary requirements" (which they specified), and "Reads and writes" were their musts. The team spent considerable time discussing the measurability of the objective, "Reads and writes." They realized that the objective was not a "must" the way they wrote it because it wasn't quantifiable. Thus they developed a simple reading and writing test based on the forms and text that they used within their section. They showed this test to the human resources department and received permission to use it in their evaluation of applicants. Because of their discussions, they rewrote this objective to state, "Passes reading and writing test."

At this point, their decision analysis looked like this:

1. Write an open decision statement.

"Select best entry-level employee for our maintenance team"

2. Develop objectives.

- *Understands basic electricity*   Want
- *Knows how to use hand tools*   Want
- *Willing to do any type of task*   Want
- *Gets along with others*   Want
- *Good work habits*   Want
- *Passes reading and writing test*   **Must**
- *Meets salary requirements*   **Must**
- *Available to work in 3 weeks*   **Must**
- *Can hardwire computer networks*   Want

Obviously some of their want objectives were more important than others. Understanding basic electricity may be a great deal more important than knowing how to use hand tools. (Teaching someone who doesn't have a clue about Ohm's law, series circuits, parallel circuits, capacitance, and inductance is difficult; showing someone how to use hand tools is likely not as hard.) Therefore, the quality of the team's selection process will be improved if they assign higher weights to more desirable objectives to reflect their greater relative importance. Using a scale of 1 to 10, and giving the highest number to the most important want objective, their list might now look like this:

1. Write an open decision statement.

"Select best entry-level employee for our maintenance team"

2. Develop objectives.

- *Understands basic electricity*   9
- *Knows how to use hand tools*   8
- *Willing to do any type of task*   6
- *Gets along with others*   7
- *Good work habits*   5
- *Passes reading and writing test*   **Must**
- *Meets salary requirements*   **Must**
- *Available to work in 3 weeks*   **Must**
- *Can hardwire computer networks*   2

Note that they didn't assign a "10" to any of the want objectives. We try to avoid assigning "10's" to our objectives. We save them for extremely important objectives that normally would be musts, but can't be because they aren't measurable.

Note also that the assigned weights will differ according to the raters. In a group, we obtain a consensus. If we're not leading a team but doing this process by ourselves, we can seek help from others by asking, "How important do you think this objective is compared to that one, and why?" Must objectives may also have a corresponding want objective. For example, if it had been important to Bill's team, they could have written a new want objective, "Can start work at any time over the next 3 weeks" and maybe rated it a "2." Here, they felt that it wasn't very important that somebody start immediately, so they did not rewrite the must objective. However, they looked at the must objective, "Meets salary requirements" and added a new want objective, "Satisfaction with salary" and rated it a "4."

 Step 3. Create alternatives.

In this step we create alternatives to fulfill our objectives. At this point, it is often helpful to think in terms of the following classifications:

- *corrective* alternatives that solve the problem;
- *interim* alternatives that don't remedy the problem, but do buy time; and
- *adaptive* alternatives that allow us to live with the problem.

Corrective action is normally the best type of alternative for fixing specific problems as it is usually the least expensive. For example, if the problem is a fire, I can take corrective action by putting the fire out with a fire extinguisher. Or I might take interim action by doing something to restrict airflow to the fire. Or I could take adaptive action by deciding to let the fire burn out—and roast hot dogs! By being aware of all three of these classes of alternatives, we can significantly increase the number of available approaches.

In developing creative alternatives, two things are helpful. First, we brainstorm a list of possibilities, and later evaluate and combine them to create workable solutions. Second, we get help! We need to talk to people whose opinions and judgment we trust. We can talk with people who are involved in the decision or play a role in carrying it out. Since we wrote out our decision, we can show others both the decision statement and the alternatives we are considering, and ask them for additional ideas.

It is much easier to make good decisions after we have clarified our objectives and created alternatives. For example, suppose Bill and the team were faced with the following applicants. Should they eliminate any of these prospective employees because he or she fails to satisfy at least one of the must objectives?

Applicant #1: Female. Great personality. High school graduate. Attended a two-year electronics technical school after high school. New to the job market. States she is willing to do any type of work. Little knowledge of work habits, as she has not been employed since school years. Fourteen years ago worked part-time after school as a maintenance person for a local grocery store chain. In the toolbox test that was devised by the team, she correctly identified 15 of the 16 tools that she was shown (missed the spanner wrench). She says that she was seldom late for work. Unable to check references since the grocery store is now out of business. Reads and writes well, meets the salary requirements. Has no knowledge of computers or computer networks. She is unemployed and states she could come to work tomorrow. Said she really needs the job and the money is fine.

Applicant #2: Male. In the interviews, seemed quiet and withdrawn—almost depressed. His job was eliminated when there was a major reorganization at his old company. He has been out of work 3 months and is having difficulty obtaining employment. He is a highly skilled maintenance person with 20 years of experience in carpentry, hydraulics, and electricity. He correctly identified all 16 tools in the toolbox test. His references check out. He has good work habits, but a history of sickness. His old organization would not specify type of illness. He said he needs a job, and would be satisfied with the starting salary though it is far less than what he had been making. He also stated that he doesn't mind doing any type of work, no matter how disagreeable. Reads and writes well. High school education. Could start tomorrow. Doesn't know anything about computers or computer networks.

Applicant #3: Male. High school graduate. Worked for his father during the summer while in high school. Father runs a small electrical contracting business out of his home. Father says his son is a hard worker, has good work habits, and never missed a single day from work. Applicant states he is not too proud to do any task that needs to be done. Reads, but writing skills are marginal. His writing sample, full of errors in basic grammar, had many misspelled words, and his handwriting is barely legible. When questioned about his writing, applicant stated that he has always had difficulty with his spelling. Correctly identified all 16 tools in the toolbox test. He meets salary requirements, and would like to start immediately. Seems like a nice guy, but very serious. Did not laugh or joke during any of his interviews with members of the team even when it would have been appropriate. He is, however, a computer whiz. Has his own computer. Talks computer talk. Is familiar with computer networks although he has never hardwired a system.

Must Bill's team eliminate any one of these three applicants from consideration because he or she fails to meet a must objective? They have a difficult decision. They cannot consider applicant #3 because he doesn't meet one of their must objectives, "Passes reading and writing test." We have pointed out that it is not desirable to have must objectives that are not absolutely necessary, because they eliminate alternatives. So, unless the team can find a way out of their dilemma by making "reading and writing" a want objective, they cannot select this alternative and must confine their attention to applicants #1 and #2, both of whom meet all their required must objectives.

This decision is typical of the ones you face at work and at home. You may want to select, or at least consider, a particular alternative, and too often consider it even when it doesn't meet a must. Decisions turn out better when we first take the time to determine objectives, rank them, create several alternatives, and then rationally evaluate each in terms of musts and wants. This process produces good decisions because it helps us determine what is really important.

The team is now ready to write down information on how well each applicant meets each objective. Usually, it is probably best to first write in the data, noting "Yes" or "No," for the must objectives. As discussed, applicant #3 was eliminated because he did not meet the must reading and writing requirement.

Their chart now looks like this:

1. Write an open decision statement.

"Select best employee for our maintenance team"

2. Develop objectives.   3. Create alternatives.

		Applicant #1	Applicant #2	Applicant #3
Understands basic electricity	9	Two years technical school	Highly skilled	
Knows how to use hand tools	8	Part-time maint. person 14 years ago. Scored 15 of 16 on tool test	20 years of experience. Scored 16 of 16 on tool test	
Willing to do any type of task	6	Says is willing to do any kind of work	Was a senior craftsman but indicates would do any task	
Gets along with others	7	Great personality	Quiet and withdrawn, seems almost depressed	
Good work habits	5	Can't verify work habits	Good work habits but has a history of illness	
Passes reading and writing test	M	Yes	Yes	No
Meets salary requirements	M	Yes	Yes	
Available to work in 3 weeks	M	Yes	Yes	
Satisfaction with salary	4	Satisfied	Salary may not meet his needs	
Can hardwire computer networks	2	No experience with computers or networks	No experience with computers or networks	

Notice that the team could have written "yes" and "no" answers for their objectives. But later, when they compare the alternatives with each other, it will be very difficult to weight a series of "yes's" and "no's." By writing in data or information they can later judge which alternative is best. (Of course, must objectives always include "yes" or "no," i.e., go or no-go, meets or doesn't meet the objective.) For example, in the objective, "Gets along with others," they could have written in "Yes" or "No" for both applicants, but the team chose to write down more detailed information.

Having previously compared and weighted their want objectives using a value scale of 1 to 10, the team will now do the same for each alternative. For each objective (each row), they will automatically give the best alternative a "10," and the other alternative something less then 10. (This will keep them from double-weighting an objective.) They will not weight the must objectives, since these objectives are really screening devices that eliminate alternatives that cannot be considered.

See the next page for the example of weights assigned to the alternatives.

1. Write an open decision statement.

"Select best employee for our maintenance team"

2. Develop objectives.   3. Create alternatives.

		Applicant #1	Applicant #2	Applicant #3
Understands basic electricity	9	**2** Two years technical school	**10** Highly skilled	
Knows how to use hand tools	8	**2** Part-time maint. person 14 years ago. Scored 15 of 16 on tool test	**10** 20 years of experience. Scored 16 of 16 on tool test	
Willing to do any type of task	6	**10** Says she is willing to do any kind of work	**8** Was a senior craftsman but indicates would do any task	
Gets along with others	7	**10** Great personality	**4** Quiet and withdrawn, seems almost depressed	
Good work habits	5	**10** Can't verify work habits	**8** Good work habits but has a history of illness	
Passes reading and writing test	M	Yes	Yes	No
Meets salary requirements	M	Yes	Yes	
Available to work in 3 weeks	M	Yes	Yes	
Satisfaction with salary	4	**10** Satisfied	**3** Salary may not meet his needs	
Can hardwire computer networks	2	**10** No experience with computers or networks	**10** No experience with computers or networks	

As shown on the next page, the team multiplies the weight of each want objective by the weight of each remaining alternative (applicants #1 and #2), and records each product (objective weight X alternative weight) in the table.

1. Write an open decision statement.

"Select best employee for our maintenance team"

2. Develop objectives.   ## 3. Create alternatives.

		Applicant #1	Applicant #2	Applicant #3
Understands basic electricity	9	**X 2 = 18** Two years technical school	**X 10 = 90** Highly skilled	
Knows how to use hand tools	8	**X 2 = 16** Part-time maint. person 14 years ago. Scored 15 of 16 on tool test	**X 10 = 80** 20 years of experience. Scored 16 of 16 on tool test	
Willing to do any type of task	6	**X 10 = 60** Says she is willing to do any kind of work	**X 8 = 48** Was a senior craftsman but indicates would do any task	
Gets along with others	7	**X 10 = 70** Great personality	**X 4 = 28** Quiet and withdrawn, seems almost depressed	
Good work habits	5	**X 10 = 50** Can't verify work habits	**X 8 = 40** Good work habits but has a history of illness	
Passes reading and writing test	M	Yes	Yes	No
Meets salary requirements	M	Yes	Yes	
Available to work in 3 weeks	M	Yes	Yes	
Satisfaction with salary	4	**X 10 = 40** Satisfied	**X 3 = 12** Salary may not meet his needs	
Can hardwire computer networks	2	**X 10 = 20** No experience with computers or networks	**X 10 = 20** No experience with computers or networks	
		Total 274	**Total 318**	

The team added the product scores and had a tentative first choice—alternative #2. But note that at this point in their analysis their choice is only tentative, because they must now consider the potential risks involved in making their decision.

☑ **Step 4. Analyze risk.**

The fourth and last step in the decision process is to consider carefully the risk involved with each of the leading alternatives. This is the most neglected step in decision-making because we tend to look at life's new possibilities and beginnings enthusiastically. However, we must examine the risks in our decisions before we carry them out. To do this, we simply ask, "What can go wrong?" Here again, we can seek help from others with experience, talk to individuals who are opposed to the decision, and talk to people who will be involved in carrying out the decision. Several individuals can often foresee future problems better than one person working alone can.

When we first consider potential risks, we deal with one alternative at a time. That is, we do not initially attempt to evaluate the possibility of each risk occurring in every alternative. Then when we have completed our list of potential risks (problems) for the first alternative, we evaluate each potential problem in terms of the probability of it happening, and its seriousness if it does happen. Again, we will use the numerical scale of 1 to 10 to assign "seriousness" and "probability" weights to each of our risks. We then multiply the two weights, add the numbers, and the resultant score will show the amount of risk involved in that particular alternative. Finally, we repeat the process with each of our other leading alternatives.

In our example of Bill's team, two alternatives were left—applicants #1 and #2. Their last step, then, was to evaluate the risks in selecting each of these alternatives by asking, "If we hire that applicant, what could go wrong?" After talking with each other and the human resources department, they developed the following "risk list" for alternative #1:

Alternative #1:	Probability of it happening	Seriousness if it happened	
1. On occasion, heavy lifting is required: about 110 lb. The applicant is not able to lift this amount.	10	1	10 X 1 = 10

Total risk for alternative #1 = 10

The team rated the probability that applicant #1 could not lift 110 pounds a "10" because it was a certainty that she couldn't lift that much weight. But, they rated the seriousness as only a "1" because 1) it wouldn't happen very often, and 2) she could always ask for help.

Then, they wrote a second risk list for alternative #2:

Alternative #2:	Probability of it happening	Seriousness if it happened	
1. Because of low salary, he may stay with job only until he finds a job that pays more.	8	10	8 X 10 = 80
2. There may be a possibility of significant lost time in the future due to illness.	4	8	4 X 8 = 32

Total risk for alternative #2 = **112**

Though we can't make the decision for the team, their evaluation of risks suggests that, although applicant #2 scored slightly higher than applicant #1 in terms of objectives, applicant #1 has a much lower estimated risk than applicant #2. Risk scores like "9 X 9 = 81" and "8 X 9 = 72" are probably a missed must alternative, i.e., they probably should have been must objectives from the start. Those "9 X 9" and other high-risk scores are rattlesnakes under the bed!

All things considered, applicant #1 appears to be the best candidate.

When we finish evaluating the risks of our various alternatives, we do not subtract the risk score from the objective/alternative scores. They are "apples and oranges," two entirely different factors. Simply compare the original objective/alternative scores with the risk scores to make a balanced decision.

OAR Approach

If we have to make a major decision, we will try to use a grid analysis similar to the one just shown. We don't always have the time when we are on the phone, in the hallway, or in the boss' office. When time is short, we can use the "O.A.R." approach of 1) developing **Objectives** by asking, *"What factors should we consider?" "What resources are available?" "What restrictions exist?"* 2) creating and evaluating **Alternatives** by asking, *"What other ways might we consider?"* and 3) analyzing **Risk** by asking, *"What could go wrong?"*

On the following page is a checklist for using the step-by-step decision-making process.

Decision-Making Process

 Step 1. Write an open decision statement.

Starting with *"Select the best way . . ."* almost guarantees an open decision statement.

 Step 2. List objectives.

- ◆ Ask questions.
  - • What factors should we consider?
  - • What are our resources (money/time/people)?
  - • What results do we want?
  - • What restrictions are required?
- ◆ Determine *musts*.
- ◆ Weigh *wants* (1 – 10).

 Step 3. Create alternatives.

- ◆ Brainstorm a list of alternatives on another sheet (do not evaluate alternatives until list is completed).
- ◆ Select best 3 or 4 alternatives.
- ◆ Write date in "Must" objective/alternative boxes first.
- ◆ Eliminate any alternative that doesn't meet any "Must."
- ◆ Write in balance of data.
  - • Use phone if necessary to obtain real information.
  - • Try to avoid "yes" and "no" data; use facts and figures whenever possible.
  - • Don't use "good/better/best" classifications—use information.
- ◆ Weigh alternatives on a scale of 1 – 10, assigning 10 to the best alternative for each want objective.
- ◆ Multiply objective weight by alternative weight and record on grid.
- ◆ Add scores for each alternative.

 Step 4. Analyze risk.

- ◆ Select top two alternative scores for risk analysis.
- ◆ Evaluate probability and seriousness of risks for each selected alternative.
- ◆ Don't subtract risk scores from alternative scores.
- ◆ Don't double load decision by rewriting an objective as a risk.

On the following page is a *Decision-Making Worksheet* that you may copy and use to make your decisions.

Decision Making Worksheet

☑ **Step 1: Write an open statement ("Select the best . . .").**
☑ **Step 2: List all important objectives.**
   ♦   Identify and separate *want* and *must* objectives.
   ♦   Weight the *want* objectives, from 1 to 10 ("10" = highest weight).
☑ **Step 3: Create and list the alternatives.**
   ♦   Brainstorm a list of alternatives on another sheet of paper.
   ♦   Select three or four alternatives for analysis.
   ♦   Write data in must objective boxes for each alternative first.
   ♦   Eliminate any alternative that doesn't meet every must objective.
   ♦   Then write in data for want objectives. Use facts, figures, and opinions, not "yes" and "no."
   ♦   Assign weights to each alternative for each want objective. (Assign a "10" to the best alternative reflecting each objective, and an appropriate lower score to the other alternatives.)
   ♦   Multiply each objective weight by each alternative weight, and record.
   ♦   Add column scores for each alternative, and compare totals.
☑ **Step 4: Taking the top two alternatives, identify the critical risk objectives.**
   ♦   Assign "probability" and "seriousness" values (1 to 10 scale, 10 = highest risk). Multiply probability and seriousness ratings.
   ♦   Add risk totals for each alternative and compare.

Decision Statement: _____

_____

Objectives:	M or W	Alt:	Alt:	Alt:

Alternative: _____
Risk: P   S
_____   ____ X ____ = ____
_____   ____ X ____ = ____
_____   ____ X ____ = ____
_____   ____ X ____ = ____

Alternative: _____
Risk: P   S
_____   ____ X ____ = ____
_____   ____ X ____ = ____
_____   ____ X ____ = ____
_____   ____ X ____ = ____

12

Leadership
The Importance of
Planning

"Tell me, please, which way it is I ought to go from here?"
"Where is it you want to go?" said the cat.
"I don't care much where," said Alice.
"Then it doesn't matter which way you go!" said the cat.

Lewis Carroll
Through the Looking Glass

After making a decision, we implement that decision by effective planning. Good planning is an eight-step process for avoiding potential problems. The eight steps are as follows:

☑ 1. Write a planning statement.

☑ 2. List the steps.

☑ 3. Identify critical steps with highest potential risk.

☑ 4. List potential problems.

☑ 5. Set priorities on potential problems.

☑ 7. Analyze each major potential problem.

☑ 8. Repeat Steps 3 – 6 for other critical steps.

☑ 9. Insert major preventive and contingent actions back into original plan.

In this chapter we will review each of these steps of successful planning. We will present each step in detail and give examples. At the end of this section is a planning sheet you can use to implement your decisions.

Obstacles to Prevent Potential Problems

In all human activity, planning is critical for several important reasons. Unfortunately, there are obstacles that make it difficult for us to do what we need to do.

1. We make decisions in the present.

Planning is for the future. We are normally more concerned about today's problems and decisions than tomorrow's plans. Yet, knowing where we are going helps us get there. As Alice said to the Cheshire cat in Lewis Carroll's *Through the Looking Glass*:

"Tell me, please, which way it is I ought to go from here?"
"Where is it you want to go?" said the cat.
"I don't care much where," said Alice.
"Then it doesn't matter which way you go!" said the cat.

If we are like Alice and don't care what we do, then it really doesn't matter which way we go. But where we are going does matter to most of us, and that is why we develop plans for the decisions we make.

If we are not moving toward a specific goal, then we have no way of knowing whether our work is productive or not. Successful people plan everything they do—every day. Plans make destinations clear. They tell how to get there. And they allow us to measure the success of our efforts.

2. We tend to overlook the critical consequences of our actions.

We seem to have a tough time imagining that our decision, which of course is perfect, has any negative consequences at all. But implementing a decision creates change, and most change produces problems. It really is not a question of "good" or "bad" decisions; it is that change in and of itself does create a high probability for future problems.

3. Future consequences are often disagreeable or unpalatable.

There are people who constantly worry about future problems. They worry so much that they lose sight of happiness in the present. This message, however, is for those individuals who are much like me—perpetual optimists. There are few problems big enough for me to worry about if they are in the future. I can just put my head in the sand, bury my body behind my desk, and let the problems take care of themselves. But I get in trouble when a problem doesn't go away. It gets bigger. And then it is often too late to do anything about it. Fortunately, I was taught this potential problem avoidance process a number of years ago, and now I can deal with my future problems in the present and go back to living my day-to-day life with much less hassle.

4. As a society, we are trained from birth by the theme: "The Power of Positive Thinking."

Some of us were told that if we think positive thoughts about our decision, then it will "manifest" (a great New Age word) itself exactly as we want it. Sorry folks, it just doesn't work that way in the real world where we live. Implementing a plan for a decision is hard work; it doesn't just happen through positive thinking. Quite the contrary, it requires us to engage in some interesting ways of looking at the possible negative results of our actions. But if we can see the consequences of our decisions in the present, there may be things we can do now to prevent the problems from occurring.

5. Future consequences may not be initially visible.

    How true! The power of the process you are about to see will help you pull out potential problems that you may well have never seen—until it was too late.

6. Individually, we may think, "Of course I understand *all* the possible problems that may occur in implementing my decision."

    Time and time again, even though I knew without doubt that there were no potential problems with my decision, there were in fact many, very real problems. By talking with others, sharing the decision and resultant plan, I have discovered the power of feedback from others.

Reasons for Planning

Now that we have looked at reasons for not planning, here are some reasons why we should plan.

1. Planning enables us to experience a daily sense of accomplishment.

    Our plans will guide us in choosing the work today that will lead to our goals—thus providing a continuous feeling of fulfillment. Distant, general aims alone don't have much influence on our immediate activities. But when we take a distant goal and specify its sub-goals, with a step-by-step plan to reach each sub-goal, then we'll see that some of these steps need to be completed today. By successfully carrying out today's steps in our plan, we will immediately feel a sense of accomplishment.

2. Good planning prevents procrastination.

    The most important things in life—like long-term goals and objectives—do not create a sense of urgency until we begin to see how they must be reached. Because they appear so far off in the future, we may feel it is alright to put off action on them until tomorrow, especially since there are so many seemingly urgent things to do right now. So, given the choice between "urgent" matters and long-term goals (no matter how important), most people go with the urgent and postpone the important. But when we bring our ultimate goals and objectives into the present by creating step-by-step plans, then we realize that acting on a distant goal is urgent now!

3. Planning allows us to involve our employees.

If we have responsibility for others, it makes a lot more sense to include these people in determining our goals, especially if they are going to play a part in carrying out the plan. If our employees participate in the development of goals and objectives, and even help formulate specific strategies, then they are more likely to be committed to the plan. This is especially true if our employees expect to be included in planning their goals.

Let's examine a process that well help us be more effective in planning and in avoiding potential problems.

☑ Step 1. Write a planning statement.

Now that we have made a decision, we are ready to write a planning statement in objective form. A planning statement is simply a description of exactly what we want to accomplish. Such a statement should have the following three characteristics:

Quantifiable. For example, the statement "To have productive cross-functional team meetings" does not communicate enough information. What does the word "productive" mean? How will I know when the team is "productive"? Since my planning statement doesn't give enough specific information about my goal, it will be hard to actually know when we are successful. To make the statement more quantifiable, I can specify behaviors, or what the team will do when it is productive. I could, for example, observe that:

- *They will use the problem-solving process that we were taught.*
- *Team members will come to the meetings.*

End Result. A planning statement that only identifies behaviors is still not an effective way of specifying our future direction. We can also include end results. For example, I could expand my initial planning statement as follows:

- *The team will use written problem-solving processes in 4 of the next 6 weekly meetings.*
- *Team members will have a meeting absenteeism rate not more than 5%.*

Completion Date. Finally, my planning statement should specify a date by which the plan will be accomplished. The planning statement would now look something like this:

Create a productive team by January the 5th by using problem solving process in 4 of the next 6 weekly meetings and reducing absenteeism to not more than 5%.

There is nothing remarkable about Step 1. It's a regular goal or objective—a planning statement that includes measurability, an end result, and a completion date.

 Step 2. List the steps.

After we have written a planning statement, we can then develop the steps we will take to achieve them. As we identify the steps in our plan, we establish completion dates for each step. But we do not assign a final number to the steps at this point, as we may need to add additional steps later.

As an example, I know a person—let's call her Elizabeth—whose planning statement was to become a manager in her organization within four years. The initial steps of her plan looked something like this:

1. Write a planning statement.

"To become a manager in this organization within four years"

2. List the steps.   Completion Dates

		Completion Dates
A.	Meet with my boss and discuss promotional goal.	Sept. 15
B.	Write 10 key development objectives on my present job.	Sept. 30
C.	Analyze my managerial skills; determine my strengths and areas of needed improvement.	Oct. 15
D.	Take a minimum of 2 management workshops each year.	Dec. 1
E.	Complete my BS Degree at night school within 3 years. Sign up this semester.	Jan. 15
F.	Determine potential management openings that may occur during the 3rd and 4th years.	Mar. 1

This part of the planning process is simple. Most people can probably write a planning statement and then list the steps in their plan. In fact, this is where most individuals stop their planning process. But wisely, Elizabeth realized that she also needed to look carefully at the steps in her plan, noting any that could cause difficulties—let's call them "critical steps."

☑ Step 3. Identify critical steps with highest potential risk.

From past experience we know that sometimes a particular step means trouble! (Maybe we took that step before and it led to a disaster.) If a step is completely new to us, we'd better look out. "Murphy's Law," what can go wrong will, may get us. Major steps, with lots of parts and pieces, are especially vulnerable, particularly if we have no experience with the step. Problems can also result when people have to communicate over distances by phone, letter, fax, or e-mail, and also when there are a number of people involved. If a step means operating close to the limits of our space, time, or money, we probably have trouble on the horizon. For example, if our plan requires that we order a new item that's exactly 3 feet wide and our door is 3 feet 2 inches, we better get an ax! Or if someone tells us the item we ordered will be here Wednesday, and we have to have it Thursday, we might be wise to assume that it won't arrive until Friday. If a step in our plan "will only cost "$9,990.00," and we have exactly $10,000.00, then we know what's going to happen!

The key question to ask here is the same one that we asked in the "Selecting the Best Alternative" chapter of this book. That is, "When we perform this step in our plan, what could go wrong?"

All this potential problem analysis may sound negative. But the good news is that if we anticipate potential problems before we carry out our plan, we can often develop solutions that will greatly increase the chances that we will achieve our goal.

In the example of Elizabeth, she selected as a critical step in her plan, "Attend night classes and get the 24 credits I need to finish college." She viewed this step as a potential problem because it was new for her (she had never attended college at night). It was also a very important one. She had worked for a boss who had once said to her, "Your chances of being selected as a manager in this organization are a lot better if you have a college degree. In fact, your chances of making it without one are zero!"

2. List the steps.

    A. Meet with my boss and discuss promotional goal.
    B. Write 10 key development objectives on my present job.
    C. Analyze my managerial skills; determine my strengths and areas of needed improvement.
    D. Take a minimum of 2 management workshops each year.
    E. Complete my BS Degree at night school within 3 years.
    F. Determine potential management openings that may occur during the 3rd and 4th years.

Critical Step

 Step 4. List potential problems.

Having identified the steps that may cause problems (critical steps), select one and list the potential problems. In Elizabeth's case, she wrote down the following potential problems with her night classes step:

3. Critical step.

    E. Complete my BS Degree at night school within 3 years.

4. List potential problems.

    a) I'll get bored and stop attending.
    b) It takes longer than 3 years to obtain the 54 credits I need.
    c) Night school will be very hard on my family.

To obtain our list of potential problems, we simply ask others and ourselves, "What could go wrong when I do this step?"

 Step 5. Set priorities on potential problems.

The next step is to evaluate the probability and seriousness of each potential problem. That is, we figure out what the probability is that the problem will occur, and then how seriously it will affect the success of our plan if it does occur. To rate probability and seriousness, use "H" for high, "M" for medium, and "L" for low.

In our example, Elizabeth felt that there was only a small chance that she would get bored and drop out (probability of the event occurring = L), but if she did, it would seriously jeopardize her plan (seriousness = H). Her boss would see her as a failure in something he considered very important (earning a college degree).

She also thought that there was only a low probability that it would take her longer than three years to obtain a degree. But, if this did happen, she might still be eligible for promotion given evidence that she was almost through with her education. When she considered her family, however, it was clear that not only was there a high probability that night school would be very hard on her family, when it occurred, it would be very serious indeed.

Her analysis now looked like this:

5. Set priorities on potential problems.

4. List potential problems.	**Probability** **P**	**Seriousness** **S**
a) I'll get bored and stop attending.	**L**	**H**
b) It may take longer than two years to get my degree.	**L**	**M**
c) Night school will be very hard on my family.	**H**	**H**

 Step 6. Analyze each major potential problem.

Next, we need to analyze our greatest potential problems by finding their likely causes, and planning preventive and contingency actions. In solving problems, we act on causes. To prevent or prepare for potential problems, we look for likely causes. After we have identified the likely causes, we ask, "What can be done to reduce the probability that this event (or likely cause) will happen?" In other words, what preventive action can we include in our plans? We also must consider: "If the worst comes to pass and the problem does occur, what can I do now to reduce the seriousness of the consequences?" In other words, what contingency action can we include in our plans from the start?

For Elizabeth, the potential problem "Night school will be very hard on my family" had a high probability of happening, and when it happened it would be high in seriousness. Thus she selected this problem for further analysis. She asked herself, her family, and others whose opinions she respected, "Why would night school be so difficult for my family?"

In real life, she received a long list of probable causes or reasons why night school might be difficult for her family. Those of you who have been through the night-school experience know that there are a number of likely causes leading to family hardship. But in order to simplify our example, we have only listed three causes. On the following page is an example of her analysis.

6. Analyze each major potential problem.

"Night school will be very hard on my family."

A. Likely Causes			
3 nights/wk away from family			
Lack of study time			
Family not aware of hardships			

Now that we have identified the likely causes, the next step is to ask, "What can we do now to reduce the probability of the event (or likely cause) occurring?" In our example, Elizabeth found there were a number of things she could do. Again, there were many more preventive actions that Elizabeth discovered she could take, but these are a representative sample.

A. Likely Causes	B. Preventive Action		
3 nights/wk away from family	*See if college has courses I can take at home*		
Lack of study time	*Buy course books now and start studying; Take courses that are easy for me*		
Family not aware of hardships	*Involve family in preplanning; have Bill talk to Joe who is also attending night school*		

The next step is for Elizabeth to say, "OK, the worst comes to pass and the cause of the problem happens. What can I do now to reduce the seriousness of the event if in fact it happens?" She was able to create a number of contingency actions that could help lessen the impact of the likely causes if they did occur.

A. Likely Causes	B. Preventive Action	C. Contingency Action	
3 nights/wk away from family	*See if college has courses I can take at home*	**Enroll Bill (spouse) in one or more courses with me**	
Lack of study time	*Buy course books now and start studying; Take courses that are easy for me*	**Get family to help me study**	
Family not aware of hardships	*Involve family in preplanning; have Bill talk to Joe who is also attending night school*	*(No action)*	

The last part of Step 6 is to ask, "What's going to trigger each major contingency action?" Often, we are the person who observes the cause occurring and act as our own trigger. At other times someone or something else must trigger the contingency action. For example:

A. Likely Causes	B. Preventive Action	C. Contingency Action	D. Trigger
3 nights/wk away from family	*See if college has courses I can take at home*	*Enroll Bill (spouse) in one or more courses with me*	**Me** *(Elizabeth)*
Lack of study time	*Buy course books now and start studying; Take courses that are easier for me*	*Get family to help me study*	**Spouse complains and says, "You're never home!"**
Family not aware of hardships	*Involve family in preplanning; have Bill talk to Joe who is also attending night school*	*(No action)*	(If there is no contingency action, there is no trigger)

Step 7. Repeat Steps 3 – 6 for other critical steps.

After analyzing the first critical step, we would then take each of the other critical steps and conduct the same analysis. That is, we would

☑ 3. Identify critical steps with highest potential risk.

☑ 4. List any potential problems concerning each critical step.

☑ 5. Evaluate each potential problem on its probability of happening and seriousness if it happens anyway.

☑ 6. Analyze each major potential problem for likely causes, preventive actions, contingency actions, and triggers.

 Step 8. Insert major preventive and contingent actions back into original plan.

The last important step in our planning process is to insert our major contingency and/or preventive actions back into our original plan. In our example, Elizabeth's plan will now look like this:

	Completion Dates
A. Have a family meeting and discuss plans.	Sept. 1
B. Ask Bill to talk to Joe. Call Joe and ask him to talk to Bill.	Sept. 2
C. Meet with my boss and discuss promotional goal.	Sept. 15
D. Call college and see if it has televised or online courses I can take at home.	Sept 20
E. Meet with my college adviser and determine elective course that my spouse would enjoy taking.	Sept. 22
F. Buy course books now and start studying.	Oct 1
G. Write 10 key development objectives on my present job.	Oct. 15
H. Analyze my managerial skills; determine my strengths and areas of needed improvement.	Nov. 1
I. Take a minimum of 2 management workshops each year.	Nov. 15
J. Complete my BS Degree at night school within 3 years. Sign up this semester.	Jan. 15
K. Determine potential management openings that may occur during the 3rd and 4th years.	Mar. 1

Note that the new steps in her plan are shown in bold print. As you can see, by adding these new steps to her plan, she has greatly increased the probability that she will successfully reach her goal. Obviously, in her real plan, she also analyzed other critical steps and added additional steps to her plan that are not shown in our example. Note too that some of her completion dates have changed to include her new activities.

Many of us spend a great deal of time dealing with a variety of problems but do very little planning. We can become so busy running from crisis to crisis that we don't take the time to plan for success.

But when we commit ourselves to analyzing our decisions and then following a proven step-by-step planning process, we will find we are not sidetracked by problems. We will surely increase our level of achievement.

On the following pages is a worksheet that you may copy for your own use.

Potential Problem Avoidance Worksheet

☑ Step 1. Write a planning statement.
☑ Step 2. List the steps.
☑ Step 3. Identify critical steps with highest potential risk.
☑ Step 4. List potential problems. Ask, "What could go wrong?"
☑ Step 5. Set priorities on potential problems. Use High, Medium, or Low to
     rate probability of event occurring and seriousness if it does.
☑ Step 6. Analyze each major potential problem. Take each high priority
     potential problem (example: a fire) and write in likely cause (a
     match), preventive action (allow only nonflammable material in
     room), contingency action (if there is a fire anyway, we have a
     sprinkler system), and then assign a trigger for the contingency action
     (the sprinklers have lead alloy valve that melts if a fire occurs).
☑ Step 7. Repeat Steps 3 - 6 for other critical steps.
☑ Step 8. Insert major preventive and contingent actions back into original plan.

☑ **Step 1. Write a planning statement.** Make the statement quantifiable,
     end terms of the end result desired, and include a completion date.

_____

_____

_____

☑ **Step 2. List the steps,** and, ☑ **3. Identify critical steps with
                    highest potential risk.**

Steps of Plan: Check critical steps
                                                         (see next page)

  1. _____ _____
  2. _____ _____
  3. _____ _____
  4. _____ _____
  5. _____ _____
  6. _____ _____
  7. _____ _____
  8. _____ _____
  9. _____ _____
 10. _____ _____
 11. _____ _____
 12. _____ _____
 13. _____ _____

☑ **Step 3. Identify critical steps with highest potential risk.**

Analyze the steps that have the highest risk of encountering problems. These are critical steps. Mark critical steps on the preceding page with an asterisk or check mark. Select one critical step and write it below. (The following analysis will be repeated later for the other critical steps.)

_____

☑ **Step 4. List potential problems.**

Ask the question, "What might go wrong with this step?" and list the potential problems below:

☑ **Step 5. Set priorities on potential problems.**
Use H = High, M = Medium, and L = Low to rate probability (P) and seriousness (S).

	P	S

☑ **Step 6: Analyze each major potential problem** for likely causes, preventive action, contingency action, and trigger if needed.

Likely Causes	Preventive Action	Contingency Action	Trigger

☑ **Step 7. Repeat Steps 3 – 6 for other critical steps** using copies of the preceding page of this worksheet.

☑ **Step 8. Insert major preventive and contingent actions back into original plan.**

Write a new plan that incorporates important preventive and contingency actions (from Steps 6 and 7) as new steps in your original list of steps. Write all steps in chronological order, and number the steps. Finally, write a completion date for each step.

Step #	Step	Completion Date

Leadership
Developing Objectives
with Employees

The purpose of the work on making the future is not to decide what should be done tomorrow, but what should be done today to have a tomorrow.

P. Drucker
Managing for Results

In the preceding chapter, we discussed how we could develop plans that have a high probability of being successful. In this chapter, we will also discuss planning, but it is *with* our employees. The process is somewhat the same, especially in the first step (writing objectives and listing steps), except that now we are helping the employee to plan his or her goals.

The step-by-step process for planning with our employees is as follows:

☑ 1. Prepare for the joint meeting.

☑ 2. Open the meeting.

☑ 3. Discuss the employee's tentative goals and determine the measurability of each.

☑ 4. Offer additional goals if appropriate.

☑ 5. Determine priorities of goals.

☑ 6. Review employee's strategies and plans to achieve key goals, and offer ideas.

☑ 7. Set follow-up dates for review session, and conclude meeting.

☑ 1. Prepare for the joint meeting.

If this is the first time we have developed mutual goals with an employee, we need to take the "mystery" out of the process by letting him or her know exactly what the meeting will be about. So we meet briefly with the employee before the interview and discuss:

- The purpose of the upcoming meeting

- How the process works:
    - Brainstorm a list of goals and identify those that are a priority.
    - Write priority goal statements that are measurable.
    - Develop a list of action steps to achieve each goal.

- Any appropriate organization/department/section goals he or she needs to know before completing his or her worksheets

- When and where the meeting will take place

Purpose of the Upcoming Meeting

Here, we can explain to our employees why doing more paperwork is a good idea. Sure, we can require them to write goals, but it is important to obtain their acceptance and commitment to the process. In order to gain buy-in from our employees, we can review and then use the "reasons for planning" that were listed in the preceding chapter. For example, "Planning enables us to experience a daily sense of accomplishment" and "Good planning prevents procrastination" are especially appropriate reasons here.

How the Process Works

Brainstorm a list of goals. First, tell the employees to find a quiet place and brainstorm a list of the most important goals they see in their job. As they list their goals, ask them not to evaluate or judge them. Ask them to write down everything that occurs to them, even if it may seem "silly." If they have a burning secret desire to accomplish something different or special, ask them to write it down! Tell them to focus on all areas of their jobs—whatever goals are important to them.

Suggest that they not worry about writing measurable goal statements at this point. As long as they know what they mean by what they write, that's fine. At this point in the process, it is their list. They shouldn't have to show it to anybody.

For example, here is a recent list of my job goals:

1) Create a graduate certificate program in leadership for my university.
* 2) Become the Academic Director of the new Leadership Program.
3) Write another book on teaching.
4) Establish a set of teaching standards for adjunct faculty.
5) Identify a world-class speaker for an in-service training day for our adjuncts.
6) Obtain contracts for two more on-site, undergraduate leadership certificate programs.
* 7) Learn more about motivating my adjunct teachers.
8) Conduct a peer-peer consulting session with colleague this semester.
9) Develop a new course for the undergraduate leadership program.
10) Create a web page for my students.
11) Teach the required load of courses, with an average student evaluation on all courses not less than 4.5 on a 1 – 5 Likert Scale.
* 12) Ensure that the capstone course for the Human Resource Management area is completed and has a major "service learning" component.

Then, tell the employees that after they have spent a few minutes freely creating their list of personal goals, they need to select the top three or four items and mark them with an asterisk or check mark (as I have).

Write priority goal statements that are measurable. Now that they have brainstormed a list of the things they would like to be and do, and identified the most important ones, tell them that they are ready to write out their highest-priority goals in an objective form using the "Goal Worksheet" found at the end of this chapter. An objective or goal (we will use these two words interchangeably) is simply a statement of exactly what they want to accomplish. Such a statement should have three characteristics.

First, we tell the employees that goal statements should be specific, not general. For example, the statement, "Learn more about motivating my adjunct teachers," (my objective #7) does not communicate enough information. What does the word "motivating" mean? How will I know when I have learned more about motivation? By what date do I want to have obtained this knowledge? Since my goal statement doesn't give enough specific information about my goal, it will be hard to actually know when I am successful—or even whether I am successful. Thus, in my goal statement I need to specify behaviors and/or identify results:

- Specify my behaviors. Decide what actions I am going to take—what I will do—to learn more about motivation. For example:

  - Attend a workshop at the university on "Motivating Today's Teachers" by January of this year.
  - Give each of the adjunct teachers in my area honest positive feedback on three different occasions by the end of the first semester.

- Identify results of my motivation efforts. For example:

  - The team of 22 adjunct teachers in my area will have average student evaluations not less that 4.5 during the next semester.
  - The adjuncts in my section will rate me 4.0 or above on the yearly 360° survey.

Second, we tell them that a good goal statement also should be measurable—*quantifiable.* "To learn more about conducting a performance appraisal session with my employees" sounds fine. But I really won't know when I have satisfactorily achieved this goal because I haven't specified my standard—or measure—of achievement. If I rewrite this goal as, "To be able to conduct a performance appraisal session with my employees by January 1 of next year," it is now measurable, in two ways. First, I have used a word that specifies behavior ("conduct," rather than "learning"). And second, I have committed myself to a specific time period. With my goal statement thus expressed in measurable terms, I can figure out when I have achieved it.

Third, we tell our employees that a goal statement should be *achievable*. There is little point in setting myself up for failure. A good goal statement will extend and improve my performance, not break me.

We tell our employees that they can develop several different types of job goals:

- First, regular or *routine* goals that simply specify the things employees normally do in their jobs

- Second, *problem-solving* goals that employees write to resolve a specific problem

- Third, *innovative* goals, written to facilitate new or creative ideas

- Finally, *personal* goals, which employees write about themselves

Most of our employees' growth on the job is connected with the last three kinds of goals. Thus, it is better for both them and our organization if they concentrate their efforts in these three areas rather than on just routine goals.

Develop a list of action steps to achieve each goal. After they have determined which goals they need to carry out, they can then develop the steps they will take to achieve them. As they identify the steps in their plan, ask them to set completion dates for each step. (But suggest that they not assign a final number to their steps at this point, as they may need to add more steps later.)

Organizational Goals

Next, in this initial meeting, we tell the employees about any specific organizational goals that they need to include in their list. For example, in the preceding list of my goals, Item 12, "Ensure that the capstone course for the Human Resource Management area is completed and has a major 'service learning' component" was my leader's goal.

We should also tell them to put their energies into only two or three goals at any one time. Their chances of success are much better if they concentrate on a few important goals rather than all of them at once. (Less important goals can usually be addressed in the future.)

When and Where the Meeting Will Take Place

Finally, in this initial meeting with our employees, we tell them when and where the meeting will take place. We should have located a meeting place that is private and where we can control interruptions. If it is impossible to hold our telephone calls for an hour meeting, then we need to go elsewhere. We can reserve the conference room, or find someone who is on vacation and use his or her office. We can even tell our boss what we will be doing, and ask not to be interrupted (if possible!) Whatever we do, we need to treat this meeting as critically important, and not allow interruptions.

After this preliminary meeting with the employee, we also need to spend some time thinking of several key objectives that we would like to see the employee achieve during the upcoming year. Using the "Goal Worksheet" found at the end of this chapter, we write out the goals as well as tentative plans and methods for how the employee will achieve them. We can share these plans with the employee in the upcoming meeting, if needed.

☑ **2. Open the meeting.**

When an employee first walks into our office or conference room, we need to explain that we wish to help him or her better understand the organization's and department's goals and objectives, improve his or her goals and plans, and explore potential problems that may exist with the plans.

Next, we can help reduce any anxiety the employee may be feeling by telling him or her the meeting agenda. For example, we might say something like,

> *"Bill, I see my role in today's meeting as being a resource for you. I may have some information you need on our department's goals, some ideas or suggestions to help improve your plans, and even some ideas about anticipating potential problems. What I'd like to do is to discuss your goals and make sure that they are measurable statements, then offer any additional specific goals if appropriate. I'll also try to help you set some priorities so you know where you need to spend your time, review your strategies and plans and offer ideas if needed, and then set up specific follow-up dates. This is your meeting, Bill, and I am here to help you any way I can."*

Of course, we will use our own words to explain generally to our employee what is going to happen, and our role in the meeting.

☑ **3. Discuss employee's tentative goals, and determine the measurability of each.**

In Step 3, we ask the employee to relate the goals he or she wrote. Here, we review only the goal statements at the top of the *Goal Worksheets,* since the specific plans and methods will be discussed later after setting priorities. As the employee reads his or her first goal, we need to make sure that it is specific, measurable, and has target dates.

As the leader, we can help the employee in identifying his or her ideas for improving the goal statement by asking questions such as:

- "How will you know when you are successful?"

- "What will you be able to do (or avoid doing) when you have achieved your objective?"

- "What conditions will exist when you finish?"

- "What tangible results will be achieved?"

- "What are you going to do to make this happen?"

During the discussion of the employee's goals, it is not necessary to determine whether the goals are feasible or appropriate. We will discuss feasibility in Step 6 when we review the employee's plans. And we can deal naturally with the question of appropriateness in Step 5 when we set priorities. Remember, what looks initially like an impossible goal may turn out to be possible after reviewing the employee's strategies and plans.

☑ **4. Offer additional goals if appropriate.**

After reviewing each of the employee's goals in Step 3, we may have additional organizational, departmental, or sectional objectives that he or she hasn't addressed. So here is where we can offer additional topics that we feel are important. Since we took the time to write out several objectives before the meeting, we will be ready at this point to make any needed suggestions.

☑ **5. Determine priorities of goals.**

Before employees start to spend time implementing their job-related goals, we should review their priorities. In conjunction with our employees, we examine which of the goals they have written are "must do," "ought to do," and "nice to do." Since we will appraise their performance on what they do, it only makes sense for them to complete the high-priority goals that meet with our approval.

Ask the employee to arrange, in order of priority, the goals that were discussed in both Step 3 (his or her goals) and Step 4 (our goals). Then, two or three key goals should be selected for the immediate future. Goals that are not selected as first priorities can be deferred to quarterly follow-up meetings, and implemented as the initial objectives are achieved. We deliberately should restrict the number of objectives initially selected for two reasons. The employee's chances of success are better if his or her efforts are concentrated on only a few key objectives. Second, we can improve our chances of following up the employee's progress if we have a reasonable number of objectives to monitor.

☑ **6. Review employee's strategies and plans to achieve key goals, and offer ideas.**

As the employee discusses his or her plans and methods, we can do several things. First, if the employee has a good plan, we will be sure we say so. Second, we ask what we can do to help the employee reach his or her goals, and offer our suggestions for how the plans could be further improved. Third, with each goal we should ask the key question, "If we do this, what could go wrong?" to elicit any potential problems. Then, we can offer suggestions or ideas for preventive or contingency solutions, and include these ideas in the original plan. Finally, we review the target dates for the goal and action steps, and adjust them to make them more realistic if indicated.

☑ **7. Set follow-up dates for review session, and conclude meeting.**

We should tell our employee that we will be available to discuss his or her plans whenever needed. But to ensure that we will really follow up with the employee's progress toward his or her goals, we should set specific dates in the employee's presence, and write them in our calendar. Normally one follow-up meeting each quarter will be sufficient, with additional meetings scheduled as needed.

In concluding the meeting, we ask the employee to provide us with a copy of the *Goal Worksheet* after the meeting. Then, we can spell out our positive expectation by saying, "I know you can do it!" Finally, we express our appreciation for the time and effort that he or she spent preparing for this meeting.

On the following page is a *Leader's Checklist* of the key steps in writing objectives with our employees. Following that is the *Goal Worksheet* that you and your employees may copy and use for each of the key goals. Remember that goals should be written in specific and measurable terms so that you and others will know when the employees have reached them.

**Leader's Checklist for Developing
Objectives with Employees**

☑ **1. Prepare for the joint meeting.**

- Tentatively complete the *Goal Worksheet* on key goals for this employee.
- Meet in advance and:
  - Discuss purpose of upcoming meeting.
  - Describe how the process works and give employee a copy of the *Goal Worksheet.*
  - Present any appropriate organizational, department, or section goals employee needs to know.
  - State when and where the meeting will take place.
- Plan minimum of one hour for meeting, and ensure:
  - Privacy
  - No interruptions

☑ **2. Open the meeting.**

- Explain our role as a resource for
  - Organizational goals
  - Our department or section goals
  - Ideas and suggestions
  - Analysis of potential problems
- Outline the meeting agenda.

☑ **3. Discuss employee's tentative goals, and determine the measurability of each.**

- Ask employee to relate his or her goal statements (do not discuss specific plans at this time).
- Ensure that each goal is specific, measurable and has a target date.

☑ **4. Offer additional goals if appropriate.**

- Offer additional goals(s) only if necessary.

☑ **5. Determine priorities of goals.**

- Ask employee to prioritize all of the goals.
- Discuss the employee's priorities and reach a consensus, if possible.
- Limit the number of goals to two or three for the initial time period.

☑ **6. Review employee's strategies and plans to achieve key goals, and offer ideas.**

- Provide specific positive feedback to the employee about any of his or her significant plans or strategies.
- Ask what we can do to help the employee reach his or her goals.
- Offer ideas and suggestions to improve the employee's list of activities.
- Analyze potential problems by asking, "What could go wrong?"
- Develop contingency or preventive actions for potential problems, and incorporate into plans.
- In light of planning analysis above, examine original target dates in each objective and adjust if needed.

☑ **7. Set follow-up dates for review sessions, and conclude meeting.**

- Tell employee that we are available to discuss his or her progress whenever needed.
- Inform employee that there will be scheduled follow-up meetings (e.g., quarterly).
- Write specific dates in our calendar (in the employee's presence) for the first follow-up meeting (approx. 3 months).
- Ask employee to provide us with a final copy of the *Goal Worksheet* after the meeting.
- Spell out our positive expectations.
- Express our appreciation.

Goal Worksheet

Goals should be **specific, measurable, attainable,** and **challenging.** They can be regular, problem solving, innovative, or personal goals. Write your goals like this: "To . . . (verb) . . . (end result) . . . (subject) . . . (time)."	**Priorities:** H = High M = Med. L = Low	**Write specific and detailed plans and methods to achieve goals:** A) Detail the steps of your plan for each goal. B) Ask, "What could go wrong?" and identify potential problems. C) Identify likely causes of potential problems. D) Develop key preventive and contingency solutions. E) Put solutions back in original plan as new (or modified) steps. F) Note new steps with an asterisk. G) Date and number all steps.

14

Leadership
Conducting Effective Performance Appraisals

When they are interviewed, employees report not having
undergone performance appraisals for several years, if ever.
Their supervisors, in contrast, report having conducted
performance appraisals regularly.

Mohrman, Resnick-West, Lawler
Designing Performance Appraisal Systems

Introduction

Some years ago, I had a boss who was truly incompetent in conducting performance appraisals. To compound the problem, he had no idea that he didn't know how to handle employee appraisal meetings. The result of his brief once-a-year session was that I felt bad about him and about my organization. And most important, I felt bad about me!

But I knew that his short annual presentation of my strengths and weaknesses was a poor way to conduct a performance appraisal. Since then, I have read everything I could about performance appraisals. I have also attended many workshops on this subject, conducted appraisal sessions with numerous employees, talked to thousands of managers, supervisors, and employees, and taught hundreds of workshops on the topic.

And only now, many years after my first unfortunate experience, do I feel comfortable—most of the time—participating in a performance appraisal session. I have learned a lot and much of it the hard way!

What's in this chapter. First, we'll review the important factors that affect the quality of performance appraisals. Next, we will look at the reasons for conducting an appraisal session. And last, there is a step-by-step approach to use in managing the performance appraisal interviews we conduct with our employees. This planned approach will help us conduct productive, balanced, and fair performance appraisal sessions.

This method is not a "sit-back-and-listen-as-the-boss-tells-the-employee-his-strengths-and-weaknesses" approach. It is participative. But there is a cost to you. It requires you to spend time preparing for the appraisal meeting. You will also find that your appraisal interviews will run longer—to your advantage. Furthermore, there may be more open disagreements during your meeting. But an open discussion will allow you and your employee to reach a better understanding of his or her actual performance.

Factors Affecting the Quality of Performance Appraisals

There are four factors that affect the quality of a performance appraisal interview. They are the environment in which the performance appraisals are conducted, the performance appraisal system that is used, the leader who conducts the performance appraisal, and the employee.

Environmental Issues

There are several environmental issues that affect the quality of a performance appraisal. These issues include executive management support, human resource department support, delegation of the task to the appropriate people, the number of employees who must be interviewed, the employee's job, whether job standards exist, and legal issues.

Executive management support. Do our executive managers support the idea of performance appraisals by conducting quality interviews with their department heads? Or do they talk about the need for good appraisals without doing them themselves? In any case, the "buck stops with us," since we are the leaders of our employees. Whatever executive managers do or don't do, we are responsible for leading our employees in the best way possible. And that means conducting quality performance appraisals regularly with our employees.

Human resources department. Has the human resource department designed the performance appraisal system and forms that help rather than hinder the process? For example, suppose our organization expects us to present completed appraisals to our employees with little or no input from them. Though two-way communication during performance appraisal meetings is essential for interviews that produce positive results, such a system is set up to encourage only one-way communications. An effective way to solve this problem is for us to conduct informal appraisal interviews with our employees shortly before the "official" appraisal sessions. This will not only produce interviews that are fairer to our employees, but also will give us better information to use later while filling out the appraisal form.

Delegation. Another environmental factor that affects performance appraisals is delegation. In other words, are the individuals who should be conducting performance appraisals allowed to conduct them? For example, a department head had two first-line leaders and twenty-one employees reporting to him. He conducted all the performance appraisal interviews with the employees to improve communications between the employees and management. He did, however, meet individually with his two leaders and discuss their employees' performances before conducting appraisal interviews with these employees. But here we have two problems because of poor delegation. First, the department head is attempting to do performance appraisals on too many people. And second, he is bypassing the leaders who are in a much better position to know the details of their employees' performance. The results are likely to be poor appraisals and first-line leaders who appear to their employees to have little real authority.

The number of employees who must be interviewed. The number of employees who report to us also has a great effect on the quality of performance appraisals that we conduct. If we have only six employees, we can spend more appraisal time and conduct more effective interviews than twenty-six employees. Quality performance appraisals take time—time to prepare for them, and time to conduct them. The more employees we have reporting to us, the harder it is to find enough time to do in-depth preparation and interviews.

The employee's job. The employee's job can have a great impact upon the quality of the performance appraisal. Obviously, if the employee's job is monotonous and not very motivating, the performance appraisal will be more difficult. Contrast this type of situation with an employee who has an exciting or challenging job. Interested and challenged employees normally are easier to talk with during a performance appraisal interview.

Job standards. Appraisals are easier to conduct if both the employee and the manager understand the job, its standards of performance, and the established goals or objectives. Sometimes we run into problems during our performance appraisal interviews because our expectations may be unclear to our employees. Most of us have heard employees legitimately say, "I didn't know that I had to do that!" We have also heard such questions as, "What is a good job?" or "When am I not doing this job well enough?" and "When am I devoting too much time and energy to this task?" These questions suggest that the employee doesn't know what to do prior to the appraisal.

To avoid such problems, the leader meets individually with his or her employees six to twelve months ahead of time to discuss their specific job responsibilities. The leader and the employee should both complete the worksheet independently of each other and then meet and discuss how they both see the job. It is amazing the number of times that the leader and his or her employee do not agree about which tasks are most important, the standards for tasks, and the authority the employee has for each task. Using this strategy helps to ensure that the employee's efforts are on track. As a result, the next performance appraisal meeting with this employee will likely be fairer and more productive.

By using a worksheet similar to the one below (see the chapter on "Establishing Employee Performance Standards"), we will be better prepared to discuss and obtain agreement on the employee's job tasks.

Job Analysis Worksheet

List the main tasks in your job.	How critical is each job task? "A" = Highest "B" = Medium "C" = Lowest	What standards are used to measure your job performance in each task?	What problems exist that handicap your performance?	Authority Levels* 1 2 3

* A "# 1 authority level" means that the employee has total authority to do the task. He or she doesn't have to ask permission to do the task, or even tell the leader that it was done. The employee simply does it because it's a routine part of his or her job.

A "# 2 authority level" allows the employee to do the task without first asking for permission; but he or she is expected to let the leader know that it was done.

A "# 3 authority level" indicates that the employee needs to obtain approval from his or her leader before doing that task.

Legal issues. Changing laws may affect the ability of leaders to stay abreast of the latest requirements regarding such matters as privacy issues or Equal Employment Opportunity guidelines on promotions/transfers based on past performance appraisal data, etc. Astute leaders keep themselves informed so that what they do obeys both the intent and letter of the law.

The Performance Appraisal System

Another factor that greatly affects performance appraisals is the appraisal system. How often are appraisals scheduled? How is the appraisal form routed through the organization and who has access to it? What information is requested?

These and other questions address the design of the performance appraisal system. Although the organization's human resource department usually establishes the system, if it doesn't work for us, there are still some important things we can do.

How often are appraisals scheduled? At a minimum, appraisals should be scheduled at least yearly for experienced employees and every six months for newcomers. If our organization doesn't follow this schedule, we can still conduct informal appraisal sessions that do.

How is the appraisal form routed through the organization? If our boss must review and sign the form before we conduct a performance appraisal interview with an employee, then our organization's system is inappropriate. A boss who must "review the form" before we are allowed to conduct an appraisal interview with our employee communicates lack of trust in our ability to complete the form properly with the employee. For effective interviews, the leader and the employee should complete the appraisal form together, and then send it through channels.

Who has access to the form? The question here is not just one of restricting confidential information only to those who have a legitimate need for it. It is also one of allowing the employee to have full and ready access to both the blank and the completed forms. The employee needs blank copies of the form to prepare properly for the interview. In addition, the employee should be given a copy of his or her completed appraisal form to use as a reference during the year.

What information is requested? Some appraisal forms list general duties, personality traits, and work habits, and then rate the employee on each. Other forms are customized for the employee's specific job, with ratings assigned for each of his or her major job duties. (This is by far the better type of form.) The more subjective the form, the more difficult it is for us to use it fairly and consistently. In addition, the more the form rates character and personality traits such as "attitude" instead of measurable behaviors, the more difficult it is to administer.

A good appraisal form can enhance the interview results. Yet skilled interviewers using poor appraisal forms can conduct excellent appraisals. So if we are required to use a form that measures personality traits, we use it. But as a part of our preparation for the interview, we should consider the employee's strengths and areas of needed improvement in light of his or her job performance. Then in the interview, we can talk about performance, not personality.

The key point is to use the system in the best way you can. Don't let the system use you!

The Leader Who Conducts the Performance Appraisal

As the individual who conducts the performance appraisal, we have a profound affect on the quality of the appraisal interviews. For example, our attitude toward this part of our job, what we know about doing it, and how well we do it (our skills) all make a big difference in the effectiveness of our performance appraisal sessions.

Our attitude. Our attitude will influence how much time we spend in preparation, the priority we give to performance appraisals over crises that may occur (and usually do), the amount of time we set aside for quality interviews, and how important our employees feel the appraisal session is. If we see performance appraisal as a major part of our job, we are likely to devote significant time and thought to it.

Our knowledge. Unfortunately, many leaders have learned how to conduct performance appraisal interviews from bosses who lacked knowledge of how they should be done. But there are very specific things that any leader can learn how to do to improve performance appraisal results. Later in this chapter there are some common sense strategies that will help most leaders to be considerably more effective.

Our skill. We can all nod intelligently as we discuss the key strategies for conducting an appraisal interview. But because we are creatures of habit, the chances are that we will not use the steps effectively—though we may want to. Thus we need to have the opportunities to develop our skill in using the new things we have learned. That is why it is essential for you to select several key ideas presented in this chapter and use them in your next performance appraisal interviews.

The Employee

The employee is the other person involved in the performance appraisal interview. And the employee's attitude toward the interview, preparation for it, and his or her performance level all affect the outcome of the session.

The employee's attitude. The employee's attitude is vital to a successful appraisal session. If the employee is hostile or feels the appraisal session is an exercise in paperwork, then the results will be poor. If we know that an employee has a negative attitude toward the appraisal interview, it is up to us to find out why he or she feels that way and then determine how we can help the employee see the positive benefits of a performance appraisal.

There are clear benefits for the employee. For example, interviews can be exciting opportunities for employees to spend private time with us to determine how well they are doing. This is a time to talk about what the employee has done well in the past and to discuss his or her future goals within the organization. Even poor performance can be discussed in a positive way, i.e., as areas that need improvement, not as "weaknesses."

The amount of time the employee spends preparing for the interview. We have discussed the need for the leader to properly prepare for the appraisal session. But if we want the employee to participate in a two-way discussion in the interview, then the employee must also be given enough time to prepare adequately.

It is up to us as the leader to help the employee in his or her preparation. We need to make sure that the employee has a blank copy of the appraisal form so that he or she knows what will be asked. We can encourage the employee to analyze his or her strengths and areas needing improvement. And we can suggest that he or she come prepared to do most of the talking.

The employee's performance level. Statistically, if we have ten employees, one will be a superstar, eight will range from "very good" to "meets minimum acceptable standards," and one will be a problem—our cross to bear. If an employee is outstanding in all categories, an appraisal is fun to conduct! When this isn't the case, the interview is more difficult to handle.

Although the strategies presented in the next section work well with all employees, they are particularly helpful in dealing with the problem employee.

Of the four key factors affecting performance appraisal quality—the environment, system, interviewer, and employee—the ones that we can influence the most are 1) us, the interviewer, and 2) our employee. As a result, the balance of this chapter will examine the reasons for conducting performance appraisals, and then our attitude, knowledge, and skills in conducting appraisal interviews. You will not see different types of appraisal forms, nor discussions of various performance appraisal systems used by other organizations. The emphasis will be on us as leaders—and what we can do to become even more effective.

One last point before looking at the reasons for conducting appraisal interviews: our ability to conduct a successful performance appraisal is far more dependent on what has been going on all year than on what we do or don't do during the interview. In other words, if we haven't been performing our job as a leader in guiding, coaching, counseling, directing, and training throughout the year, then the most impressive interviewing skills in the world won't make our interviews successful. A performance appraisal session is not a substitute for ongoing leadership. It is the result of good leadership!

Reasons for Conducting a Performance Appraisal Interview

The reasons for conducting performance appraisal sessions affect the way we conduct appraisals. The main reasons that some leaders conduct performance appraisals is because their organizations require them. I often wonder how many of us would really conduct performance appraisals on a regular basis if we weren't required to by our organizations.

We also utilize performance appraisals as an opportunity to obtain information to use in making future decisions on salaries, promotions, or demotions. And some leaders use performance appraisal interviews to tell their employees what they have done right or wrong. This first group of reasons for doing appraisals is the traditional one that initiated many performance appraisal systems. And they are important reasons. But there are other, sometimes even more important, reasons for conducting performance appraisal interviews.

For instance, we may want to develop subordinates through coaching and counseling by creating a mutual understanding of the employee's strengths and areas of desired improvement and then create action plans for implementation. Or we may want to do career counseling by determining where the employee wants to go, whether he or she can get there, and what plans we can help the employee develop to achieve these goals. In addition, we may want to conduct an appraisal interview to have an opportunity to provide recognition and motivation for an employee.

The first set of traditional reasons above requires that we, as the leader, play the role of a *judge*. And if we take on the role of a judge, the employee will quickly assume a corresponding role. A new employee may become passive and do very little talking. And an older employee may react strongly, defending him or herself when being judged. The focus of this type of interview is on the past: we are reflecting on what has already happened.

The second set of reasons requires that we talk with our employee as a *counselor*. When we do this, we will find that he or she will be more active and participative during the interview. This group of reasons looks at where the employee is presently and what can be done in the future.

The problem here is that it is extremely difficult to play both roles in the same interview. If we play the role of judge, and, in effect, tell the employee to "sit down, shut up, and listen while I tell you your strengths and weaknesses," then it will be very difficult for us suddenly to shift gears and say, "I'm here to help you in any way that I can."

It's not impossible to play both roles in the same interview; it's just very difficult. It is all in where we choose to put our emphasis. And for real change to occur in the employee's behavior following the interview, we must place our emphasis on coaching, counseling, guiding, leading, training and helping—not judging. It is not so much what the employee has already done, but what he or she will do in the future that is important.

Nine Key Steps in Performance Appraisal

Ninety-eight leaders in five different organizations were selected by their subordinates as very competent in conducting performance appraisals. In closed-door sessions, these leaders were extensively interviewed. It was quickly discovered that they had certain common values or guidelines:

1. Talk about performance, not personality. It's what has or has not been done, not what he or she *is*.

2. Offer insight into the employee's problems, not indictment. Offer understanding and help, not blame.

3. Focus on development, not discipline. Focus on the future, not the past.

4. Discuss with the employee, rather than present. Talk *with* the employee, not *at* him or her.

These ninety-eight leaders were also asked what they did and didn't do, and specifically how they proceeded in a performance appraisal interview. Following are the nine key steps that these leaders identified as critical for conducting an effective performance appraisal interview.

☑ 1. Prepare for the interview.

☑ 2. Introduce the meeting.

☑ 3. Determine the topics the employee wants to discuss.

☑ 4. Discuss concerns not mentioned by the employee.

☑ 5. Develop written action plans for carrying out key solutions in a specific time period.

☑ 6. Give specific feedback on any positive performance that has not already been discussed.

☑ 7. Summarize the interview and discuss ratings.

☑ 8. Set follow-up dates.

☑ 9. Thank the employee.

A number of years ago I was in Houston, Texas, leading a performance appraisal workshop. One participant sitting in the back hadn't said much, and from his attitude two things were evident. First, he didn't want to be there, and second, his boss had made him come anyway! I had just presented the nine key steps for conducting performance appraisals. This individual then said sarcastically, "Don't you think this is nothing more than a canned approach to a performance appraisal?"

But before I could say anything, a new leader in the group challenged the gentleman. What she said made a powerful impact on this individual, who from that point on became an active workshop participant. (In fact, he participated almost too much, although now positively.) She said, "A football team spends a great deal of time practicing specific plays before a big game. Does that mean it's a 'canned approach'? Or a *planned* approach?"

The following nine key steps, and sub-steps, will enable us to plan and conduct effective performance appraisal interviews. We can use these steps as a guide, a road map, to help us achieve our objectives.

Although each step is important, there may be times when it is appropriate not to use a particular step, or to use them in another order. For example, if, in Step 3, the employee has raised all the concerns about his or her performance that we had on our list, we will not have to use Step 4, "Discuss concerns not mentioned by the employee." Or the model suggests that we talk about all the concerns (ours and the employees), and then develop written action plans for all the important areas that need improvement. But on closer inspection, we can see that doesn't make sense. Far more effective would be for the employee (or us) to bring up one area of needed improvement. Then we immediately develop an action plan for that first concern before moving on to another area of discussion.

Let's now look at each of the nine performance appraisal steps in more detail.

☑ **1. Prepare for the interview.**

Approximately two to three weeks before the scheduled performance appraisal interview, we should meet with the employee and state briefly where and when the discussion will be held. At this time, we need to give the employee a copy of the performance appraisal form and ask that it be completed before the appraisal meeting. We should ask the employee to examine his or her ideas about the job and how well he or she is performing in each area. Then we request that the employee consider any special problems or recommendations for discussion and develop some specific plans for further improving job performance.

Filling out the form in advance will help the employee better prepare for the performance appraisal meeting. Normally, we should not ask to see the employee's completed form before or during the actual session. It's the employee's "worksheet," and is used only as an aid for him or her to plan for the meeting.

In addition, we also should tentatively complete the performance appraisal form—in pencil. Filling out the form in advance gives us the opportunity to obtain additional data if required. We list the employee's key strengths and areas of needed improvement. And for the areas where the employee needs improvement, we first analyze potential causes of problems by asking

- Is he or she aware of what was expected?

- Is he or she aware of his or her performance?

- Are there uncontrollable factors?

- Does he or she lack ability or knowledge?

- Is there lack of motivation? If so, why?

Then, we develop possible solutions and tentative action plans. The causes, solutions, and plans we identify are all tentative, because our information is not complete until we gain additional information in the interview from the employee. We also want the employee, during the interview, to develop his or her ideas and solutions in order to increase his or her acceptance.

In planning for the performance appraisal session, we need to set aside sufficient time—normally an hour. But we don't schedule it for the last hour of the day or the hour just before another critical appointment. Since we may need to take longer than an hour, we schedule the session so that extra time is available if necessary. It is also our responsibility to ensure that the employee can meet us in privacy, with no interruptions. If we can't control possible interruptions at our office, we need to go somewhere else.

☑ 2. Introduce the meeting.

When the employee first enters our office (or a neutral area such as a conference room), we can relieve the employee's tension by greeting him or her warmly. We might help him or her feel more at ease by sitting across the corner of our desk or by sitting in front of the desk with our employee. This will reduce the "I'm-the-Boss" problem and help the employee communicate more openly.

The objective of this interview is to assist, guide, and help the employee to develop professionally. A judgmental role, as indicated earlier, can produce passive and/or defensive employee behavior that is not conducive to development. Thus, as the interview begins, we should stress our role as a counselor, not a judge; e.g., "During this interview, I'd like to offer any assistance I can give, and answer any questions you may have. This is your interview. I'm here to help in any way I can."

☑ **3. Determine the topics the employee wants to discuss.**

In the past, most performance appraisal interviews began with the leader telling the employee what he or she did "right" and "wrong." Asking the employee for the topics that he or she wants to discuss is a radical departure from this older method. But there are four reasons why this is an excellent way to begin the interview:

1. The employee may raise an issue already on our list. It's much easier to deal with an area of needed improvement if the employee brings it up.

2. The employee may not be prepared to talk about a topic that we bring up, which will increase his or her tension.

3. We may discover areas of concern that we weren't aware of.

4. We want the employee to enter actively into a discussion, not just to listen to what we have to say.

To open this part of the interview, we simply ask, "What topic would you most like to discuss today?" or "What's first on your list for today's discussion?" Note that both questions are "neutral," i.e., they do not initially ask for a concern or a problem, but allow the employee to respond with whatever topic he or she wishes to bring up.

When we ask a question such as those above, we will usually receive one of three possible responses from the employee:

1. An area of concern (i.e., something the employee feels he or she needs to improve)

2. An area of his or her positive performance

3. A decision not to respond, e.g., "I don't know. What do you want to talk about?"

Let's look at each of these three possible responses.

Area of Concern

If the employee brings up a performance problem or other area of concern, it is likely that the first statement made by the employee will be very general. General statements such as, "I have trouble getting along with Jane," or "Those people over in information services won't communicate with me!" are difficult to problem-solve. Thus we may need to ask questions to help the employee be more specific. For example, "Could you give me an example?" or "Can you be a little more specific?" will provide us with more information to use to help the employee solve the problem.

When we feel the problem is defined in specific terms, the next step is to pose questions that help the employee explore the cause of the problem. Questions such as, "What do you think is the cause of this situation?" or "What other causes do you see?" should be asked even if you think you already know the answers to the questions. You do this for three reasons:

1. The employee will be more open to your suggested solutions if he or she believes we understand the cause(s) of the problem.

2. Identifying the most probable cause(s) increases the chances that proposed solutions could work.

3. The employee may be closer to the problem and thus able to see causes that we can't see.

Last, when we are comfortable that the employee has identified the cause of a problem, we ask further questions to obtain his or her solutions—even if we believe we know the solution. The purpose in asking for a solution, rather than offering ours, is that an employee who helps find the solution to a problem will more readily accept the changes which that solution will require. In addition, there is always the likelihood that the employee may have a solution that is better than ours.

To elicit an employee's suggested solution, we simply ask, "What ideas do you have for developing a solution to this situation?" or "What suggestions do you have for increasing your performance in this area?" or "What else can you do?"

But be cautious here. The employee's response might be, "Well, I guess I'll just have to try harder!" The problem with this solution is that even though it communicates a willingness to change, it says nothing about how that change will occur. We will find it is very difficult to later follow up an "I'll-try-harder" solution. It is better for us to say, "Well, I appreciate your willingness to try harder. But how do you see yourself doing that?" or "What things can you do?" When we get specific solutions, we can better follow up and provide appropriate feedback. Surprisingly enough, in Step 3 an employee will bring up an area of concern (a performance problem) more often than a positive performance, or an "I don't know" response.

Now let's look at the second most frequent response to the leader's request for a topic of discussion: a positive performance statement.

Positive Performance

When we ask, "What topics would you like to discuss first today?" the employee may bring up something that he or she feels especially proud of. When this happens, we should immediately provide specific positive feedback, e.g., "I'm glad you mentioned that! I've noticed several instances where you've done extremely well. For example . . . (describe events)." The reason for providing specific feedback is to increase its positive impact to the employee as well as to give believability to the compliment. If we can describe specific times and situations, the employee knows that we really have noticed his or her positive performance.

No Response

Occasionally an employee may choose not to respond to our question, "What topics would you like to talk about first?" This sometimes happens with a new employee who is still anxious, or an employee who has had bad experiences with past performance appraisal interviews. If we feel the cause of the reluctance is nervousness, then we can take the initiative and comment positively on a strength we have noticed. This will help reduce the tension the employee may be feeling and set the stage for a productive interview. After we have discussed the employee's positive performance, however, we do need to follow up again with, "What other topics would *you* like to discuss?"

☑ **4. Discuss concerns not mentioned by the employee.**

After dealing with the topics the employee has brought up for discussion, it is now time for us to bring up any of our concerns that have not already been mentioned by the employee. This step uses a four-step sub-model as follows:

A. Describe the employee's specific performance.

First, we introduce the topic by describing in specific terms the employee's actual performance. A specific statement helps reduce arguments with the employee because it describes behavior, not personality. For example, we don't say, "You make too many errors!" (what is "too many"?); or "You're always late!" ("always" is probably not true). Instead, specify the behavior, e.g., "There were six errors made on the January report"; or "The record shows that you have been fifteen minutes late five times during the past thirty days."

B. Describe the expected standard of performance.

Next, we need to state exactly what the employee should be doing that he or she is not doing, or what the employee should not be doing that he or she is doing. We should try to avoid nonspecific statements like "You've got to improve your production," "I expect you to improve your attitude!" or "You need to reduce the number of errors you're making." Examples of better performance standard statements are "I expect a minimum of ten percent increase in your production," "This job requires attendance at or before eight o'clock each morning," or "The performance standard for this job is zero defects."

C. Ask employee to identify cause(s) of the situation.

As suggested in Step 3, it is important to probe for the cause of the problem for the following reasons:

- Employee identification of causes helps in later acceptance of solutions.
- The employee may see causes not seen by us.
- Identifying the most probable cause increases the quality of the solution.
- It keeps the discussion focused on the cause of the problem in order to prevent premature focus on solutions.

To help the employee analyze the cause of the problem, we ask, "What do you think is the cause of this situation?" or "What other causes do you see?" Note that in the first question the word selected was "situation," not "problem." Employees tend to react less defensively to analyzing situations rather than problems.

D. Ask employee for his or her suggested solutions.

Here again it is important to ask the employee for his or her solutions. If the employee is going to play a role in making needed changes, it is better to gain acceptance by guiding him or her to identify the solution.

The leader and the employee should explore each solution to reach one that will correct the problem. We also can make suggestions based on our general knowledge or experience that might improve the quality of the solution. Then we can encourage the employee to select the solution(s) that will be employed.

Because of the difficulty of handling too much change at once, we can help the employee select only a few solutions. We are looking for quality and degree of improvement in important areas, not small improvements in many. After selecting a solution or solutions, the employee will develop an action plan for each solution, in Step 5.

☑ **5. Develop written action plans for carrying out key solutions in a specific time period.**

Some solutions will not need action plans. For example, the employee who is constantly tardy doesn't need a full-blown action plan to get to work on time. But for more complex solutions, a written goal statement with step-by-step plans will greatly increase the likelihood that the employee will accomplish the positive change.

If this is the first time a particular employee has written an action plan, we may have to put on our "training hat" and assist in writing a planning statement. However, we need to be careful about who holds the pencil! If we write it, it's our plan, not the employee's. Letting the employee write a planning statement encourages ownership, acceptance, and future results.

But even though we want it to be the employee's plan, we can increase its quality by offering our suggestions or assistance. We can provide help by saying, "I wonder if this might be something you could consider doing . . .?" "What can I do to help?" or "What would you like me to do?"

☑ **6. Give specific feedback on any positive performance that has not already been discussed.**

A performance appraisal interview provides us with an excellent opportunity to give employees positive feedback on their accomplishments. We should plan to spend a significant amount of time on this step so as to balance the interview between the employee's needs and strengths.

To provide positive feedback that is meaningful to the employee, we can use the following model (similar to the one presented in the chapter on motivation):

A. Describe the employee's specific behavior and illustrate with examples.

By being specific and giving examples, we make our feedback credible. Also, the employee then knows exactly what he or she did that we like and appreciate. This will increase his or her motivation to repeat the behavior in the future.

B. Give reasons why the employee's strength is important.

When we plan for this meeting, we analyze why a particular strength of the employee is important to us, the organization, and to him or her. By giving all the reasons why the employee's strength is important, we reinforce the desired behaviors.

C. Spell out our future expectations.

By spelling out our expectations of continued high performance, we inform the employee that we expect such performance in the future.

D. Express our appreciation.

Most employees have a need to feel appreciated by their leaders.

E. Develop written action plans for further use of the employee's strengths (if appropriate).

Leaders often spend much time discussing how an employee can improve, and developing written action plans for improvement in particular areas. Similarly, we should spend time discussing an employee's strengths, and develop written action plans for better using those strengths if possible. Leaders sometimes overlook the fact that good performance can be made even better, thus building on an employee's strengths.

7. Summarize the interview and discuss ratings.

In Step 7, we highlight the key areas discussed to ensure clear understanding. Misunderstandings result when two people think they clearly understand what was said and agreed upon, when in fact they don't. In addition, if we summarize the key points each of us made in the interview, then both of us will have a solid feeling of accomplishment.

After we have summarized the highlights of the discussion, we share with the employee our perception of his or her ratings. If we discuss ratings first in an interview, the employee cannot see the reasons for our ratings. The employee may then become defensive, and we will find ourselves defending the ratings. By summarizing the interview and discussing your ratings at the end of it, we will focus attention more on the job performance, rather than on the ratings.

 8. Set follow-up dates.

Now we set follow-up dates with the employee and mark the date and time on our calendar in the employee's presence. This shows that his or her performance is important to us and clearly commits us to follow up, and the employee to meet expectations as agreed.

 9. Thank the employee.

Thanking the employee for the time and energy he or she devoted to preparing for and taking part in a performance appraisal interview is simple common courtesy and will be greatly appreciated.

If you want to experience greater effectiveness and success in conducting performance appraisals, this tested nine-step process is for you. But it will require that you give it the needed time and effort to prove itself. Any human interaction process tends to look easy when reduced to its key steps on paper. Some hard work is necessary when learning a new system, however. If some step in this process doesn't seem to work for you, feel free to alter it. Shape the system to fit your needs. But, give it a full and honest try before judging it. If you do, you will find this basic nine-step method as effective for you as it is for the successful leaders who utilize it.

On the following pages you will find a *Preparation Guide* and a *Leader's Checklist* to copy and use in planning for and conducting your next performance appraisal interview.

Leader's Checklist

☑ **1. Prepare for the interview.**

    ☐ Give employee a copy of the performance appraisal form and discuss it with him or her 2 to 3 weeks before the actual interview.
    ☐ Ask employee to complete a copy of the form before the interview.
    ☐ Reserve an area for the interview where you can control interruptions.
    ☐ Review incident files, and analyze specific areas to be discussed in the interview.
    ☐ Tentatively analyze causes and solutions and create tentative action plans.
    ☐ Tentatively fill out the performance appraisal form on the employee.

☑ **2. Introduce the meeting.**

    ☐ Put the employee at ease.
    ☐ Reduce physical barriers to communication.
    ☐ Stress your role as a counselor, not "judge."

☑ **3. Determine topic(s) employee wants to discuss.**

If employee brings up an area of concern:
    ☐ Ask questions to help employee be specific.
    ☐ Ask questions to explore causes.
    ☐ Obtain employee's solutions.

If employee brings up area of positive performance:
    ☐ Provide positive feedback.

If employee does not offer topic:
    ☐ Comment positively on strengths you have noticed.
    ☐ Ask again for topic.

☑ **4. Discuss concerns not mentioned by the employee.**

- ☐ Describe employee's specific performance.
- ☐ Describe the expected standard of performance.
- ☐ Ask employee to identify causes of the situation.
- ☐ Ask employee for his or her suggested solutions, and discuss.

☑ **5. Develop written action plans for carrying out key solutions in a specific time period.**

- ☐ Let employee select key solutions for development.
- ☐ If necessary, assist the employee with writing a planning statement.
- ☐ Offer suggestions or ideas as employee develops specific steps that he or she will take over the next six months.

☑ **6. Give specific feedback on any positive performance that has not already been discussed.**

- ☐ Describe the employee's specific behavior and illustrate with examples.
- ☐ Tell him or her why it was important to you, your organization, and to the employee.
- ☐ Spell out your future expectations.
- ☐ Express your appreciation.
- ☐ Develop action plans for the employee's strength(s) if appropriate.

☑ **7. Summarize interview and discuss ratings.**

☑ **8. Set follow-up dates.**

☑ **9. Thank employee.**

Preparation Guide

Preparing for Your Actual
Performance Appraisal

In each step below, write what you would actually say or do when you conduct the interview with your employee. Feel free to look at the text for ideas on what you can say in each step.

☑ **1. Prepare for the interview.**

Have you met briefly with the employee one to two weeks in advance to prepare him or her for the interview by

a. Giving him or her a copy of any form(s) that will be used in the interview? _____

b. Discussing the form(s) with the employee? _____

c. Asking that the employee prepare for the interview by filling out the form(s) before the meeting? _____ (Don't ask to see the form(s). They are to be used privately by the employee.)

Have you prepared for this interview thoroughly by

a. Reserving an area where you can control interruptions? _____

b. Reviewing incident files on this employee and carefully analyzing specific areas to be discussed during this session? _____

☑ **2. Introduce the meeting.**

What will you do? _____

_____

_____

What will you say? _____

_____

_____

_____

☑ **3. Determine topic(s) employee wants to discuss.**

What are you going to say to encourage the employee to talk first?

_____

_____

When employee brings up area of concern:

a. What questions will you ask to determine cause(s)?

_____

_____

b. What questions will you ask to determine his or her solution(s)?

_____

_____

What questions will you ask to obtain a second or even third issue for discussion from this employee?

_____

_____

☑ **4. Discuss concerns not mentioned by employee.**

a. Describe the employee's specific performance.

_____

_____

b. Describe the expected standard of performance.

_____

_____

c. What questions will you ask to determine cause(s)?

_____

_____

d. What questions will you ask to determine his or her solution(s)?

_____

_____

Discuss concerns not mentioned by employee. (Used when there are two concerns. Repeat Step 4 if there are two concerns.)

a. Describe the employee's specific performance.

_____

_____

b. Describe the expected standard of performance.

_____

_____

c. What questions will you ask to determine cause(s)?

_____

_____

d. What questions will you ask to determine his or her solution(s)?

_____

_____

☑ **5. Develop written action plans for carrying out key solution(s) in a specific time period.**

a. What questions will you ask the employee to get him or her to relate his or her key solution(s)?

_____

_____

b. What will you say to get him or her to write an action plan?

_____

_____

☑ **6. Give specific feedback for any positive performance that has not already been discussed.**

a. What specific example will you use to describe the positive performance?

_____

_____

b. What reasons will you give this employee why the positive performance was important?
    To you? _____
    To the organization? _____
    To the employee? _____

c. What can you say to let him or her know that you expect this positive strength in the future?

_____

_____

d. What will you say that is genuine in expressing your appreciation?

_____

_____

e. How can this employee's strength be even better utilized?

_____

_____

_____

_____

☑ **7. Summarize the interview and discuss ratings.**

What will you say to lead into the actual summary?

_____

_____

☑ **8. Set follow-up dates.**

What will you say?

_____

_____

☑ **9. Thank employee.**

What can you say that is genuine?

_____

_____

_____

_____

Personal
Leadership Skills

15

Leadership
Managing Our Time

*Our time is a very shadow that passeth away, and after its end,
there is no return. For it is fast sealed that no man cometh again.*

The Wisdom of Solomon, 2:5
Apocrypha

Remember when we were young, and those lazy summer days stretched on and on? Remember when the closer it got to summer vacation, the longer it took to arrive? Remember when the time from one holiday to the next seemed endless?

And now, why do our days seem hurried, almost mysteriously shortened? What happened? What happened to time?

Certainly our perception of time is dependent on what we're doing. We all know how waiting for something we want to happen seems like forever, and how a disagreeable task seems to take so long.

But that's only part of the answer. Our perception of time is also affected by the number of new events we're conscious of in a given period of time. For example, a drive from point A to point B on an unfamiliar road may seem to take forever. But if we travel that same distance on a familiar road, the trip seems shorter.

Similarly, when we engage in familiar, habitual tasks, we often wonder at the end of the day where the time has gone. The danger here is that we may not be aware of the way we have managed (or haven't managed) much of this routine time.

Most of us want to become increasingly effective in what we do. But the desire to improve is not all that is necessary. We also need to become aware of how we have been managing our time, so that we can understand what positive change can be made, and why.

Time management is actually a matter of asking ourselves some personal questions. The first is, "What are the things that are truly important to me?" Second, "How much of my time am I giving to these things?" And third, "What takes up my time while contributing very little to my goals or to the quality of my life?"

Time management also means accepting responsibility. It's easy to say, "I have trouble managing my time because . . .

- Other people always interrupt me.
- There is too much paperwork.
- Others misfile reports.
- My boss changes his or her priorities.
- Others won't cooperate with me.
- There are too many emergency project requests.
- The computer is always down.

- It always seems like I have to wait for others.
- My employees require too much of my time."

Agreed—many of these problems do occur. But they occur to everybody! And we know that some people, facing these same problems, are much more productive than others.

Good time managers will surely appreciate Reinhold Niebuhr's prayer:

> *. . . give us grace to accept with serenity the things that cannot be changed, courage to change the things which should be changed, and the wisdom to distinguish the one from the other.*

Effective leaders have learned to accept the things they can't change, and to take responsibility for the things they can. And they recognize the difference. If we can exert some control in our lives, make certain decisions, and accept part of the responsibility for what we do or don't do—then we can do something about our lives. And it's our choice!

Awareness of Time

Note that everything that follows is written for leaders to use in managing their time more effectively. But what follows is also extremely helpful in those situations where we, as leaders, have an employee who also needs help in managing his or her time.

Given that we have a positive attitude, that we want to be increasingly effective, and that we are willing to accept responsibility for change, what's next? What are some things we can do, and help our employees do, to manage time more productively?

First, we need to look closely at what we've been doing with our time. Peter Drucker said, "Memory is treacherous; don't trust it." That is, what we think we did and what we've really done are often two different things. So we need to have some way of obtaining accurate data about our past actions to use in decisions for the future. The best method is to use a "Time Log" to record accurately where we are spending our time.

Reproduce copies of the Time Log on the following page, and use it to record your daily time expenditure. Record everything you do. Write down when someone interrupts you, and when you interrupt yourself. Note telephone calls, incoming and outgoing; email contacts; visitors; trips to the water fountain; a coffee break. Write it all down. To obtain enough data for a complete analysis of your time, you should plan to record a minimum of three full days, both at work and at home.

Time Log

Name: _____   Date: _____

Time	Activity	Time Consumed
_____	_____	_____
_____	_____	_____
_____	_____	_____
_____	_____	_____
_____	_____	_____
_____	_____	_____
_____	_____	_____
_____	_____	_____
_____	_____	_____
_____	_____	_____
_____	_____	_____
_____	_____	_____
_____	_____	_____
_____	_____	_____
_____	_____	_____
_____	_____	_____
_____	_____	_____
_____	_____	_____
_____	_____	_____
_____	_____	_____
_____	_____	_____
_____	_____	_____
_____	_____	_____
_____	_____	_____
_____	_____	_____
_____	_____	_____
_____	_____	_____
_____	_____	_____
_____	_____	_____
_____	_____	_____
_____	_____	_____

When you have finished collecting information on how you actually spend your time, add up your time in categories. This will be a major help in determining whether the way you spend your time is really how you want to spend it. Using the following chart, categorize and record each day's information from your Time Log sheets.

Weekly Time Analysis

Work	Day 1	Day 2	Day 3	Day 4	Day 5	Total	Percent
Unscheduled Visitors (Pleasure)	___	___	___	___	___	___	___
Unscheduled Visitors (Business)	___	___	___	___	___	___	___
Scheduled Visitors (Pleasure	___	___	___	___	___	___	___
Scheduled Visitors (Business)	___	___	___	___	___	___	___
Visitors Subtotal						___	___
Outgoing Telephone (Pleasure)	___	___	___	___	___	___	___
Outgoing Telephone (Business)	___	___	___	___	___	___	___
Incoming Telephone (Pleasure)	___	___	___	___	___	___	___
Incoming Telephone (Business)	___	___	___	___	___	___	___
Email/web Pleasure	___	___	___	___	___	___	___
Email/web Business	___	___	___	___	___	___	___
Communication Subtotal						___	___
Time with Boss	___	___	___	___	___	___	___
Meetings with an Employee	___	___	___	___	___	___	___
Group Employee Meetings	___	___	___	___	___	___	___
Other Meetings	___	___	___	___	___	___	___
Waiting	___	___	___	___	___	___	___
Breaks and Lunches	___	___	___	___	___	___	___
Reading	___	___	___	___	___	___	___
Writing/Typing	___	___	___	___	___	___	___
Faxing	___	___	___	___	___	___	___
Planning	___	___	___	___	___	___	___
Physical Work	___	___	___	___	___	___	___
Other Work	___	___	___	___	___	___	___
Work Subtotal	___	___	___	___	___	___	___
Total of All Work						___	___

Home	Day 1	Day 2	Day 3	Day 4	Day 5	Total	Percent
Meditation	_____	_____	_____	_____	_____	_____	_____
Spouse	_____	_____	_____	_____	_____	_____	_____
Children	_____	_____	_____	_____	_____	_____	_____
Friends	_____	_____	_____	_____	_____	_____	_____
Chores	_____	_____	_____	_____	_____	_____	_____
Eating	_____	_____	_____	_____	_____	_____	_____
Sleeping	_____	_____	_____	_____	_____	_____	_____
Civic	_____	_____	_____	_____	_____	_____	_____
Business	_____	_____	_____	_____	_____	_____	_____
Recreation	_____	_____	_____	_____	_____	_____	_____
Hobbies	_____	_____	_____	_____	_____	_____	_____
Telephone	_____	_____	_____	_____	_____	_____	_____
Television/Video	_____	_____	_____	_____	_____	_____	_____
Computer	_____	_____	_____	_____	_____	_____	_____
School	_____	_____	_____	_____	_____	_____	_____
Total of All Home Categories						_____	_____
Total of All Work Categories						_____	_____
Grand Total						_____	_____

After categorizing and recording your Time Log information, decide which time expenditures you wish to change. To do this, you'll need to ask some tough questions, including,

1. Did I use any time to plan for the future?
2. Have I recorded activity—or "results"? (Activity = what I did. Results = what I accomplished)
3. What was the longest period of time spent on one thing without interruption?
4. Which interruptions were most costly?
5. What can be done to eliminate or control these interruptions?
   - Which telephone calls were unnecessary?
   - Which phone calls could have been shorter yet equally (or more) effective?
   - Which visits were unnecessary?
   - Which visits could have been shorter yet equally (or more) effective?
6. How much time did I spend in meetings?
7. Did I find myself jumping from task to task without completing the previous one?
8. Did crisis work push more important things aside?

9. Did I notice a self-correcting tendency occurring as I recorded actions throughout the week?
10. How much quality employee development time did I spend?
11. How much quality time did I spend with my family? What, if anything, do I want to change?

When we have answered these questions, we are in a much better position to decide what we should change to save time in our work and personal life. Of course we may discover that what we are doing is exactly what we want to do; if so, our final decision will be to do nothing. In either case, the information will help us make the right decision.

And when we make changes, we should be aware of two points:

1. Increasing the amount of time spent on one activity will take time from another activity.

2. Changes can sometimes cause problems that, in turn, take even more time to fix.

What is Urgent?

Dr. Charles Hummel once wrote an article entitled, "The Tyranny of the Urgent." In it he distinguished things that are truly important from those that seem "urgent." When important things and urgent things occur simultaneously, which usually wins our attention?

Let me give you an example. Many years ago, I made a decision to leave the organization I worked for in St. Paul and move my family back to my home state of Virginia. I planned to be my own boss as an independent training consultant. After a couple of grim years, I finally achieved my bottom line financial goal— i.e., we weren't starving!

At the time, my office was in our converted garage. Because we had many children, I had a business telephone line and a family line.

One Friday evening at 5:30 we were sitting down for supper when the business line rang. I asked the children to quiet down, and answered the phone. "International Training Consultants. Dick Leatherman speaking. How can I help you?" I said.

The caller was the program director of a local university's management center. He was extremely agitated—so much so I could hardly understand him. Because I was also getting some noise in the kitchen, I put him on hold and went down to the garage to continue the call. "What's wrong?" I asked.

His story was a program director's nightmare. He was at the end of a weeklong seminar for about a hundred purchasing agents from up and down the eastern seaboard. The keynote speaker for Saturday morning was the dean of one of the country's leading law schools. But because the dean had the flu, he wouldn't be there in the morning.

So the program director pleaded, "Dick, will you be our keynote speaker tomorrow morning? We don't care what you do. Just come in and do something!" Let me tell you, that request made me feel good. He had called me first!

But let's put him on hold for a minute so I can tell you about several things I had already scheduled for the Saturday in question.

First, because my office was at home we had some pretty strict rules about the children bothering me when I was working. A week before the program director's call, I had been working in my office when Matthew Leatherman (he was about seven years old at the time) careened in with a big emergency. Well, he wasn't broken or bleeding, and the interruption irritated me. As a result, I wasn't very nice to him. And as he sulked out of my office, he said under his breath (but just loud enough for me to hear him), "Daddy doesn't have time for me anymore since he has his own business." And Matthew was right. I wasn't spending as much time with him as I once did. So I said, "Hold it, Bud. You're right. I don't spend as much time with you as I used to. But I'll tell you what— let's you and me have a turtle day next Saturday morning. How about it?" "Oh, yes!" he exclaimed, and I got a big hug.

Do you know what a "turtle day" is? It's when you take a seven-year old boy out to look for turtles. The fact that you probably won't find any is not the point. It's what you can talk about while you look! One-on-one, private time between a daddy and his son. That's the point!

And there was another important thing I had scheduled for that Saturday. On the Wednesday before, Laurie, my 16-year old (going on 21), had asked me if I would teach her how to drive. I said, "Hey, Honey, my tax dollars help pay for you to get professional driving instruction at your high school! Besides, you don't want to learn my bad driving habits." (I'm a lousy driver.)

"But Daddy," she replied, "I've never driven a car, and I get my 'behind-the-wheel' instructions next week. The other kids will be in the car too, and I don't want to make a fool of myself in front of them!" "Oh, I see," I said. "I'll tell you what—let's spend some time next Saturday at the shopping center parking lot, and you can scare me to death!" "Fantastic!" she said. And I got a big hug for that, too.

The last thing I had scheduled for that Saturday was time with my youngest daughter, Leanne. Her "Uncle Frank" had made her a giant dollhouse. It was a marvel to see! It was carpeted, and it had real windows. It also had a low-voltage lighting system with a miniature chandelier hanging in the dining room.

Well, Leanne's house had an attic fire. Somehow the low-voltage wiring had shorted out, and the transformer had burned up. She had been "reminding" me to fix it for a couple of months. And the Tuesday before the Saturday in question, she had asked, "Please, please, please," (or were there four "pleases"?) "fix my dollhouse?" I said, "Tell you what I'm going to do. I'll put the transformer in your dollhouse this coming Saturday. At the same time, I'll teach you how to solder wires." I got another big hug for that!

Remember, we still have the program director on hold. What do you think I told him when he frantically said that Friday evening, "Dick, we don't care what you do. Just come in and do something!" Yes—I said, "Okay." Then I walked up to the kitchen and said, "Guess what, gang? Daddy has a seminar at the Hyatt House tomorrow morning!" There was dead silence.

Then my oldest daughter said, "Daddy!" and walked out of the room.

Matthew said, "But . . . but . . . what about turtle day?"

And Leanne, with all the faith and trust of a young child in her father, said, "That's OK, Daddy. I know you'll fix my dollhouse someday."

I did eventually fix the dollhouse, go turtle hunting with Matthew, and give Laurie some hints on driving. But not that day—when I let the "urgent" win out over those things that were truly important to me.

Two lessons can be learned from my experience. First, there is no end to it: the "tyranny of the urgent" is a battle we all will fight day after day. Do you imagine this was the last time I let a crisis get in the way of something that was really important? The thing we must try to do at home and on the job is to choose well when the urgent tries to displace the truly important.

Secondly, as Peter Drucker has said, "Learn to say 'no' nicely if you can, but nastily if you must. But learn to say 'no' so that you have time for the really important things in your life."

If saying "no" is difficult for you, recognize that you can't say "yes" to everything. In other words, you have a right to say "no." A simple, "No thank you" is often sufficient and appropriate for those situations where a personal relationship with the other person is not important to you. And sometimes you must say "no" more than once.

Here's an example:

It's 6:30. You're in the middle of eating supper. The phone rings and you answer it.

You:	"Hello."
Caller:	"Is this Ms. Olson?"
You:	"Yes."
Caller:	"Wonderful! This is William Applebee from the Easy Glide Home Appliance Company. I am happy to inform you that you have won a matching set of stainless steel kitchen knives with genuine molded handles. One of our representatives will be in your area next week to deliver your prize. When would it be convenient for her to stop by?"
You:	"Thank you, but I'm not interested."
Caller:	"Ms. Olson, our computer selected you at random for this free set of superb knives that I know you will love having in your home. It won't take but a minute to have them delivered to you. So when would be the best time for you, Monday or Tuesday of next week?"
You:	"Thank you, but I'm really not interested."
Caller:	"I'm sorry, but I don't understand. Why aren't you interested in owning this free set of fantastic knives?"
You:	"I'm not interested."

At this point, if the caller continues to be a pest, say, "Goodbye," and hang up. But, if the relationship with the other person is important to you, first acknowledge the request, then say "no," and last add an explanation. For example, suppose you are a great typist. You have a good friend who is taking evening classes at the local college. The conversation goes like this:

Friend:	"Do you have a minute?"
You:	"Sure, Jack. What's up?"
Friend:	"I really hate to ask you, but I've got a special paper due Friday. I can't find anybody who can type it for me. Would you mind doing it?"
You:	"It sounds like you're facing a tight deadline. I'd really like to help you, but I can't. I don't have time to do it."

Friend:	"I know you are busy, and I really hate to ask. But you type so fast. It's only ten pages. Isn't there some way you could squeeze it in?"
You:	"I'm really sorry, Jack, but I can't. I have other plans."

Note that you acknowledged his needs ("It sounds like you're facing a tight deadline"), said "no" tactfully (I'd really like to help you, but I can't), and gave a reason ("I don't have time to do it"). Note too, that when your friend persisted in his request, you said "no" again.

But how do we know when to say "no"? By realizing what is important to us. And how do we ensure that important things are not pushed aside by "urgent" things?

By planning! Planning allows us to identify important goals, and put them into action. The resulting activities generated by this analysis then become a part of our daily planning.

Daily Planning

Daily planning is making a "to-do" list for each day. This list should include the priority items that should be done immediately, as well as things that we can do today to help carry out our long-range goals. It doesn't have to be anything fancy—just a small piece of paper we carry in our pocket or purse to jot down the things we have planned for that (or the next) day. It doesn't make any difference when we do it, whether we do it first thing in the morning, or at the end of the day. Just so we do it daily!

But keeping a to-do list daily may involve a significant amount of time. For example, even if we spend only 10 minutes a day making our list, that adds up to 3650 minutes, or 60 hours a year! So there is a cost for doing a daily to-do list. And thus there must be a compelling reason to lead us to do such daily planning.

In fact, there are many good reasons why effective people plan daily. First, when you visibly identify all the things you feel you need to do today, you can establish your priorities by seeing what's important, and what's only urgent. Since everything on our list can't be a #1 priority, try using the categories of:

1 = Must Do   2 = Should Do   3 = Could Do

Daily planning also helps our boss set priorities with us. For example, if our boss constantly interrupts us with new crisis requests, it's strategically helpful to hold up a daily to-do list and say, "OK, boss, where does that fit on my list?"

Third, a to-do list acts as a memory aid. I, for one, have reached an age where, if I don't write it down, there is only a very small chance I'll remember what it was that I said I absolutely wouldn't forget!

I use a daily to-do list for yet another reason. It tells me what to do next after finishing a task. I am a very task-oriented person. While I'm working on a task, I'm usually not thinking of other things that need to be done. Then when I finish a job, because I can't think of what I wanted to do next, I may simply take a break. But if I have a to-do list in front of me, I can see exactly what I need to do next.

Others who keep daily to-do lists report that it simply feels good to scratch tasks off their list as they are completed. In other words, we have set up a way of giving ourselves immediate positive feedback as we complete each task.

Finally, I save my lists for a month or so and review them to see if I can discover any way that I can further improve my time management. For example, if I haven't completed a task that I had planned to do that day, I immediately rewrite that task on the next day's list. And if I see that I rewrote a particular task more than once, I realize that I may be procrastinating.

If you don't already use a daily to-do list, try it! It will be time well invested. Or simply commit yourself to keeping a list for 20 working days. When you see that it pays off, you will continue to use such a list, without difficulty—because you've gotten into the to-do habit.

On the next page is an example of a to-do list. Make as many copies as you need and then stack the sheets and staple them at the top to make your to-do pads. Or, there are some terrific computer programs that can help keep track of the demands on our time.

We have presented several concrete strategies for managing your time well:

- Time logs
- Prioritizing "important" things over "urgent" ones
- Daily planning with "to-do" lists
- Creating a plan for the future

Using these techniques will allow you to do key tasks on schedule and have more time for creative thinking, for your boss, for your employees, and for yourself. To become a better manager of your time, you need to spend it on those things that are really important. In short, you need to take control of your life!

Daily To Do List

Tasks To Do	Priority	Time	Date

Daily To Do List

Tasks To Do	Priority	Time	Date

Daily To Do List

Tasks To Do	Priority	Time	Date

Daily To Do List

Tasks To Do	Priority	Time	Date

16

Leadership
Managing and Conducting Meetings

Nero fiddled while Rome burned. Nero was in a meeting.

Dick Dunsing
You and I Have Simply Got To Stop Meeting This Way

"You mean you expect me to stand up in front of a group and lead a meeting?" You bet! Good meeting leaders are not born knowing how to lead meetings well. They learn! And they usually learn the hard way. For example, one well-known research study of five organizations found that they ranked ineffective meetings as one of their top five time-wasters.

But we don't have to learn how to conduct successful meetings the hard way! We can learn by studying topics such as meeting preparation, facilitation skills, and meeting follow up. And we can learn by examining the different types of meetings, and the knowledge and skills required for each.

There are four basic types of meetings: providing information, instructional, problem solving, and obtaining information. In looking at the graph below, we can see how each of these meetings is a function of the flow of communications between the leader and the meeting participants. Notice that on the far left, the leader is doing most of the talking (providing information), and on the right, the meeting participants are doing most of the talking (obtaining information).

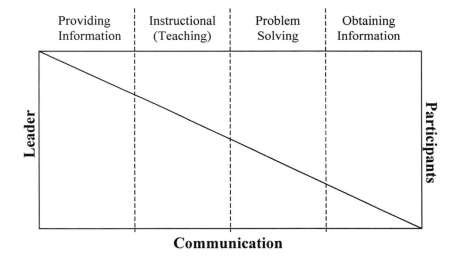

This concept is important because, although there are common skills that are useful in all types of meetings, there are specific skills that are more applicable to one type meeting than another. For example, the ability to thoroughly prepare and organize meetings is useful for all four types, but the skill of asking probing questions is usually not used when "providing information."

Listed below are some of the skills and knowledge needed in each of these four meeting types. Note that this is not an all-inclusive list. You can probably think of other skills that belong here.

Providing Information	Instructional	Problem Solving	Obtaining Information
• Prepares/ organizes	• Prepares/ organizes • Sets priorities	• Prepares/ organizes • Sets priorities	• Prepares/ organizes
	• Uses active listening skills	• Uses active listening skills	• Uses active listening skills
• Has expert knowledge	• Is a subject-matter expert	• Has some knowledge	• Communicates expectations
	• Asks probing, open questions • Uses Socratic skills	• Asks probing, open questions • Identifies source of problem • Resolves conflict	• Asks probing, open questions
	• Solicits feedback • Accepts/interprets feedback	• Solicits feedback	• Uses recording skills
	• Uses nonverbal skills	• Uses nonverbal skills	• Uses nonverbal skills
• Knows target audience	• Has knowledge of instructional needs of audience	• Uses basic problem solving, decision making, planning, and consensus processes	• Sorts important information out • Uses summarizing skills
• Anticipates questions about content	• Anticipates questions about content	• Anticipates questions about processes	
• Uses strong presentation skills	• Uses excellent teaching skills • Is interactive	• Uses good facilitation skills	• Uses excellent facilitation skills
• Creates takeaway handouts	• Creates takeaway handouts	• Creates handouts on processes used	• Has methods to compile info
• Has excellent A/V skills	• Has good A/V skills		

It's much easier to learn how to manage and conduct meetings if we break down this activity into its steps, and examine each one, keeping in mind the four basic types of meetings. There are six key steps:

1. Prepare for the meeting.

2. Open the meeting.

3. Use the appropriate process (in problem-solving meetings).

4. Obtain acceptance.

5. Close the meeting.

6. Follow up.

Let's look at each of these steps in detail.

 1. Prepare for the meeting.

Leaders who prepare for their meetings conduct better meetings. It's as simple as that. You will find in this chapter the proper method of preparing for any meeting. But note: unless you are willing to invest time in doing so, your meetings will be less effective than they can be. So it's up to you. If you want real results in your meetings—and you want your employees to feel good about them—then you must prepare. Here's how.

Start Early

We can't leave preparation for important meetings to the last minute. Waiting too long to start the preparation process drastically reduces what we can accomplish. We may find that we need a couple of overhead transparencies, but don't have time to get them made. We discover at the last minute that our old PowerPoint® presentation has out-of-date information. We learn that a key member can't come because he or she didn't have enough advance notice. Or we realize we should have a written agenda to hand out, but don't have time to have it typed, much less copied. These, and many other problems, can occur if we wait until too late to prepare for our meeting. But by taking a few minutes to think through the things that need to be done, we can usually determine how much time we need to prepare. Included at the end of this chapter is a *Meeting Preparation Checklist* that you can copy and use to help yourself prepare for your meetings and have plenty of time to do what needs to be done.

Communicate

We need to let those who are to attend the meeting know, in writing, the "who, what, when, where and why" of the meeting. If this is not a regularly scheduled meeting, it is especially important to confirm in writing (or orally for small groups) the meeting time and place. For all meetings, routine as well as special, we need to make sure that the members receive the meeting objectives and agenda in advance. In general, the more details the members have about the meeting ahead of time, the better prepared they will be.

Meeting Objective. Some meetings really get crazy because the leader didn't think through in advance what was supposed to be accomplished—and no one else knew either! If we don't know where we are going in a meeting, how will we achieve our goal? So one of our key tasks in preparing for a meeting is to think through why we need the meeting. What do we want the members to do in the meeting—and do as a result of it? What do we want them to learn? To consider? To decide? To act on? What do we want to achieve in the meeting? What should happen when the meeting is over? Answering these questions will result in clear objectives for our meetings. If we don't know the answers, we should think about not having the meeting—and save everybody a lot of time!

A meeting objective is simply a description of what we, or the members, want to accomplish as a result of the meeting. For example, we can hold a meeting to provide or obtain information, identify problems, determine the cause of a specific problem, make a decision, create a plan, or train employees. In other words, an objective expresses the purpose of the meeting and describes the desired outcome.

Meeting Agenda. The agenda lists the topics that will be covered to achieve the meeting objective(s). It describes what we will do in the meeting—the activities that will take place to accomplish the desired results. For example, if the objective of the meeting is to make a group decision, the announced agenda of topics/activities might look like this:

A problem-solving meeting will be held on January 5 at 8:30 AM in conference room "B" to determine our priority problem areas for analysis.

Objective:
The group will select, by consensus, our three most pressing problems.

Agenda:

1. *Discuss the need for a decision.*
2. *Determine the factors we should consider in making the decision.*

3. *Brainstorm a list of problem areas.*

4. *Make a final decision, using a consensus process.*

5. *Assign responsibilities to specific individuals to carry out our decision.*

Prepare the Content

After we have written our meeting objective(s) and established the agenda, we are ready to examine our role in the meeting. We consider, first, what we need to do in the meeting, and second, what we need to do to prepare for our part in it. For example, if we were in charge of the meeting described above, we would probably talk to our boss to see what problems he or she sees in our section. We will also need to spend time thinking about the major problems as we see them. Then we make a list of these problems in case others do not bring up some of them for discussion in the meeting.

Or we may want to prepare handouts, have reference material available, design a PowerPoint® presentation, or even invite a subject matter expert to sit in on the meeting. The key is that whatever needs to be done will take time. And the time to begin is usually long before the day of the meeting. Next, we consider what we want the members to do in the meeting and determine if any of them need to do something in preparation for it. Certain individuals may need to know in advance that they will be asked to offer their expertise or to bring their records and files for reference. Or we may wish to assign specific meeting roles to key members, such as "Recorder," "Facilitator/Observer," or "Leader." We can communicate with these members before the meeting so that they will have time to prepare for their part in it.

Assign Meeting Roles

One of the best ways to manage and conduct successful meetings is to assign specific meeting roles to the members in advance. Assigned roles will not only get people more involved in the meetings, but will also create more productive meetings. Involving our participants by assigning roles is especially important in "Problem Solving" and "Obtaining Information" meetings. So let's look at our role in these meetings, and then at four other roles that we can assign to our employees.

Our Role as the Boss. I've stayed away from using the term "boss" throughout most of this book. In this chapter, however, I don't see any way of avoiding this term in order to distinguish us as the formal leader (supervisor, manager, or executive) from the Meeting Leader. The "boss" and the Meeting Leader might be the same person—but they don't have to be. As the boss, we don't always have to lead our meetings—we can delegate that responsibility to one of our key employees! We might even choose not to be present at the meeting. Many organizations today elect to have their employees meet without the boss in order to solve production problems, increase quality, or help their non-exempt employees become more involved in and challenged by their work.

Of course, even if we don't attend our employees' meetings, we are still in the communication loop. We will be asked to offer our input, obtain resources for the team members, and make decisions. We don't need to worry about "giving away our power" by delegating responsibility and authority to our people to hold their own meetings. We will likely be surprised at how new (and more important) tasks will arise to fill the time made available for us by appropriate delegation of meeting responsibility. We will also find that our people will become much more excited about their jobs; and it is amazing to hear the ideas they come up with—if we just turn them loose! Someone once said that a boss's job is to give employees what they need to do their jobs—supplies, tools, training, authority, and responsibility—and then to stand out of the way!

Of course, the first time we choose not to attend an employees' meeting, we will need to provide them with helpful, clear guidance on how to conduct their meetings. We can suggest they assign meeting roles to the attendees, use an easel or whiteboard, and utilize the best process for the task at hand. We can also tell them that we need to be informed of the meeting results, and that we will help them in any way we can.

If my anxiety over allowing my employees to hold meetings without me is too strong, then I can try attending the meeting as a participant and ask one of my employees to be the Meeting Leader. This satisfies my need to keep some control and also gives increased responsibility to my people. I find that my biggest problem is keeping my mouth shut and letting my employees run the meeting.

Meeting Leader. Whether we choose to lead the meeting ourselves or to delegate this responsibility to someone else, someone needs to take the leadership role. So let's look at what a good Meeting Leader does.

First, effective Meeting Leaders should establish and send out the meeting agenda, prepare needed handouts, arrive early, start on time and end on time, and use a flipchart or whiteboard to keep the meeting on track. Second, Leaders need to be able to handle problem participants.

Here are some common problems the Leader may encounter with his or her group and some suggested solutions.

1.   One team member monopolizes the conversation.

Possible Cause:

Possible Solution:

You—the boss—talk too much.	Ask a peer (another supervisor, manager, or executive) to attend your meetings to give you feedback.
The member has expertise in the subjects being discussed.	Ask the member to submit a position paper to all of the group members prior to the meeting.
The member doesn't know he or she has a problem.	Ask the member for permission to conduct a frequency count of the number of times he or she speaks.
The Leader doesn't exert control because he or she isn't the boss (but is an assigned Leader).	Tell the Leader that he or she has management's full support and needs to control a monopolizing speaker.
	Tell the group members that others are going to have a chance to serve as Leader, and that they should treat the present Leader the way they would want to be treated.
	Provide members with training on group roles and rules.
The Leader doesn't know how to manage the situation tactfully.	Teach the Leader how to

- Interrupt tactfully and shift the discussion to others by using a question.

- Express his or her concern to the employee privately, describe the negative results of monopolizing, and ask for cooperation.

2. A member does not participate.

Possible Cause: *Possible Solution:*

The member is shy.   Assign him or her the role of Recorder (see definition that follows).

                                     Involve the member in the discussion by asking him or her questions.

                                     Give positive reinforcement for any contribution.

The member is bored.   Assign him or her the role of Recorder, Facilitator/Observer, or Meeting Leader.

                                     Get him or her more involved by assigning tasks for later completion.

The member is angry.   In private discussion, determine the cause of his or her anger. Attempt to identify solutions to resolve the problem and counsel if needed.

3. A member is continually tardy or absent.

Possible Cause: *Possible Solution:*

The member has a bad habit of lateness/absenteeism.   Stress the importance of being present and on time (tardiness and absence are not fair to the group).

                                     Require performance by taking disciplinary action.

There is a work-environment problem   Change the employee's environment so that he or she can attend the meetings and be on time.

The member doesn't know what is expected of him or her.   Communicate expectations.

The above problems and related causes include most of the difficulties a Leader will encounter in conducting a meeting. Leaders also need to be familiar with and comfortable using a variety of meeting processes like problem solving, decision making, and planning. (These group processes and others will be discussed later in this chapter.) Finally, astute Leaders are not bothered by conflict. They know that disagreements are expected, are healthy, and can be managed.

Recorder. The Recorder is responsible for recording who attended (and did not attend) the meeting, the topics that were discussed, the key points that were made (not every word that was spoken) and who made them, and who agreed to do what (and when) as a result of the meeting. At the end of the meeting, the Recorder should also summarize the topics and task assignments, copy all easel paper and items that were written on the board (after the meeting), and follow up by promptly sending out minutes of the meeting to all group members. The Recorder should also keep files on all meetings.

Facilitator/Observer ("F/O"). Next to the Leader, the Facilitator/ Observer often plays the most crucial role in a meeting. Members who take on this role need to be insightful, knowledgeable, tactful, and courageous. They must be insightful in order to keep their focus on the *processes* taking place in the meeting, not the topics or content of the discussion. They must therefore be knowledgeable about group meeting processes. They need to be tactful when providing feedback in a non-judgmental way about members' performance. They also need to be courageous in order to provide us, the boss, with feedback when we are in the role of the Meeting Leader and make mistakes, or talk too much as a group member.

Facilitators/Observers need to make an agreement with us (the boss) and the members as to what they will and will not do in the meeting. For example, should the F/0 interrupt discussion when it is off track, or wait until the meeting is over? Should he or she suggest an appropriate process for a topic that is going to be discussed? What will be the specific nature of the F/O's involvement in the meeting? Questions such as these need to be answered prior to the meeting.

Most groups and leaders want their F/0's to be active in the meeting as a facilitator. In other words, if the group gets off course, the F/0 lets them know it. And when the group is uncertain about which process to use, the F/0 makes suggestions. However, most groups agree that the F/0's feedback should be directed to the *group,* not to individuals, and that personal feedback to us (as the boss) as Leader should be given privately. The majority of groups want their F/0's to focus upon how the group is functioning, not on the content of the meeting. Thus, the F/0 normally does not get involved in the topics under discussion. When the groups are small, however, it may be advisable for the F/0 to have some input into the topic being discussed.

Because of their great influence, F/0's also need to refrain from sending nonverbal signals as they observe the meeting. Utterances (saying "Uh-oh!") or facial contortions (rolling the eyes upward, snorting, or laughing) that indicate displeasure, or any other kind of gesture or sound can affect the conduct of the meeting. The basic role of the F/0 is to observe, and to facilitate only as agreed.

Some typical F/0 questions are

- "I have noticed that during the past hour only three of you have been involved in the discussion. Would it be possible to obtain input and involvement from everyone?"

- "It seems like we have gotten off the subject. How does the present discussion relate to our stated objective (or agenda)?"

- "Before we jump to conclusions and take action, do you think we have identified the real cause of the problem?"

- "Rather than settling on that solution now, should we consider other alternatives also?"

- "Have we looked at the risks in our plan? In other words, if we adopt it, what could go wrong?"

Members. The group members also have specific responsibilities in the meeting. For instance, they need to schedule their work so that they can attend all meetings and arrive on time. They need to cooperate with the other members of the group, i.e., they should listen to one another; avoid interrupting others; and refrain from putting down another member's ideas.

Members also need to accept the responsibility of being involved. Although the problem of a bored member needs to be addressed by the Leader, it is that member's responsibility not to become bored in the first place! On the other hand, too much involvement by one member should also be avoided. Members need to be very sensitive to "air time" and not monopolize the discussion.

Members should also be honest with one another. They need to take the responsibility to say what they really think and feel. And if you, the boss, are present, you need to strongly encourage the members to "tell it like it is."

Finally, every group member should seek to become proficient in performing all four group roles—Leader, Facilitator/Observer, Recorder, and Member.

Equipment, Materials, and Facility

Some parts of this section will already be familiar to us—and some won't. But even in those topic areas in which we are already competent, we need to remember that the best can become even better. Following are some tested ideas that can help us further improve our skills, especially when conducting "Providing Information" and "Instructional" meetings. And if we discover just one helpful new idea that works for us, then our investment of time has been valuable.

Check Out Equipment. May I give one piece of advice that I have learned through experience? Arrive at the training room early. "Murphy's Law" will catch up with us, eventually—what can go wrong will go wrong! And most things that go wrong take time to fix. I have walked into a meeting room and found tables and chairs missing. I have found projectors missing, video equipment borrowed, and the electrical power off at the outlets. Meanwhile, the meeting attendees were looking at me like I was a complete idiot for not having the place set up properly.

Before the meeting begins, we need to check out the equipment, materials, and facility. If we plan to show a videotape, does the player work? Does the overhead projector project properly, and is there an extra bulb? Have the overhead transparencies been cleaned since the last time they were used, and are they in the correct order? Is the overhead projector screen in the room and is it properly positioned? Is the screen positioned so that ceiling lights do not shine directly on it? Is the projector focused? Does the electronic projection system (PowerPoint®) work, and does it have a remote control that works? Can the image be clearly seen by participants in the back of the room? Do the AC outlets work? Will we need an extension cord?

Next, if we need an easel, and don't have one, can we hang blank easel paper on the wall? Is there extra paper? Do we have magic markers and are they usable? Is there masking tape to hang up the completed charts? Are our handouts ready for distribution, and do we have extra copies? Occasionally a sheet is left out of a handout, so it is wise to have an extra set or two.

The whole idea is to run a professional meeting. Our participants can't help but judge us by how well we are organized. So we spend time—before the meeting—being absolutely certain that everything that is needed is in place.

Overhead transparencies. Having used overhead projectors for over thirty years as an important tool in conducting meetings, and having worked for the 3M Co. where they were developed, I'll admit my bias. If we aren't already using this method, we are being deprived of an important tool for learning.

I always had the feeling that my meetings were more effective when I used overheads. Then the Wharton School of Business and the 3M Company conducted an interesting study that supported what I had intuitively believed. They asked 136 master's degree candidates to conduct 36 meetings for the purpose of introducing a new "product," Crystal Beer.

The case for Crystal Beer (a make-believe product) was cleverly written so that the reasons for and against accepting the product were statistically even. The variable in the study was the method of presentation—overhead transparencies vs. whiteboard (a whiteboard is like a blackboard, except that it has a white, glossy finish and can be written on using dry markers). The participants in the meetings were asked to listen to the presentations and then approve or disapprove the new product. The meetings and their outcomes are listed in the following table:

Number of Meetings	Presenters' Position	Presentation Method	Outcomes
12	Pro Crystal Beer	Overheads	67% "Go with the beer."
	Con Crystal Beer	Whiteboard	33% "No beer."
12	Pro Crystal Beer	Whiteboard	33% "Go with the beer."
	Con Crystal Beer	Overheads	67% "No beer."
12	Pro Crystal Beer	Whiteboard	50% "Go with the beer."
	Con Crystal Beer	Whiteboard	50% "No beer."

As the results indicate, the use of overhead transparencies had a positive impact on the subjects' decisions. Even more interesting was that the audience perceived the presenters who used transparencies as being more professional, persuasive, credible, interesting, and better prepared. The researchers also found that the whiteboard resulted in presentations that tended to be monologues, while the overhead transparencies produced more group discussion. Last, the meetings that were conducted using overhead transparencies were much shorter, because the groups made their decisions faster. For all these reasons, transparencies (or a multimedia presentation) are the medium of choice for most meeting leaders today.

Transparencies are great for us, as the Meeting Leader—and for the participants. They make it easier to maintain eye contact with the participants while presenting information. They also give us flexibility in presenting information, as they allow us to delete one or more transparencies if we see that we are running out of time. We can leave the lights on without dimming them and still get a usable image. And last, they increase the amount of information that can be presented in a given period.

But the most important reasons for using transparencies have nothing to do with us as meeting leaders. The major reasons for using them are to 1) improve participant retention of the program's ideas and concepts, 2) make it easier for them to remember training instructions, and 3) reduce the chances of misunderstanding.

The following are some key points on using the overhead projector:

- In many cases, we can control the group's access to the information by using the "reveal" technique, by placing a sheet of 8 ½" x 11" paper on the transparency, and then turning the light on. We can reveal each point by holding the transparency frame with one hand and pulling the paper out with the other hand, revealing one point at a time. We reveal whole thoughts or paragraphs at one time, not line-by-line.

- Too much revealing can create a feeling of being controlled in the audience. Therefore, we use this method only when we really need to limit the participants' access to the information that is being presented. For example, if I had a transparency that simply outlined the three topics that were to be covered in the meeting, I would probably not use the reveal technique. Or if I had a visual that gave detailed instructions for group work on an assignment, again, I would likely not reveal the information line-by-line. If, however, I needed to focus attention on each item of a list, I would probably reveal each item in turn as I discussed each one.

- For projectors with long tabletops, it is usually easier to put the paper on top of the transparency when using the reveal technique. For projectors with small tabletops, however, paper placed on top may fall off when we move away from the projector. To avoid this, we can place the paper under the transparency before turning the light on.

- The projector light should be off unless an overhead transparency is on the projector in order to avoid the distracting white glare of the direct transparency light. With this in mind, we can turn the projector off between transparencies. On the other hand, it can also be distracting if we are showing a series of brief visuals and turn the light off each time we change from one to the next. As in most things we do, it's a balance. With a series of short transparencies, I usually leave the light on and remove the first one while at the same time placing a new visual on the projector.

- In almost all cases, we can leave the room light on when using the overhead. Most overhead projectors are deliberately designed so that we can keep the room lights on as we present information. This helps us maintain eye contact with the group and allows them to see—and interact with—each other.

- We are to avoid turning around and reading from the screen except on the rare occasion when we may wish to strongly emphasize a specific point. Instead, we read the information directly from the transparency as we reveal it. This allows us to maintain better eye contact with our group.

- We can use a pencil, pen, or small pointer to indicate specific items on a transparency. A finger as a pointer looks strange when enlarged ten times on the screen!

- If possible, we should mount or insert our transparencies on or in frames. We can write our notes on the white-frame margin of the transparency. An ordinary fine-point permanent transparency pen will write on white plastic frames, and an ordinary ballpoint pen can be used on cardboard frames. Caution: if we need to later erase what we have written, we should use *nonpermanent* pens for writing on the transparency itself.

- We usually read each word of a transparency as it is shown on the screen, instead of turning the overhead on and silently standing there while the group reads.

- We need to ensure that we have an extra lamp bulb that fits our specific projector, and that the extra bulb in the machine is not already burned out. Avoid moving or jarring the projector when the lamp is on. The lamp's filament is soft and easily broken when the projector is on.

- For best participant viewing, we can position the overhead screen in the right hand corner of the room (as we face the participants), and the projector in the front center of the room at an angle so that the light is centered on the screen. If we are left-handed, we simply reverse the above (i.e., position the screen in the left-hand corner of the front of the room).

The overhead projection system offers these advantages over most other forms of imaging:

- Allows normal room light
- Is simple to operate
- Allows eye contact with our group
- Saves presentation time
- Is flexible
- Is readily available in almost any meeting room

An overhead projection system, when properly used, creates an exciting and professional presentation and is enjoyable to use. To appear professional, however, overheads not only need to be used well, they also need to be constructed well.

Almost any commercial print shop can produce professional transparencies. The only problem is cost. The work is usually expensive, especially if there are large numbers of visuals. But if we don't know how to use a word processing program (such as PowerPoint®) and we have the budget, it is considerably easier to have a professional lay out our transparencies than to try to make them ourselves. We can hand print or type our "visual" on an 8 ½" x 11" sheet of paper, and take it to a print shop to be typeset and printed. Or we can type them up on our word processor, save to a disk, and take the disk to the print shop. If the transparencies are to be mounted on frames, we can also take a transparency frame of the size that is used so that the image can be set clearly within the margins of the frame.

But making our own transparencies can be fun! All the needed materials are available locally in a wide selection of films and colors. There are two main ways of producing a transparency—use a paper master with a standard copy machine, or feed the computer image directly to a printer.

We can make transparencies using a regular copy machine by creating an image on the transparency film in the same way we would make a regular plain-paper copy. The film is loaded in the paper holder of the copy machine, our original is placed under the mat, and the result is a printed film. Using a color copier can produce color transparencies. Using a black-and-white copier produces, you guessed it, black-and-white transparencies.

A better version of this same process is to use a laser printer and feed the image directly from our computer to the printer. In general, using a computer to print a transparency directly to the printer is easier to do and makes sharper images. These computer desktop publishing systems can also be used to create great transparencies. For example, a program like PowerPoint® enables us to use the output with standard overhead transparencies or with a multimedia projector. If, however, we don't already know how to use a computer desktop system to make transparencies, learning to use one will require a considerable investment of time.

Here are some hints in making professional-looking transparencies using a word-processing system.

1. A "Times New Roman" type with a font size of 24 points (not less than 20 points) and larger point-size for headings (28-48 points), depending on the amount of information, will result in clear, professional transparencies that can be seen from the back of the room.

2. Avoid the overuse of graphics—in other words, don't use graphics just for the sake of having graphics. Any illustration that is used on a visual should serve a purpose. Also, avoid using the popular, limited selection of graphic images that are included as part of the common word-processing programs that most of us use. The problem is that they are so overused that they lack impact. We have all seen them, perhaps even used them ourselves, and probably are pretty tired of seeing them again. There are dozens of high-quality graphic programs available at reasonable cost, and they are well worth the investment.

3. Felt-tip *permanent* pens for use on transparencies can also be purchased in a variety of colors and tip widths. These can be used to highlight key statements, or to box in an important paragraph—permanently. The pens should be of the permanent type designed specifically for use with transparencies. *Temporary* pens will smear badly, destroying the

appearance of a finished transparency, and regular felt-tip pens made for writing on easel paper usually don't work at all (the ink beads up). On the other hand, if what is needed is a temporary notation on an existing transparency, we use a transparency pen that is labeled "temporary" and can be rubbed off with a damp cloth or napkin.

4. In most cases, we mount transparencies on a frame. Frames make handling our transparencies easier and also provide space for us to write our "cheat notes" on the margins. This will free us from our trainer's guide and allow us to make better, more consistent eye contact with the participants. Frames also allow us to make horizontally-lettered transparencies, since the frame will mask the light that would normally spill out the top and bottom.

This discussion is not complete without mentioning the two major problems in designing transparencies: 1) trying to put too much on one transparency; and 2) using print that is too small to be read by the participants. The first is confusing. And the second is frustrating, especially to those seated toward the back of the room.

When we make transparencies, we use the "KISS" formula: "Keep it simple, stupid!" Usually, "6 x 6" is a good rule of thumb—a maximum of six words across and six lines down will keep our transparencies from being too "busy." Transparencies are used to illustrate key points, or serve as outlines, and don't require the program's complete content. The "6 x 6" rule is only a guideline, however. If, for example, we want to present complete instructions to our meeting members, we may need to create a very detailed transparency that can contain over fifty words.

Video Projection Systems. Using a PowerPoint® electronic system is, as my generation would say, cool! It appears very, very professional. It eliminates the fuss of changing overhead transparencies. We can click from one point to the next on the screen as we build fancy images. Our points can fly in from the left, from the right, grow from a spot in the center to a large image, and then fade to the next. We can have prerecorded sound and/or recorded video within the CD. It can be a complete multimedia package presentation.

That last word, presentation, is the concern. Electronic projection systems do lend themselves more for "Providing Information" meetings than for any of the other types. This system can be used, and used impressively, when presenting information. If I want to make a presentation of information and wish to move from point "A" to point "Z," then an electronic PowerPoint® presentation is my first choice.

This system does, however, have its limitations. Many of the older models, especially some of the portable units, have light images that are too dim to be easily seen with full room lighting. When the lights are dimmed, not only do we have to stop our discussion in order to dim them, we also have a more difficult time maintaining eye contact with the participants. Electronic projection systems also work well as they move forward, step-by-step. But some systems are difficult to reverse in order to go back and look at prior images. We are also stuck with the order. With overhead transparencies, if we see that we are running out of time, we can toss out some of the visuals and move on to the close. With PowerPoint®, we are stuck flashing through images we no longer have time to discuss. Yes, it is possible to navigate around unwanted images, but it is usually a clumsy operation at best. Finally, the system is much more complicated than an overhead. I have observed potentially outstanding presentations go down the flusher because of Murphy's Law.

If we choose to use the PowerPoint® projection system, it is our responsibility to arrange to have it in the room (if it is not already a part of the room's equipment). It is also our responsibility to make sure we know how to set it up, and how to use it! It is very distracting to begin the meeting, discover the system won't work, and then have to wait for somebody to go get an A/V person.

PowerPoint® images are designed much the same way as overheads, and the same general rules apply. For example, I avoid using a font size less then 24 points; I use light colors and red only for accent, not for extensive text; if I use graphics, I ensure that they are appropriate; and I use animation only where it is needed, not just to show I know how to do it. One last point: I avoid the stock templates used in the PowerPoint® program like the plague. Yes, they are easy to use for beginners, but I find them restrictive (they force me to use a preset style). In addition, everybody uses them, which creates a sameness of presentations. Finally, all the images in my presentation look the same. In creating PowerPoint® images, remember the rule of architecture also applies here, i.e., "form follows function"! Or, if you were raised in the country like I was, "don't let the tail wag the dog." The PowerPoint® program is the tail, your image and resultant message is the dog.

Flip Charts. When presenting information to participants for discussion, the overhead projector is probably best. This is because the Leader normally has time to plan what information will be presented to the participants, and has time to create transparencies to use in communicating these ideas. Presenting concepts and ideas using an overhead transparency or a PowerPoint® system is usually much quicker than writing out the information on flip charts during the presentation.

To manage our "Obtaining Information" meetings effectively, a flip chart is almost a *must*! When we are receiving information from our meeting participants, a flip chart is probably the tool of choice for most meeting leaders. Recording our group's thoughts and suggestions on easel paper during the meeting will help keep them focused on the topic at hand. A flip chart makes it easier to review key points at any time; and it permits recorded ideas to trigger new thoughts as the meeting progresses. Also, a flip chart enables a group to use problem-solving processes in a logical, step-by-step way. And it will give us more control and, thus, better management, of the meeting.

One problem in using a flip chart to record discussions is that it can slow down the meeting, since our members can obviously talk faster than we can write. While brainstorming a list of ideas, for instance, we will need to write them down and allow them to trigger new ideas. And we may get writer's cramp with the fast flow of thoughts. But groups will usually pace their suggestions to give us time to write.

When using flip charts, here are several ideas that can help make us even more effective in conducting meetings.

- Dark marker colors work best for writing on the easel paper. Black, dark brown, or dark blue are the most legible. Lighter colors like yellow, orange, or green are difficult to read. Surprisingly, red is also difficult to read, and should be avoided.

- Block printing on the easel paper is much easier to read from the back of the room than script.

- Easel paper with light, preprinted "grid" lines will help make our printing more legible, and will look more professional.

- Low-tack masking tape for taping easel paper to walls is preferable, since some types of adhesive tape will pull paint right off the wall when removed.

There are a great many types and styles of easels available for holding flip chart pads. Unfortunately, many are too flimsy, or heavy, to be useful. (After working with—and working on—easel stands for many years, the best one I've found is the Oravisual #A502. It is sturdy, has a back plate to support the easel pad, and folds up for storage.)

Handouts. I am a firm believer in handouts! They allow participants to focus on the discussion, rather than on taking notes. And if we use overhead transparencies or PowerPoint® to present information, then handouts are a must to keep from presenting faster than participants can write. Thus, providing handouts prevents the meeting participants from becoming frustrated by frantically trying to copy down the information being presented. Handouts also enable participants to better utilize the information back on the job by serving as memory aids.

People tend to judge a product's quality by the way it is "packaged." And this is also true for handouts. Participants in an important meeting will hear our points; but they see the media. They observe the quality of the transparencies or PowerPoint® images, the flipcharts, and the handouts, and this, unfortunately or not, influences their judgment about the meeting. The information that we present might be outstanding, but if we have poorly prepared handouts, full of typos and misspellings, our meeting will be negatively evaluated by some before we even have a chance to present all the information.

If we have twenty or more pages of handout material, it is usually best to collate and assemble them by stapling, or to use some form of binding. By leaving the back side of each page blank (or lined), the participants in the meeting will be able to use that space for taking additional notes that are needed or desired.

To conduct an important, critical meeting, we should decide to spend what is necessary to have presentable handouts. We can typeset and format them using one of the more common word processing programs. Print them on a high-quality, 24-pound, bright-white laser paper. For handouts with less than one hundred pages, we can use a spiral binding so the pages lay flat. If there more than one hundard pages, we use three-ring binders—either silk-screened (more expensive and normally used only when quantities are large) or with clear covers that will accept pre-printed inserts. Indexes, tabs, and numbered pages result in easy reference. In short, we want our participants to say, "Wow! Are these ours to keep?"

When the participants later use their handouts for reference, they appreciate it if they are easy to read and understand. Clear writing usually consists of short sentences, written in the way we speak. Most of us are much better writers than we imagine—if we can forget some of the self-consciousness and negative self-perceptions many of us have experienced from the time we entered school.

For example, because I was born dyslexic, I always thought that I was a terrible writer. I can't spell. I mix up lower case *b's* and *d's*, and even write my *2's* backwards on occasion. And I failed the sixth grade at Beverly Manor Elementary School in Staunton, Virginia.

So my natural conclusion was that I couldn't write. Fortunately, I met a remarkable teacher—Bill Griffin, a Professor of English at Virginia Commonwealth University. After looking at an article I had written, Bill said, "Dick, you are a wonderful writer! You've learned the secret of writing like you talk." Was that an exciting day for me! That was some twenty-five years ago, and since that time I have written thousands of published pages.

Don't misunderstand me. I still need the help of a proofreader, since my spelling, grammar, and syntax are awful. But I'm not afraid to write! I'm not afraid of being me as I write for you. And the end result, I have been told by many, is more than adequate. If you feel that writing is hard, or that you lack ability to write well, get some help with the mechanics of writing. But if you will write like you talk—and you must be a fairly effective speaker, or you wouldn't be a leader—you will likely be a good writer.

One of the toughest topics any leader can write about is safety training! So, below is an example on how our writing style can make this normally boring topic more interesting.

Formal Writing Style	**Suggested Writing Style**
It is the policy of AAA Power, Inc. that accident prevention be considered of primary importance in all phases of operation and administration.	Here at AAA Power, we believe that accident prevention is important!
It is therefore the desire and intent of the company to provide safe and healthy working conditions, and to establish and insist upon safe practices at all times.	It's the company's job to provide you with safe and healthy working conditions. It's your job to *always* work safely.
The prevention of accidents is an objective affecting all levels of the organization and its activities.	Preventing accidents is everyone's concern, from top executives to associates on the plant floor.
It is a basic requirement that each manager and team leader make the safety of associates an integral part of regular management functions.	Managers and team leaders are responsible for your safety.
It is equally the duty of each associate to accept and follow established safety regulations and procedures.	You are also responsible. Accepting and following safety regulations and procedures is part of your job.
This is the responsibility of each associate at AAA Power, Inc. regardless of position or area of responsibility.	Everyone here at AAA Power is responsible for safety. Everyone!

If we evaluate the readability statistics on the preceding examples, we will see that the formal writing is at a grade level of 13 (a freshman in college should understand this). The less formal example has a grade level of 10.1 (a sophomore in high school). Considering our audience, in this example, we would likely choose to write less formally.

Let's take a look at one more example. Suppose I was designing a handout to use in an "Instructional" meeting to teach team leaders how to be more effective in conducting orientation sessions for new associates. I would start the handout by writing in the following style:

> Do you remember what your first day on a "real" job was like? Do you remember the way you were treated? I do! I was told to report to my new boss at 9:00 sharp for my "orientation." When I got there, he told me to "Have a seat and I'll be with you in a couple of minutes." He was busy! So I sat and waited. After about 30 minutes, I felt like maybe he had forgotten me. I certainly did not feel like I was very important. Finally, I saw him glance at the clock, and look over at me. As he hurried by, he said, "Give me just a couple of more minutes." I sat there another 15 minutes.

> Not a very good way to start my new career! And we have all seen or experienced examples worse than mine. Think about your first day. What was it like?

> Turnover is expensive. New associates who are not treated appropriately on their first day often don't stay. Because labor is a significant cost of doing business, it is critically important to our success that new associates are properly trained. And our new associate's training starts the moment he or she walks into our organization.

Again, to make our writing interesting to the participants in the meeting who have to read it, we need to write like we talk.

I have written almost seventeen pages on Step 1, preparing for the meeting. This gives you some indication how important I believe preparation is in conducting effective meetings. Now, let's move on to the next step, "Opening the meeting."

☑ **2. Open the meeting.**

It's time to begin the meeting—on time! We can't punish the early arrivals and reward latecomers. If we delay starting the meeting, several things are going to happen—none of them desirable. First, we will develop a reputation for starting meetings late, and (guess what!) our members will begin arriving late. Second, some people may strongly feel that we are wasting their time by not starting on time. And third, we are going to end up having trouble meeting our time schedule.

The agenda should be recorded on the easel paper ahead of time and posted on the wall. If we are conducting a Problem Solving or Obtaining Information meeting and we haven't already assigned the roles of Recorder and Facilitator/Observer to key members, now is the time to do so. The Leader, the Recorder, and the Observer/Facilitator should know the processes that will be used. And if we plan to have one of our group members serve as the Meeting Leader, he or she should know this well in advance to allow him or her time to prepare. We can begin the meeting by reviewing the meeting objective(s) and agenda, and move to the first order of business.

☑ **3. Use the appropriate process (in Problem Solving meetings).**

For "Problem Solving" meetings, we need to select the appropriate process for the work the group is going to do. There are four types of meeting process tools we can select from.

A. Problem Identification. Some meeting processes are used to gather and arrange data in a systematic way in order to identify problems. Note that these processes don't solve the problems—they provide information that tells what, where, and how serious they are. In other words, they help us and our employees pinpoint and describe problems, and set priorities. They can also provide information for management to use in justifying funds needed to fix a particular problem.

Such processes include

Situation Analysis. This tool—sometimes called a "Cause-Effect Diagram"—has replaced the earlier "fish-bone" technique. It is used by teams to identify each of the causes and effects of a particular problem. It also provides a simple way of setting priorities on the problem's causes. (See Chapter 10.)

Pareto Chart. This is nothing more than a bar chart that is used to show the frequency of occurrence for each of a particular set of problems. For example:

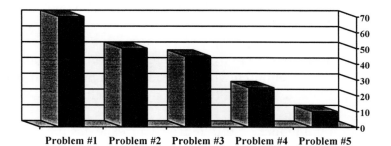

Number of Times Problems Are Occurring

Problem #1   Problem #2   Problem #3   Problem #4   Problem #5

Histogram. This is a bar chart that usually plots problem-frequency against some form of measurement, in contrast to the Pareto Chart that plots frequency against identified categories. For instance:

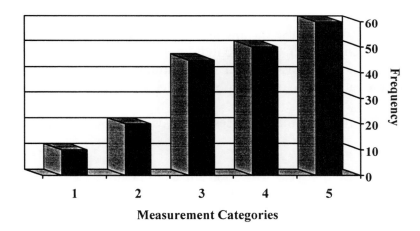

Measurement Categories

For example, suppose we conducted a survey to determine employee satisfaction of their jobs. One of the questions was, "How satisfied are you with your job?" The employees were asked to rate their satisfaction on a scale of 1 to 5, with 1 = "Not at all satisfied" and 5 = "Extremely satisfied." Note that on the above histogram around sixty employees rated their job satisfaction a "5," about fifty employees rated it a "4," somewhere around forty-five employees gave it a "3," around twenty employees rated it a "2," and only about ten employees out of all the people surveyed rated it a "1."

Correlation Analysis. A correlation analysis is used to examine the relationship between two different things. For example:

- Does it really rain every time you go to the beach? Simply correlate a number of consecutive trips to the beach and rainy weather (probably not much correlation).

- Do children who are read to by their parents become avid adult readers? Correlate children who are read to with number of books they read per year as an adult (likely a good correlation).

- Does teller training make a difference? Correlate customer complaints, or any other measure, with tellers who have received training and those who have not (probably a medium correlation).

Note that most problem identification groups need to be able to use basic statistics to analyze their data. They must understand such measures as mean (an average), median (the middle number), mode (the most frequently appearing number), and standard distribution (the old "bell-shaped curve"), and be able to calculate standard deviations (S.D.) and Chi-Square.

B. Causal Analysis. Causal analysis is used to discover the cause of a specific problem. A group can use this method to analyze data to determine where the problem occurred (versus where it did not occur), and when it happened (versus when it didn't). After answering these questions, a team can often identify the most probable cause of the problem. (See Chapter 10.)

C. Decision Making. Two major processes are used by teams to make decisions.

Evaluation of Alternatives. This tool is used to identify the best of several alternative solutions. Selecting the best computer or choosing the best way to do a task are examples of decisions that can be made through evaluation of the merits of each alternative. (See Chapter 10.)

Force Field Analysis. This process helps make a decision when there are only two alternatives, e.g., to buy a computer or not, or to change the way to do a task or not. Thus it is an especially good tool to use when there are two sides, pro and con, to an issue. (See the chapter on managing change.)

D. Planning. A planning process is used by a team to do just that—plan. A goal statement is written, and then the team helps to develop appropriate steps in the plan. Next, a technique called "Potential Problem Avoidance" is used to examine problems that might occur when the plan is implemented. (See Chapter 11.)

☑ **4. Obtain acceptance.**

Involvement. In "Instructional," "Problem Solving," and "Obtaining Information" meetings, involvement is usually the best way to obtain acceptance. We encourage the team members to offer ideas or suggestions. As the boss, we should not offer to do everything ourselves, but delegate assignments to others. We can assign the key roles of Facilitator/Observer and Recorder, and even that of Leader.

Consensus Management. Another way to obtain involvement and, thus, acceptance is to use a tool called *consensus management*. It is a technique often used in conjunction with other processes to help teams make better group decisions. It produces more agreement among team members than traditional voting does—which usually end up with "winners" and "losers." In consensus management, everyone "wins," resulting in greater acceptance of the group's decision. Consensus management also generates more creative ideas than does a traditional voting process.

Consensus management is employed at any point where a traditional vote would be taken. It is used to identify which problem(s) a group wants to address, or which topic(s) to consider at a future meeting; to analyze a list of alternative solutions to a problem, to select those the group wants to explore further, and to choose the best solution; or to determine which steps to use in a plan.

Since consensus management is so critical to the functioning of an effective team, let's look in detail at how it works.

1. Write the question to be considered on easel paper.
2. Brainstorm a list of ideas relating to the question (topics, suggestions, alternatives, etc.). When the group brainstorms, we don't stop to evaluate each idea—we simply write exactly what each person says on the easel paper. We try to obtain everyone's suggestions without allowing discussion at this time.
3. When all the members have had an opportunity to present their ideas, we ask if any of them can be combined or eliminated.
4. We then ask each person to explain *briefly* the reasons for his or her suggestion. (These presentations are limited to not more then two minutes per person.)
5. Next, we ask each member to select and write down his or her first three choices, in order of preference, from the ideas listed.

6. The members now assign three points to their first choice, two points to their second, and only one point to their third.

7. The Leader then calls on each person in turn, recording on the easel paper list his or her point-value rating.

8. Finally, the Leader adds up the total score for each item and announces the group's selection.

If the list of items happens to be long (fifteen or more), it is preferable to have the members select their top four, or even five, and assign four or five points to their first choice, and so on. This decision process is usually superior to traditional voting methods because, among other reasons, it better reflects the relative strength of the group's preferences for the particular ideas that have been generated.

 5. Close the meeting.

One of the Leader's jobs is to keep track of time. If a meeting is scheduled to end at ten o'clock, then unless there is a major reason not to do so, the Leader should end the meeting at ten by announcing, "We are out of time." The members will have other appointments, places to go, and job tasks to finish. If someone still has an issue to discuss, the Leader should suggest that it be covered at the next meeting (and ask the Recorder to make a note of it). Or, the Leader may invite those who are interested to stay for a short time after the meeting.

The Leader also needs to make certain to leave enough time to

- Ask the Observer/Facilitator for his or her comments on the group's process.
- Ask the Recorder to summarize the meeting, and review any tasks that need to be assigned.
- Ask for volunteers or assign people to complete these tasks.
- Announce the time and place of the next meeting.

 6. Follow up.

To follow up, the Leader needs to check that the people who were assigned tasks are completing them on schedule. As the Leader, we also need to ensure that we complete any tasks that we agreed to do!

Finally, we privately thank the group members who served as Observer/ Facilitator, Recorder, and Leader (if assigned) for their work in making the meeting a success.

The ideas and strategies presented in this chapter won't, of course, solve every meeting problem. But they will help us resolve most of them. And they will help us plan and organize our meetings so that we can conduct and manage them with significantly greater productivity and success.

On the following page is a "Meeting Preparation Checklist" that you can use to assist in the planning of important meetings.

Meeting Preparation Checklist

Meeting Date: _____   Location: _____

Time: Start _____   End _____   Lunch _____

Meeting Objective(s): Describe what you, or the members, want to accomplish as
a result of the meeting.

_____
_____
_____
_____
_____
_____
_____

Topics (or Agenda):

_____
_____
_____
_____
_____
_____
_____
_____
_____
_____
_____
_____
_____
_____
_____

Who Should Attend?

_____   _____
_____   _____
_____   _____
_____   _____
_____   _____
_____   _____
_____   _____

Checklist (Check tasks required)	Notes (Person to contact; person responsible, etc.)	Date Completed

Pre-Meeting Communications

_____ Agenda	_____	_____
_____ Handouts	_____	_____
_____ Assignments	_____	_____
_____ Attendees confirmed	_____	_____
_____ _____	_____	_____
_____ _____	_____	_____

Speakers

_____ Approval received	_____	_____
_____ Contacted	_____	_____
_____ Advance copy of outline and/or speech	_____	_____
_____ Confirmed in writing	_____	_____
_____ Advance copy of handouts	_____	_____
_____ Lodging	_____	_____
_____ Invoice from speaker	_____	_____
_____ Speaker fees paid	_____	_____
_____ _____	_____	_____

Meeting Leader

_____ Outline of day's events	_____	_____
_____ Notes for commentary	_____	_____
_____ Handouts	_____	_____
_____ Prizes, awards, etc.	_____	_____
_____ Transparencies:	_____	_____
_____ • Prepared	_____	_____
_____ • Clear write-on film	_____	_____
_____ • Marking pen	_____	_____
_____ Prepared flipcharts	_____	_____
_____ Videotape(s)	_____	_____
_____ Slides	_____	_____
_____ PowerPoint® disk	_____	_____
_____ CD's	_____	_____
_____ Evaluations (if appropriate)	_____	_____
_____ _____	_____	_____
_____ _____	_____	_____

Checklist (Check tasks required)	Notes (Person to contact; person responsible, etc.)	Date Completed

Lodging for Out-of-Town Attendees

	Rooms confirmed	_____	_____
_____	Transportation	_____	_____
_____	_____	_____	_____

Meeting Room

	Room reserved	_____	
_____	• Room key	_____	_____
_____	• Appropriate size	_____	_____
_____	• Loading entrance	_____	_____
_____	• External noise checked	_____	_____
_____	• Incoming phone calls held	_____	_____
_____	• Restroom location	_____	_____
_____	• Tables	_____	_____
_____	• Chairs	_____	_____
_____	Room layout drawing for setup person	_____	_____
_____	A/V Equipment	_____	_____
_____	• Overhead projector and spare bulb	_____	_____
_____	• Slide projector	_____	_____
_____	• Large screen	_____	_____
_____	• Video player	_____	_____
_____	• Video monitor	_____	_____
_____	• Video recorder	_____	_____
_____	• PowerPoint® projector	_____	_____
_____	• Computer	_____	_____
_____	• Laser pointer	_____	_____
_____	• Public address system	_____	_____
_____	- Microphone	_____	_____
_____	- Wireless mike	_____	_____
_____	- Volume control	_____	_____
_____	• Flipcharts	_____	_____
_____	- Extra paper	_____	_____
_____	- Marking pens	_____	_____
_____	- Masking tape	_____	_____
_____	• Writing board	_____	_____
_____	- Chalk	_____	_____
_____	- Dry markers	_____	_____
_____	- Erasers	_____	_____

Checklist (Check tasks required)	Notes (Person to contact; person responsible, etc.)	Date Completed

Meeting Room (Continued)

_____	Electrical outlets	
_____	Room lighting	_____
_____	Extension cord(s)	_____
_____	Temperature controls	_____
_____	Note-taking	_____
_____	• Scratch paper	_____
_____	• Pencils/pens	_____
_____	Nametags	_____
_____	Desk tags	_____
_____	Direction signs	_____
_____	Refreshments	_____
_____	• Morning	_____
_____	• Afternoon	_____
_____	Meals	_____
_____	• Menu selection	_____
_____	• Written orders when to serve	_____
_____	• Cost	_____
_____	• Gratuities	_____
_____	• Billing	_____
_____	_____	_____
_____	_____	_____

Travel for Meeting Leader (if meeting is out of town)

_____	Plane reservations	
_____	Plane ticket	_____
_____	Motel reservations	_____
_____	Travel money	_____
_____	Business cards	_____
_____	Materials shipped	_____
_____	Return address labels	_____
_____	Tape for repackaging	_____
_____	Laptop and/or Palmtop	_____
_____	Wireless phone	_____
_____	_____	_____

Notes:

_____

_____

_____

_____

_____

_____

17

Leadership

Interviewing and Selecting

Managers do not spend enough time making selection decisions, yet they often spend a great deal of time with problem employees, correcting mistakes or working out problems. If a small amount of that time had been spent in better selection, the problems might well have been avoided, and the managers could spend their time in the areas that would have a higher impact on the organization.

Bill Byham
"Recruitment, Screening, and Selection"
Human Resources Management & Development Handbook

Our objectives in conducting an effective selection interview are to

1. Determine what a candidate can do.
2. Determine what a candidate is willing do.
3. Determine whether a particular job fits the candidate's values, interests, and preferences.
4. Present the job and organization realistically to the candidate.
5. Leave the candidate with a good impression of our organization and us.
6. Reinforce or enhance the candidate's positive self-image.
7. Conduct our interviews legally.

It is impossible to understand interviewing and selection without dealing with some legal issues. But a word of caution: although I feel that the legal information presented here is accurate, it is nonetheless *my understanding. I am not a lawyer!* In addition, both the laws and their enforcement are constantly changing. Therefore, I cannot assume responsibility for any legal implications arising from what is presented here, and therefore I urge you to talk with an attorney about any legal problems that you may encounter concerning an applicant.

The Cost of Poor Hiring Practices

Some of the costs of replacing employees when they don't succeed are obvious: the initial cost of recruiting, interviewing and training; our time; and then having to do it all over again if the person that is hired doesn't work out.

But ineffective interviewing and selection also involve some costs that aren't as obvious. For example, suppose we look at our employees as an investment. As with any investment, we need to realize a return. During an employee's career in our organization, the investment, in terms of salary and benefits, can be a figure that easily exceeds one million dollars. When we stop and realize that we literally make million-dollar investment decisions, often based on only an hour or so spent interviewing and selecting an employee, it's kind of scary.

Problems also result because organizations operate within a larger community. And communities are very quick to judge organizations whose hiring practices result in high turnover because people and jobs were poorly matched. When the word gets around—and it doesn't take long—it becomes harder and harder to find good candidates because we don't get good applicants!

Problems may result, too, from litigation and lawsuits for wrongful discharge. Here again, nobody wins. In most states, we can still terminate an employee who doesn't have a contract, written or implied, for almost any reason. But if the employee feels that hiring promises weren't honored and/or that he or she was unfairly terminated, then whether or not we "win" a resulting lawsuit, we still lose. Have you ever had to sit for hours while an employee's attorney takes your deposition? I have, and it's no fun!

In addition, the morale in our section or department will—note *will*, not *may*—suffer when an employee leaves, either voluntarily or involuntarily. Indeed, we will be caught either way: if we don't terminate an employee who was poorly hired, we will see morale fall. And when we do terminate him or her, morale will suffer because of the termination. It's a lose-lose situation, we lose no matter what we do. Therefore, it's tremendously important to spend the time and effort necessary to hire the right candidate in the first place. We will greatly improve our chances of hiring the best person for the job if we prepare properly for the interview.

Note that the following information about preparing for and conducting selection interviews is presented in a logical, step-by-step order. But, as you will discover, it does not always work this neatly, particularly because some steps must be done simultaneously.

Let's look at how to do this critical part of our job by first examining 1) all the things that need to be done in *preparation* for the interview, then 2) the *interview* itself, and finally 3) the *selection* process.

In order to see how all the parts and pieces of planning for and conducting selection interviews go together, each step is illustrated with an example. We will take the job of an administrative assistant as our example.

Preparation

There are five basic steps to follow in preparing for an interview. They are

☑ 1. Analyze the job to be filled.

☑ 2. Review interview plan to ensure that it complies with the law.

☑ 3. Determine who will interview the applicants.

☑ 4. Establish an interview area.

☑ 5. Prescreen with telephone interviews.

Let's look at each of these in more detail.

 1. Analyze the job to be filled.

The first step in preparing for our selection interview is to take a long, hard look at the job we want to fill. To do this, we first need to list the major tasks of the job and then to determine key knowledge, skills, and interests that the future employees will need for each task. We should also decide which tasks applicants must already be able to perform when they apply, and which they can be trained to do after they are hired. Next we will need to write out the questions we plan to use to determine the applicant's knowledge, skills and interests for each task. And finally we need to have a strategy to discover whether the applicant is likely to be satisfied with the job conditions—salary, benefits, working hours, etc.

List the major tasks of the job.

Now let's take our example of interviewing for the administrative assistant's position. Here's how the task listing of this job might look:

Interview Planning Worksheet

Position: *Administrative Assistant*

Tasks:

1. Files
2. Types using Windows®
3. Mails correspondence
4. Handles supplies
5. Answers phones
6. Faxes messages
7. Makes copies

Determine job knowledge, skills, and interests.

Now we need to examine each task to determine what an applicant should know, be able to do, or be motivated to do. For example, concerning the task of "filing" in the Administrative Assistant's position, the applicant must 1) have basic reading skills, and 2) know the rules of filing (where do you file the "The 3-M Company" folder?) From this task detailing, we will later determine how well the applicant fits the job.

Interview Planning Work Sheet

Tasks	Job Knowledge, Skills, and Interests
Files	- Applies rules of filing - Has basic reading skills
Types using Windows®	- Types min. of 45 wpm with only 1% error rate - Likes using Windows® - Proficient with Microsoft Word® and Excel®
Mails correspondence	- Operates postage meter - Demonstrates understanding of the US postal rates
Handles supplies	- Fills out purchase order requests - Can lift a min. of 25 lbs. (box)
Answers phones	- Has pleasing telephone personality - Knows telephone etiquette
Faxes messages	- Knows how to dial a long-distance fax number - Can position documents in machine and start/stop the operation - Loads paper into the machine
Makes copies	- Turns machine on/off - Loads paper - Troubleshoots machine - Loads toner

Decide whether the applicant should already have the required knowledge/ skills/interests.

I like to list the knowledge, skills and interests required for a specific job even though I am very willing to (or even plan to) teach the employee some tasks. For example, the Administrative Assistant's task of "making copies," is not one I would ask an applicant about; I would likely plan to teach the employee how to do this part of his or her job. But by task detailing, I am able to determine prerequisites. For example, an employee who will be required to spend most of the day typing must already know how to type—I can't teach this skill on the job. In the worksheet example that follows, "R" stands for "Required" when hired, and "T" means I can "Train" the employee after hiring.

Interview Planning Worksheet

Tasks	Job Knowledge, Skills, and Interests	R/T
Files	- Applies rules of filing - Has basic reading skills	R R
Types using Windows®	- Types min. of 45 wpm with only 1% error rate - Likes using Windows® - Proficient with Microsoft Word® and Excel®	R R R
Mails correspondence	- Operates postage meter - Adds and subtracts correctly - Demonstrates understanding of the US postal rates	T R T
Handles supplies	- Fills out purchase order requests - Can lift a min. of 25 lbs. (box)	T R
Answers phones	- Has pleasing telephone personality - Knows telephone etiquette	R R
Faxes messages	- Knows how to dial a long-distance fax number - Can position documents in machine and start/stop the operation - Loads paper into the machine	T T T
Makes copies	- Turns machine on/off - Loads paper - Troubleshoots machine - Loads toner	T T T T

Identify prescreening questions.

Now we need to determine 1) which job knowledge, skills and interests an applicant absolutely must have in order to qualify for an interview, and 2) what questions we will ask the applicant on the telephone to obtain this information. The idea is to create "knockout" questions that will keep our applicants and us from needlessly wasting time in an interview. For example, if typing is a required skill for the job, we are probably not going to teach someone that skill after he or she is hired. So, in a telephone prescreening interview we need to ask about the applicant's typing skills (if this is not already indicated on the application blank), and terminate the conversation if the applicant can't type.

Therefore, in the third column of the *Interview Planning Worksheet,* note "P" to indicate that a prescreening question should be asked; "I" to denote that the information should be obtained during the regular interview; or "P/I" if the same question should be asked both in the prescreening phone conversation as well as during the interview itself.

"Open" Questions. A critical technique required in prescreening—and later in the formal interview—is the ability to ask questions effectively. Normally, we can write our key questions in advance. When we write—and later ask—questions, we need to make them *open* rather than *closed* questions. That is, we should start our questions with "Who?" "What?" "Where?" "When?" "Why?" or "How?" Closed questions, in contrast, usually start with "Do you?" "Could you?" "Will you?" "Have you?" or "Can you?" and are normally answered with a "yes" or "no." Open questions, therefore, help us obtain more information than closed questions. And that is our objective—information. For example, the question, "How do you feel about typing?" is likely to get more information than, "Do you like to type?"

"Leading" Questions. Think of a movie or TV courtroom scene in which one of the attorneys jumps to his feet and shouts, "Objection! Objection, your Honor! The opposing council is *leading* the witness!" Whereupon the Judge says, "Objection sustained. Council will please rephrase the question."

I'd like you to imagine that there is a "judge" present when you are interviewing, listening to your questions. And every time you ask a question beginning with "Don't you?" "Couldn't you?" "Shouldn't you?" or "Can't you?" this judge is going to jump all over you! Questions like these—termed "leading" questions—ask the applicant to agree with our preconceived opinions, and will usually bias his or her response. For instance, the question, "Don't you think that it is very important to have good work habits?" quite clearly telegraphs the answer we seek, and can invalidate the information we obtain. So don't "lead the witness." If we really want to know what applicants think or how they feel, we can ask them using open questions.

Looking at the fourth column of our *Interview Planning Worksheet* concerning the Administrative Assistant's position, I briefly have indicated my prescreening questions next to any "P's" in the fourth column ("P" = prescreening question required) using open questions wherever possible.

Interview Planning Work Sheet

Tasks	Job Knowledge, Skills, and Interests	R/T	P, I, or P/I	Prescreening Questions and Samples Required
Files	- Applies rules of filing	R	P/I	*How well do you know the rules of typing?*
	- Has basic reading skills	R	P/I	*How well can you read?*
Types using Windows®	- Types min. of 45 wpm with only 1% error rate	R	P/I	*How fast do you normally type? Please bring three samples of papers or letters you have typed.*
	- Likes using Windows®	R	P	*How do you feel about using Windows®?*
	- Proficient with Microsoft Word® and Excel®	R	P/I	*How well can you use Microsoft Word® and Excel®?*
Mails correspondence	- Operates postage meter	T	I	
	- Adds and subtracts correctly	R	P/I	*What is your skill level in basic math?*
	- Demonstrates understanding of the US postal rates	T	I	
Handles supplies	- Fills out purchase order requests	T	I	
	- Can lift a min. of 25 lbs. (box)	R	P	*Can you lift a box that weighs a minimum of 25 lbs.?*
Answers phones	- Has pleasing telephone personality	R	P	Listen to how he or she sounds during the phone call.
	- Knows telephone etiquette	R	P	Listen for key behaviors during the phone call.
Faxes messages	- Knows how to dial a long-distance fax number	T	I	
	- Can position documents in machine and start/stop the operation	T	I	
	- Loads paper into the machine	T	I	
Makes copies	- Turns machine on/off	T	I	
	- Loads paper	T	I	
	- Troubleshoots machine when the red light flashes	T	I	*What experience have you had in troubleshooting copy machines?*
	- Loads toner	T	I	

Decide how we will determine the applicant's knowledge/skills/interests.

We can obtain information in a variety of ways. These include asking questions in the interview, requiring the applicant to perform certain tasks, having the applicant bring in samples of relevant work, and reviewing the applicant's résumé and/or application form for specific information and questionable areas. Let's look at each of these techniques.

Asking Questions. Our interview questions normally should be composed at the same time we develop our telephone prescreening questions. While writing questions to ask in the interview, we follow the same guidelines that were given for writing prescreening questions—use open questions while avoiding closed and leading ones. Note, too, that we may want to ask the same question in the interview that we asked in the telephone prescreening call. As an alternative, it is sometimes revealing to ask the same question in a slightly different way.

Demonstrating Performance. One of the best ways to find out if applicants can do what they say they can do is to ask them to do it! It is remarkable how often interviewers ask job candidates about their skills—but don't ask them to demonstrate them. I suspect that the reason why many people in organizations today can't read (and no one knows it until a serious problem occurs) is because 1) people lacking basic reading skills are often adept at disguising this fact, and 2) they were not asked to read in the selection interview.

So, if I want to know if applicants can type, I ask them to type. If I need to know if they can use "Ohm's law," I give them voltage ($E = 10$ V) and current ($I = 2$ A) and ask them to derive resistance ($R = ?$) If I need to know how well they can answer the phone, I have them role play with me, or, after brief preparation, answer an actual incoming phone call. If a particular job skill is important and I don't plan to teach it on the job, then I need to figure out a way for the applicant to demonstrate his or her degree of expertise for me.

Securing Samples of Past Work. There are times when it is appropriate and extremely helpful to ask the applicant to bring samples of past work to the interview. For example, if I were hiring someone to teach a one-day interviewing and selection workshop, I would ask for a videotape of him or her conducting an actual workshop on this subject. If I wanted to hire graphic arts people, I would certainly ask them to bring samples of their work. And if I were looking for a writer, then I'd want to see some things that he or she had written. If computer programmers were needed, I would ask them to bring hard copy samples of their work, as well as disks that I could run on my computer. So, if creative work that can be seen or heard is involved, we ask the applicant to bring samples of that work to the interview.

The Résumé and Application. Résumés are often written to present information in the best possible way—and this is a problem as well as an asset. We seldom see on a résumé, "I really didn't like my boss, so I quit." Or, "After I work for an organization for a year or two, I need to move on to greener pastures." Yet, these are two of the main reasons that people actually quit. Or when was the last time you read a résumé that said, "I am so desperate for work that I'll take any job. Even yours!" Therefore, interpret what you see on a résumé by realizing that the applicant has positioned the information in its best possible light.

An experienced eye can tell us a great deal. Does the work history show much too frequent moves? What does this say about the applicant's intention of staying with our organization? Are there gaps in the employment history? What questions do we need to ask about those gaps? And is the applicant's work history actually a good fit for the job we are trying to fill?

Are there any blanks in the application form? If so, why were they not filled out? What questions do we need to ask to obtain the missing information? Has the applicant been unemployed? How long? Why did he or she leave one job before finding another?

The applicant's handwriting can tell us something not only about neatness, but also about carefulness. If an application is typed, do we also need to ask to see a sample of the applicant's handwriting?

Let's return again to our *Interview Planning Worksheet* for the Administrative Assistant's job to fill in the questions, demonstrations and samples we will use where "I" (Interview) is indicated.

Interview Planning Worksheet

Tasks	Job Knowledge, Skills, and Interests	R/T	P, I, or P/I	Prescreening Questions and Samples Required	Interview Questions, Demonstrations, and Samples Examined
Files	- Applies rules of filing	R	P/I	*How well do you know the rules of typing?*	*Please put these files in order.*
	- Has basic reading skills	R	P/I	*How well can you read?*	(The above also tests for reading ability.)
Types using Windows®	- Types min. of 45 wpm with only 1% error rate	R	P/I	*How fast do you normally type?* *Please bring three samples of papers or letters you have typed.*	*Please type this letter using Microsoft Word®.* *May I see the samples of papers you have typed?*
	- Likes using Windows®	R	P	*How do you feel about using Windows®?*	
	- Proficient with Microsoft Word® and Excel®	R	P/I	*How well can you use Microsoft Word® and Excel®?*	*Type these numbers into a spreadsheet using Excel®.*
Mails correspondence	- Operates postage meter	T	I		*What's been your experience in using a postage meter?*
	- Adds and subtracts correctly	R	P/I	*What is your skill level in basic math?*	*Add and subtract these numbers.*
	- Demonstrates understanding of the US Postal rates	T	I		*What is the current postage required for a 1 oz. letter to Canada?*
Handles supplies	- Fills out purchase order requests	T	I		*Please fill out this sample form.*
	- Can lift a min. of 25 lbs. (box)	R	P	*Can you lift a box that weighs a minimum of 25 lbs.?*	
Answers phones	- Has pleasing telephone personality	R	P	Listen to how he or she sounds during the phone call.	
	- Knows telephone etiquette	R	P/I	Listen for key behaviors during the phone call.	Conduct a role play with hypothetical customer.
Faxes messages	- Knows how to dial a long-distance fax number	T	I		*What's been your experience with fax machines?*
	- Can position documents in machine and start/stop the operation	T	I		*Show me how you would send this document.*
	- Loads paper into the machine	T	I		*How would you install new paper?*
Makes copies	- Turns machine on/off	T	I		*What's been your experience with copiers?*
	- Troubleshoots machine	R	P/I		*What experience have you had in trouble-shooting copy machines?*
	- Loads toner	T	I		*How would you load toner in this machine?*

Determine Other Job Requirements. Before the interview, we also need to plan questions that will help us determine whether the applicant is appropriate for other aspects of the job. For instance, if the salary was advertised, then the applicant has applied for the job knowing what the position pays. But if salary has not been mentioned, we will need to decide how well the applicant's expectations match what the job pays.

One way to determine how satisfied the applicant might be with the salary requirements is to review past salaries indicated on his or her résumé, as we ask appropriate questions during the prescreening telephone interview. If prior pay is not noted in the résumé or application, we can simply ask, "What was your salary in your last (or present) position?" Or, "What kind of salary range are you looking for?"

We may also need to ask questions about the applicant's desires and expectations concerning working conditions, work hours, vacations, holidays, benefits, and insurance. If the job requires that the employee normally work alone, then we need to determine whether the applicant likes to do so. If the job hours are unusual, then we may need to ask questions to make sure that the hours will not be a hardship.

At the end of this chapter is a blank copy of the *Interview Planning Worksheet* we have been using as an illustration. You may copy and utilize it in planning and conducting your prescreening contacts and selection interviews.

☑ **2. Review interview plan to ensure that it complies with the law and our organization's policies.**

There are two key areas that we should evaluate to ensure compliance with the law in our interviewing and selection practices. The first has to do with questions that should not be asked either on the application form or during the interview. The second area concerns employee ratios with regard to minority status, sex, and age. Let's look at each of these in more detail.

Questions Asked. The questions on our application form, as well as those asked in interviews, must be unbiased in terms of the race/ethnicity, religion, sex, age, handicap, and national origin of applicants. Most employers today are aware that asking informational questions of job applicants in the above areas can be illegal. But we cannot assume that everyone is familiar with the law and legal guidelines in this regard, and so we are going to examine in some detail each of these areas. It should also be noted that we are frequently unaware of what we don't know—and that it is not always obvious that asking certain questions of applicants can pose legal difficulties.

Of course, some of the questions discussed below are okay when asked *after* the candidate has been offered and has accepted employment. For instance, the human resource department will need to know the age of the new employee for retirement purposes, and family information needs to be obtained for insurance purposes. On the other hand, questions about religion are not legally proper at any time.

Race/Ethnicity. If the purpose and result of an organization's hiring procedure is to deliberately hire minorities, then most questions concerning race/ethnicity are legal. But if the intent, *or effect,* of the hiring procedure is to exclude minorities, if the organization's present minority-to-non-minority ratios are suspect, or if a rejected applicant feels that he or she has been excluded due to race/ethnicity, then questions such as the following can place us in very serious trouble:

- "What is your race?"
- "Where were you born?"
- "Where did your family originally come from?"
- "Are you a naturalized citizen?"
- "How did you learn to speak Spanish?" (or any foreign language)
- "What was your wife's maiden name?"

Asking applicants for a photograph, a birth certificate, or a baptismal record as proof of age is also illegal prior to hiring.

Religious Preferences. As indicated, questions concerning an applicant's religion are always illegal. Simply do not ever ask questions such as the following:

- "What is your religious affiliation?"
- "What church do you go to?"
- "What religious holidays do you observe?"

Marital and Family Status. Questions concerning marital or family status are normally illegal—unless we ask the same question of both sexes, and we have a job-related reason for asking. Questions such as the following may result in trouble for our organization and us

- "How does your spouse feel about your need to travel in this job?" (a potentially serious problem when asked of a female applicant)
- "Are you married?"
- "Do you plan to get married?"
- "Have you ever been divorced?"
- "What are your plans about having children?"
- "What are you going to do about your children during working hours?"

Height and Weight. Unless height and/or weight information is clearly relevant to a job's requirements, questions about them are usually illegal. The issue here is why you, or your organization, would want to know? If particular height and weight qualifications are absolutely critical to a job—and we can prove it—then the questions may be OK. Otherwise, it's none of our business. Don't ask questions such as,

- "How tall are you?"
- "How much do you weigh?"

Age. Most interviewers today do not ask an obvious age-inquiry question like "How old are you?" But I have heard disguised ("clever") questions asked to secure approximate age information—which are not clever at all. In fact, the following questions (asked before hiring the applicant) would be very obvious to an opposing counsel in a courtroom:

- "How old is your oldest child?"
- "What year did you graduate from high school/college?"

Other Questions. You should be aware that there are other questions that are inadvisable because they are potentially related to the above issues even though they may not appear to be. For example,

- "Do you have any friends or family working for us?" (A hiring preference for friends or family members of your employees could restrict opportunities for minorities.)
- "Have you ever been arrested?" "Have you ever spent the night in jail?" (Since some minorities have higher rates of arrest or incarceration than others do, these questions may discriminate.)
- "Tell me about your credit rating." "Do you own your own home?" "What kind of car do you have?" (I call these questions "stupid questions" because anyone asking them has got to be marginally intelligent and in the wrong job. Unless these socioeconomic questions are clearly job related, don't ask them because they tend to discriminate against certain minorities.)

In general, then, the rule is that if your questions do not clearly relate to specific job requirements, they are potentially illegal because they may be viewed as tending to discriminate on a basis other than job qualifications.

Minority Representation. Are the applicants appropriately representative in terms of race or ethnicity and sex? If the effect of our hiring action is to either institute or perpetuate a policy of noncompliance with the law concerning race/ethnicity and gender, we may be in serious trouble. So we need to take the initiative, either with our human resource department or management, to ensure that we are appropriately encouraging minority applications and interviews.

If we are located in an area with a thirty-five percent minority population, for example, it is reasonable that we seek to interview minority applicants reflecting at least this percentage.

☑ 3. Determine who will interview the applicants.

There are some very good reasons why we might wish to involve others in the interviewing and selection process. For example, we could include other leaders who are our peers in order to gain additional insight into an applicant's suitability for the job.

Multiple interviewers can also protect us from ourselves. I remember interviewing an applicant whom I nearly hired on the spot when he informed me that he attended the same college I did. Fortunately, others were also involved in the hiring decision and helped me see my bias.

Of course, involving others will significantly increase your cost of hiring. But if we are talking about million-dollar decisions—as we are—then it could be a good idea to invest additional up-front time and money to ensure that we make the best possible selections.

If the applicants are going to be interviewed by more than one person, we can provide all interviewers with copies of an *Interview Planning Worksheet* that spells out the knowledge, skills, and interests needed for each task and the questions to be asked. We decide in advance who will focus on what aspects of the job, and which questions each interviewer will ask the applicants. Then we set up a schedule and notify each interviewer by interoffice mail as to who will be interviewed, when, and where.

An excellent strategy being used more and more today is to involve the potential employee's future coworkers in the interviewing and selection procedure. After all, if our employees are going to work with—and probably help train—the new person, they will feel much better about who is selected if they have had a hand in the decision. In addition, the chances are that our current employees know the work better than anyone else, and they can even assist us in developing the interview questions. Finally, new employees appreciate knowing that their coworkers were involved in choosing them.

4. Establish an interview area.

Since interviews are important, we need to schedule them in private locations where we can control interruptions. We can use a conference room, with a sign on the door stating "Interviews in progress. Please do not interrupt." Or find the office of someone who is on vacation. We can use our office if necessary, but we can't allow interruptions! We can tell people who might normally interrupt us that we will be interviewing and do not want to be interrupted, and that our phone calls are to be held.

We need to arrange the interview seating so that it is conducive to sharing information. In other words, we should avoid an "I've got all the power" arrangement if we really want information from an applicant. We can meet in a neutral area if possible—again, a conference room is preferable. If we must use our office, we don't sit behind the desk. We can sit across the corner of the desk, or in front of it, using a guest chair. Whatever we do, we should set up the interview area so that it helps create a true conversation with the applicant, not an "interrogation."

Finally, we can place a small clock where we can see it while we are looking at the applicant, or where it can be seen as we look down at our notes. If we glance away from the applicant to check our watch or a clock, he or she will feel that we are pressed for time.

5. Prescreen with telephone interviews

After we have identified the job requirements, examined the résumé or application form, written prescreening questions, examined the application forms and decided what they should bring with them to the interview, we are ready to conduct brief telephone interviews. These will allow us to separate those applicants who are not suitable for the job from those we will wish to interview further.

If we determine that an applicant is a possible fit, we can let him or her know what must be brought to the interview (work samples, etc.). We can also advise the applicant where, when, and with whom the interview will take place.

As you schedule prescreened applicants for interviewing, plan at least forty-five minute interviews with a minimum of fifteen minutes between appointments. Interviews are exhausting to conduct. (Wait until you conduct ten forty-five minute interviews, and see how you feel at the end of the day!) A fifteen-minute interval between interviews will give you time to complete your notes and reorganize before the next candidate arrives. It will also give you extra time in case you go beyond your scheduled time with an applicant.

The forty-five minutes of allotted time can be flexible, depending on the level of the job being filled, as well as on the experience of the applicant. If we are conducting an interview for a job that requires extensive experience, for example, then the chances are good that we will need significantly more interviewing time to allow the candidate to present the needed information.

On the following page is an *Interviewing Planning Worksheet* that you may copy for your needs.

Interviewing Planning Worksheet

Position: _____

* R = Required, T = Can train him or her to do this task, P = Determine information in prescreening, I = Determine this information in interview, P/I = Both

Tasks	Job Knowledge, Skills, and Interests	R T *	P, I P/I *	Write out all important prescreening questions to ask applicant. Note samples applicant should bring to the interview.	Write interview questions, specify what demonstrations are needed, and what samples will be examined.

Interviewing

In this section, we will look at the actual interview and the steps that can be taken to obtain the information we need. The following are the five steps that will help ensure an effective exchange of information:

☑ 1. Conduct the opening of the interview.

☑ 2. Determine the candidate's suitability for the job.

☑ 3. Describe the job—honestly.

☑ 4. Ask for additional questions.

☑ 5. Close the interview.

Let's examine each of these in more detail.

 1. Conduct the opening of the interview.

A number of years ago, I wrote a book for employees titled, *Is Coffee Break the Best Part of Your Day?* I sent the manuscript to some possible publishers, and received three contracts. Two of the three were from large, old-line publishers. And they were not very friendly, even a little bit arrogant—like they were doing me a favor by offering to publish my book. The third publisher was quite a bit smaller. But the representative was personable, flexible, and in our discussion said, "I want this book. I want to be your publisher!" Guess whom I chose? Right! Not one of the big publishing houses, but the smaller one who genuinely wanted my book.

It's the same way with job candidates. All too often we see leaders acting like the old-line publishers I encountered: stern, distant, interrogative, superior, and not very friendly! But remember, our good candidates are likely to receive a number of job offers. So if we want them to accept our offer, we need to treat them the way we would want to be treated—with interest, respect, and friendliness.

There is also a direct correlation between our candidates' willingness to share information openly and the consideration we show them. So we should treat all candidates the way we would want to be treated. (Who knows, it might be us or our children out there job hunting some day.)

We should also avoid saying, "I'm Mr. . . ." "Ms. . . . or "Dr. . . .." It will sound very formal and unfriendly! Instead, we can use our first name. If a candidate uses a title in speaking with me, I gently say, "Dick, it's Dick Leatherman." If the candidate continues to use the title, then that is his or her choice.

Establish Trust

The greater the level of trust between the job candidate and us, the greater the quality and quantity of information we are likely to receive. And we need information in order to make a good decision. First, a trusting environment is established by following the suggestions made earlier concerning preparing for the interview: scheduling interviews at a private location where we can control interruptions, not allowing ourselves to be interrupted, having our phone calls held, and arranging the seating so that the candidate is comfortable.

But trust is also established by what we say. If we begin the interview by openly stating why it is important for both of us to be honest in the interview, it is much less likely that the candidate will say only what he or she thinks we want to hear. For example, we can tell our candidates at the outset that it is important for us to let them know exactly what the job is, its good points, and its bad points, and what it *isn't*. Indicate that it's important that we level with them because if they are offered the job and accept it, they will expect it to be as we described it in the interview. If it is not, then the new employee will have a serious problem, and consequently, we will have a serious problem, too.

On the other hand, if the employee provides us with "fantasy information" based on what he or she thinks we want to hear, we may have the makings of a disaster, such as a new employee who is totally unsatisfactory in performing the work. And unsatisfactory employees make for unhappy employees—and unhappy bosses.

Here is an example of what an interviewer might say to a candidate:

> *Jack, before we start the actual interview, I need to say something very important. I think that you and I should try to be as honest as possible with each other. Not that I think you would be deliberately dishonest. But there is a natural tendency for applicants to try to appear as qualified as possible in the interview—as well as for me to make this organization sound great, and the job even better. Sure, I'm proud to*

work here. And I know you are proud of your accomplishments. But we're both going to get in trouble if we don't level with each other. You, by telling me what you're really all about; and me, by telling you what the job actually is—warts and all! If we don't do this, you may end up with a job you can't stand, or aren't truly qualified for. And then I will end up dealing with all the problems which that will cause.

If the leader and the candidate can both be straight with one another, then they both will win. If not, they both will lose!

Ask for Permission to Take Notes

If we do not take notes during our interviews, it will be impossible to remember what the candidates have said, even by the end of the day. Our temptation may be to use a tape recorder, or, conversely, not to take notes at all. The former inhibits the candidate. And the latter, as indicated, makes it very difficult to remember what was said. Making handwritten notes is the best procedure. We can tell the interviewee that we will be interviewing a number of people, and that, unless we take notes, it will be difficult for us to remember the important things that were said. Then, we can ask the candidate if it will be alright for us to take notes.

But a caution here: if we try to write down everything that is said, we will inhibit the conversation and slow down the free flow of information. Therefore, we make brief notes and flesh them out immediately after the interview. We will then be able to maintain better eye contact and rapport with the candidate, and enhance communication. This will allow us to be aware of important visual cues that might otherwise go unnoticed.

If the candidate says something that might be viewed as negative, we should avoid immediately writing it down. The candidate may be aware that what was said was not positive, and if we quickly note it, he or she may begin to feel inhibited. So we need to wait a moment or two before making such a note.

Describe the Interview Format

In general, there are two ways to proceed with your questioning. The traditional method is to ask candidates prepared questions about their experience, knowledge, skills, and interests; and then to describe the job. The other approach is to show the candidates our list of job tasks and related knowledge/skills/interest requirements, and then ask them to describe how their experience matches each task area. Both formats have advantages—and disadvantages.

Ask—Then Tell. The traditional approach to interviewing holds that we should obtain information from the candidate before describing the job. This "ask—then tell" format, of course, allows us to learn about the candidate's background before he or she is fully aware of the requirements of the job. The theory is that keeping candidates "in the dark" about the specifics of the job will allow us to obtain more honest information from them—i.e., will keep them from slanting what they say toward the just-learned job requirements. And it is obviously true that human nature will lead candidates who want a job to present themselves in the best possible light in relationship to that job. (Candidates often do so even when they really don't want the job, because it feels good to be made an offer.) Using the "ask—then tell" approach, we could say:

> *Sue, here's how we'll spend our time today. First, I'd like to ask you some questions about your experience and interests. Next, I'll tell you about the job, and you'll have a chance to ask questions. Finally, I'll let you know our decision within approximately a week. So, the first thing I'd like to ask you is . . ..*

The disadvantage of this approach is the amount of work it requires of us (although some see the extra effort as producing an advantage). We need to design a considerable number of relevant questions ahead of time, worry about their legality, and then ask them in such a way as to elicit the information we will need later in making our selection decision. It's not an easy job.

Show—Then Ask. A different—and many feel, better—interview format is to begin by showing candidates our list of job tasks and required knowledge, skills, and interests (but not our prepared questions with each of these). Then, we ask them to describe how their experiences and abilities relate to each task item, and sit back and listen. We will likely need to ask a few clarifying questions, but for the most part, the candidate will do the talking.

This approach has several advantages. First, it is a lot easier since we don't have to spend so much time and effort designing and asking prepared questions. Second, candidates are usually more comfortable because they will not perceive themselves being "interrogated," but are simply talking about themselves. And since they are more comfortable, we will probably get more information. Third, the information we obtain will likely be more useful. If candidates know what we want them to be able to do, they are better able to tell us their relevant experiences, which provides the information we need to make our selection decision.

To use this approach, we might say something like,

> *Dan, first I'll give you some specific information about this job. Next, you will have time to tell me about yourself and how your experience fits the needs of the job. Then, I'll answer any other questions you may have. Last, I'll let you know what happens about a week after the interview.*
>
> *So, let's look at the job. Here's a list of the major tasks in this position, as well as the knowledge, skills, and interests we feel are required for it. What I'd like you to do is to take, one at a time, each task, and its related knowledge, skill and interest requirements, and describe how your experience fits that part of the job. I have a copy of this list that I'll use as a reference as you talk. And I'll ask any questions I have as we go along. So why don't you take the first task, and go from there.*

The main disadvantage of this approach has already been indicated: telling the candidate about the job first can result in biased information.

 2. Determine the candidate's suitability for the job.

At this point (Step 2) we will follow the more traditional interview method of asking prepared, task-related questions, and then describing the job (Step 3). But keep in mind that the general format that you use, whether "ask—then tell," or "show—then ask," is up to you.

Ask Questions

Having opened the interview and described the procedure we will follow, we now ask our prepared questions to determine the candidate's knowledge, skills, and interest. We have discussed in detail how to design effective questions based on our task-listing and detailing. But we also need to say a word about the way that we ask our questions.

Asking Questions About Sensitive Topics. At certain points in the interview we may need to explore sensitive topics. Such questions will yield more useful information if they are carefully prefaced. For example, "In confidence, could you tell me more about . . .?" Or, "If you don't mind my asking, what can you tell me about . . .?" And if what we are told is confidential, we treat it as such.

Avoid Asking Questions the Candidate Can't Answer. When trying to determine factual information, we need to avoid embarrassing candidates by asking questions they may not be able to answer but feel they should. For instance, if we ask, "Exactly how many days were you absent from your job last year?" the candidate will feel that we expect him or her to have that information at his or her fingertips, as well as feel somewhat threatened by the question. It is much better to begin such factual questions with words like "Approximately," "Usually," "Normally," or "Generally," e.g., "Approximately how many days were you absent from your job last year?"

Repetition. Another strategy to encourage a candidate to talk is termed *repetition.* We simply repeat the last words of what the candidate has said, ending with the tone of a question in our voice. For example, suppose we are interviewing candidates for an office clerk's position. We have just asked about the candidate's experience in taking incoming telephone calls. The candidate responds by saying, "Well, several years ago when I was with the Intrusive Care organization I spent a lot of time on the phone." Then just repeat the candidate's key words in the form of a question: "So when you were with Intrusive Care, you spent a lot of time on the phone?" The candidate will usually respond by giving us additional information. In this case the candidate might add, "Yes, I was a telephone solicitor responsible for selling perpetual burial plots. It was a tough business. I really had to push for a sale!"

Probing Questions. When we ask a prepared question, we may need to follow it up with another question in order to obtain more information. These *probing questions* include questions such as:

- "Can you tell me more about that?"
- "What else?"
- "Why did that happen?"
- "What happened next?"
- "Then what?"

But when we ask probing questions, we need to avoid using too many in a series. Like a detective, we may begin to sound "interrogative"!

- "Where were you on the night of the murder?"
- "What time did you leave the party?"
- "What happened next?"
- "Then what?"

We need to avoid making our candidates feel like they are suspects in a murder investigation. Remember, helping the candidate feel at ease is the best way to secure information. So all of our questions should be designed to produce confidence and relaxation by showing our positive interest.

What-If Questions. Sometimes an excellent way to obtain information is to ask a hypothetical *What-if question.* For instance, we might ask, "Patricia, if you were given the responsibility for running this section, what would you do?" Or, "Suppose that you got this job, Ann. What strengths would you bring to it?" Such questions offer much insight—both about the candidate's approach to situations as well as his or her ability to "think on one's feet." But keep in mind that what-if questions are asking candidates to generalize from their own experience to a specific situation, and this can make some people nervous. So be supportive in asking what-if questions.

Listen

Asking questions is only part of the skills we need to conduct interviews. We also need to listen. It is especially important to practice good listening skills during the interview! We should avoid interrupting candidates while they are speaking. (There are exceptions, of course, even to this rule—e.g., dealing with a nonstop talker.) Normally, the more we listen the more we learn. We maintain good eye contact, and remember that we can process the information we hear more quickly than the candidate can speak. So we need to be careful that our attention doesn't wander as the candidate talks. Instead, we can use the "extra time" to consider and note questions we should ask when we have an opportunity.

Respond. A successful interview is one in which the candidate does most of the talking and the interviewer most of the listening. But good listening is not just sitting there in frozen silence! There are many things that we can do and say to facilitate a natural flow of communication. For example, as we listen, we can use verbal prompts, such as, "I see," "That's interesting," "Good," "Uh-huh," or "I didn't know that," to encourage candidates to continue to talk. Often these comments elicit even more information than asking another question.

We should also note that silence is a powerful communication tool. It's alright for us not to talk! We simply wait a moment to see if the candidate wants to say more about his or her thoughts—just as long as the silence doesn't become awkward for the candidate.

Posture. When actively listening to someone, our posture is called *attending.* We *attend* a person when our body communicates that we are interested in being with them and hearing what they have to say. To attend candidates in the interview, we can simply lean forward as they talk, and encourage them by nodding our head and using verbal prompts.

Clarifying and Summarizing. *Clarifying* and *summarizing* are effective and useful listening tools. Clarification (sometimes termed "paraphrasing") is nothing more than repeating, in our own words, what we understood the candidate to have said.

Summarizing what has just been said is also a good way to ensure that what we heard was what was really stated. Summarizing will also improve our retention. After our summary, we quickly return to listening, and the candidate will often provide more information on what he or she was saying. Both of these tools, clarifying and summarizing, cause us to listen better, and allow us to check our understanding.

Provide Positive Feedback. When candidates say something positive about themselves, it is important for us to respond in a positive manner by saying, for example, "That was quite an accomplishment," "You must have been very proud of that," or even just "Very good!" and "That's great!" So we need to listen carefully for things the candidate is especially proud of, whether it is the way that a job was done, recognition that was received, or accomplishments in school. Providing positive feedback helps increase our rapport with the candidate, and usually helps obtain more information.

Ask for a Task Demonstration. As mentioned earlier, if we want to know if a candidate can perform a task properly, the best way to find out is to ask him or her to do it.

Let me tell you a humorous "parable" to illustrate: suppose that I had a lifelong ambition to become a medical doctor, but my dream had not been realized. Then one day while reading a *Popular Mechanics* magazine I saw a classified ad that said, "Make big money!!! Learn to be a physician at home on your own time through our approved correspondence training program!"

So I signed up, sent in my check, and began receiving my reading assignments. As it turned out I was pretty good at learning the material, and made high grades on all my open-book exams. I found the section on "Removing the Appendix" especially fascinating, and even made an A+ on that particular lesson.

Now the question is, how would you feel about hiring me to take out your appendix? Too often we only ask candidates if they can "take out an appendix," rather than asking them to demonstrate their ability as we observe. Arranging simple hands-on task performances is not difficult to do, and is well worth the effort in what we will learn about the candidate.

Ask for Samples of Past Work. Asking candidates to bring particular samples of their past work with them is also a concrete way to examine their ability to perform a task. (Be aware, of course, of the possibility of a candidate submitting someone else's work!) We have already given examples where work samples are appropriate and helpful.

Tactfully Conclude the Interview. If the candidate is not suitable for the position, we should tactfully conclude the interview. Even after careful prescreening of candidates we may discover in the face-to-face interview that a candidate's qualifications are inadequate. When this occurs (and it will), we should not waste our time or the candidate's with further interviewing. We can diplomatically end the interview by providing a brief, general description of the job, answering any questions, and then standing as we indicate that all candidates will be notified promptly by mail. Then we can walk toward the door and shake hands goodbye. If we do get questions from the candidate, we answer them briefly and continue to end the interview.

For example, we might say:

> *Well, Betty, in closing, I really appreciate your time in meeting with me. As we stated in our ad, the job is for an office clerk. We are looking at a number of candidates and will notify each of you by mail of our decision. You should hear from us in about a week. Do you have any other questions?* (Note this is a closed, not open, question.)

Succinctly answer any question(s) that the candidate may have, and then stand and say,

> *Thanks again for coming in.* (Walk toward the door and shake hands.) *Goodbye.*

The objective in concluding the interview early is to save everyone time. We need to conclude in such a way as not to insult the candidate or hurt his or her feelings. So we avoid giving the candidate the feeling that he or she is being given the "bum's rush." We need to try to leave all candidates feeling that we are genuinely interested in them (which we should be), and that we have courteously answered all of their questions.

 3. Describe the job—honestly.

In conducting interviews, our overriding objective is to obtain information and then to tell the candidates enough about the job so that if they receive a job offer they will be able to make an informed decision about accepting the job. If we try to "sell," "persuade," or "convince" the candidate that this is the best job in the country in the best organization in the world, we may be successful in getting a short-term employee, but we might have trouble converting this person into a long-term worker!

In my experience, most leaders spend too much time in the "telling" mode. It's almost as if we say to job candidates: "OK, I've asked you all these questions, and I've listened to everything you've said. Now it's *my* turn to talk!" And we talk . . . and talk. But when we take the time to properly prepare, making and copying an *Interview Planning Worksheet* (minus our prepared questions), then it is a simple matter to show and discuss with the candidate the list of job tasks and their detailing in related knowledge/skills/interests. At this time, we also need to review the good and not-so-good points of the job. As pointed out, it's important that the candidate have a realistic view of the position so that he or she can later make an informed decision if the job is offered.

This doesn't mean, of course, that we should be negative about the job—far from it! We should begin by clearly presenting the positive features of the job. Then we can discuss any drawbacks. Here's a capsulated example of what I say when interviewing potential sales managers for our organization:

> *This job is exciting and challenging. The people are fun and easy to work with. Our customers are truly wonderful. Your new boss (me) is a leader who delegates both responsibility and authority.*
>
> *Downside? The starting salary plus commission is low, though the job does have a high future earning potential. (Then smiling.) But for a job like this, maybe you should pay us!*

☑ 4. Ask for additional questions.

Now we need to give the candidate a full, final opportunity to ask questions. In soliciting questions, we avoid the wording, "Do you have any questions?" Not only is this a closed question (inviting only a "yes" or "no"), but it actually makes it more difficult for the candidate to respond. Instead, say, "What questions do you have?" This assumes that the candidate does have questions and encourages him or her to ask them.

☑ 5. Close the interview.

End your interview by 1) stating that your time is up, 2) summarizing the highlights of the interview, and 3) telling the candidate what comes next. We might say something like this:

Sam, it looks like our time is just about up. I appreciate your openness in this interview. I feel that I've learned a lot about you and your work experience. In particular you like working with people, you enjoy doing paperwork, and you are efficient in managing your time. You don't care much for working evening shifts. And you feel that planning is not presently one of your strengths.

Now, we are interviewing a number of candidates for this position. We should be finished in about two weeks; and at that time we will notify all candidates by mail.

Thanks for coming in.

Do not tell any candidates at this time that they are not qualified for the job. Do it later by mail. This will eliminate unwanted and unnecessary defensiveness or "bargaining" by candidates at the close of the interview. Also remember that the person we finally choose may not accept the position, and we might need to reevaluate the other candidates.

Selection

 1. Schedule a follow-up selection meeting with all of the people involved.

It is generally true that involving more people in the actual selection process will produce a better decision. However, we must strike a balance here. If only one person is involved in the decision, it will have a high probability of being biased. But if there are too many people in the selection meeting, it can become difficult to get anything done. If we used multiple interviewers, then all of these should be part of the decision process. And we may wish to invite two or three of our peers to discuss the candidates and offer their opinions. As mentioned earlier, there is also great value in inviting a candidate's future coworkers to participate in the decision.

 2. Use a decision-making process.

A structured decision-making procedure usually leads to a better choice. I often use the Kepner-Tregoe (KT) decision-making grid to select the best candidate for a job. It is an excellent method for sorting out data and arranging it so that it makes sense. It is also a good tool for making a final selection decision.

As explained in Chapter 10, the KT process consists of four steps: 1) write a decision statement; 2) develop and weight our objectives; 3) identify alternatives and write data; and 4) evaluate the risks. Let's see how we would use the KT procedure to select the best candidate for our administrative assistant's position.

Step 1: Write a decision statement.

In most cases, Step 1, writing a decision statement, is straightforward. For example, "Select best person for the administrative assistant's position."

Step 2: Develop and weight your objectives.

The next step is to list all the factors (KT terms them "Objectives") we should consider when we evaluate the candidate. These factors can be obtained from the *Interview Planning Worksheet* that we completed in our initial preparation for interviewing. For example, a list of key factors for the administrative assistant's job might look like the following on a *Selection*

Worksheet. (An example of this *Worksheet,* for you to copy and use, is found at the end of this chapter.)

Factors
Knows filing
Has basic reading skills
Types 45 wpm
Operates postage meter
Adds and subtracts
Lifts 25 lbs.
Has pleasant telephone personality
Has good telephone etiquette
Troubleshoots office equipment
Meets salary requirements
Can start work now
Has good work history

Having listed the important factors in our decision, we now give them weights. We begin by noting those that are "must" factors (labeled "M")—i.e., any requirement that a successful candidate *must* fulfill. On the next page is an example of how we can designate some of the Administrative Assistant's job factors as "musts."

Factors	Weight
Knows filing	
Has basic reading skills	M
Types 45 wpm	M
Operates postage meter	
Adds and subtracts	M
Lifts 25 lbs.	M
Has pleasant telephone personality	
Has good telephone etiquette	
Troubleshoots office equipment	
Meets salary requirements	
Can start work now	
Has good work history	

Next, since some of the remaining factors are more important than others, we weight each of them using a scale of 1 (least important) to 10 (most important). If other people are involved in the selection process, we ask them to help us weight these factors by assigning priority numbers.

I normally begin by choosing the most important factor on the list, and assign it 10 points. Next, I pick the least important factor, and give it 1 point. Then I assign relative weights to the other factors. As the example continues on the following page, note that the assigned weights are ones I have determined. If you were doing this for an administrative assistant's position in your organization, of course, these weights and the factors themselves might be quite different.

Factors	Weight
Knows filing	10
Has basic reading skills	M
Types 45 wpm	M
Operates postage meter	1
Adds and subtracts	M
Lifts 25 lbs.	M
Has pleasant telephone personality	9
Has good telephone etiquette	7
Troubleshoots office equipment	2
Meets salary requirements	5
Can start work now	8
Has good work history	8

Step 3: Identify alternatives and write data.

Now suppose that of the people who were interviewed for the administrative assistant's position, three stood out—Sam, George, and Edith. (KT terms these finalists "Alternatives.") We will then write data about each finalist for each factor. We should try to write in *specific* data—not just "Yes," "No," "Good," "Poor," etc. When we later compare our candidates with each other, the more information we have, the clearer the comparison will be.

Note in our KT grid that we have used "Yes" when marking the must factors. Since these candidates are finalists, then by necessity they have all passed the must requirements. (Remember that the must factors were used as "knockout criteria" when the candidates were prescreened.) The question then arises as to why we would list must factors at all in our decision-making grid of finalists. There are two reasons. First, this lets others know all the factors that were considered, as we may need to keep good interview and selection records for up to two years—sometimes longer, depending on our organizational policy and/or laws.

Second, sometimes we may wish to take a must objective and rewrite it as a new factor. For example, suppose a candidate's ability to type *more* than the required minimum 45-wpm is a factor we would like to consider in our selection decision. We would then rewrite "Types minimum of 45 wpm" to make the new factor: "Maximum typing speed." This added factor will be assigned a weight, and then considered in the selection decision. In the following example, suppose we felt that typing speeds above 45 wpm were not important for this job, so we have not rewritten this factor. It is often wise, however, to examine each must factor to see if rewriting it in a way that will distinguish your final candidates from one another would be important in your decision.

Factors	*Weight*	*Candidates*		
		Sam	**George**	**Edith**
Knows filing	10	6 years experience	Never filed	Some filing experience
Has basic reading skills	M	Yes	Yes	Yes
Types 45 wpm	M	Yes	Yes	Yes
Operates postage meter	1	Never used one	Used daily in old job	Has seen it used
Adds and subtracts	M	Yes	Yes	Yes
Lifts 25 lbs.	M	Yes	Yes	Yes
Has pleasant telephone personality	9	Acceptable in role play	Aggressive in role play	Very good personality on phone
Has good telephone etiquette	7	Didn't know the "rules"	No mistakes	Super! One of the best we've seen
Troubleshoots office equipment	2	Experienced troubleshooter	Lacks even the basics of trouble-shooting	Did well after seeing the service manual
Meets salary requirements	5	Last job earned less	Last job earned more	Earned quite a bit less in old job
Can start work now	8	Yes	Yes	Needs to give 4-week notice
Has good work history	8	Excellent	Some gaps between jobs	Excellent

After writing down specific information for each alternative's factor, the next step is to assign weights. In this case, we will assign a "10" automatically to the best alternative for each factor, and some number less than 10 to the other two alternatives. For example, for the factor "Knows filing," we would assign Sam a weight of 10 because Sam has had more experience than George or Edith. Then, we would give Edith a "5" because she has had some filing experience, and George would receive a "1" because he has never filed.

After all the weights have been assigned, we will then multiply each alternative weight by its original factor weight as shown below.

Factors	*Weight*	*Candidates*		
		Sam	**George**	**Edith**
Knows filing	10	X 10 = 100 6 years experience	X 1 = 10 Never filed	X 5 = 50 Some filing experience
Has basic reading skills	M	Yes	Yes	Yes
Types 45 wpm	M	Yes	Yes	Yes
Operates postage meter	1	X 1 = 1 Never used one	X 10 = 10 Used daily in old job	X 2 = 2 Has seen it used
Adds and subtracts	M	Yes	Yes	Yes
Lifts 25 lbs.	M	Yes	Yes	Yes
Pleasant telephone personality	9	X 6 = 54 Acceptable in role play	X 1 = 9 Aggressive in role play	X 10 = 90 Very good personality on phone
Has good telephone etiquette	7	X 2 = 14 Didn't know the "rules"	X 7 = 49 No mistakes	X 10 = 70 Super! One of the best we've seen
Trouble shoots office equipment	2	X 10 = 20 Experienced trouble-shooter	X 1 = 2 Lacks even the basics of trouble-shooting	X 8 = 16 Did well after seeing the service manual
Meets salary requirements	5	X 8 = 40 Last job earned less	X 1 = 5 Last job earned more	X 10 = 50 Earned quite a bit less in old job
Can start work now	8	X 10 = 80 Yes	X 10 = 80 Yes	X 7 = 56 Needs to give 4-week notice
Has good work history	8	X 10 = 80 Excellent	X 3 = 24 Some gaps between jobs	X 10 = 80 Excellent
Total Scores		**389**	**189**	**414**

Having multiplied each of our candidate's factor (job task) ratings by that factor's weight and totaled the scores, we can see that Edith and Sam appear to be fairly equal candidates and that George comes far behind. Our KT decision-making grid has helped us organize and evaluate a great amount of data on three very different individuals, and led us to quite a clear (and measured) comparative ranking of them—a much-desired finding that is difficult to achieve without a systematic decision-making procedure.

But now we need to decide between Edith and Sam. So let's look at the last step in our selection process.

Step 4: Evaluate risk.

Finally, we need to ask the question, "If we hire candidate 'X,' what could go wrong?" When we have identified the possible risks for each candidate, we will evaluate each risk in terms of the *probability* of it happening and the *seriousness* if it does, again using a scale of 1 to 10. A "1" probability rating means the event is not likely to happen, while a "1" seriousness rating means that if it does happen, it won't be very serious. A "10" probability rating indicates that the event appears certain to happen, and a "10" seriousness rating means that if it does happen it will be a disaster! When we have assigned our probability and seriousness ratings, we will multiply them to get a risk rating for each candidate. If there is more than one risk with a candidate, we will add the risk ratings for a composite score.

Since two of our office clerk candidates (Edith and Sam) are closely ranked at this point, and are far ahead of the third (George), we will do our risk evaluation only on these two. (Note that "P" = the probability of the event occurring, and that "S" = the seriousness if it does occur.)

Candidate: Sam

Risk	*P*	*S*	*P X S =*
Poor attendance record due to several health problems. He may develop the same attendance problems here. (Not Americans with Disability Act health problems.)	3 X	7	21
Has been out of work for several months. He may be seeking this position only because he needs a job, rather than really wanting this one. We couldn't get a handle on this in the interview.	2 X	5	10
		Total composite risk:	31

Notice that we are analyzing the risks with each candidate separately because different candidates will have different risks. If we find a risk that is common to more than one candidate, the chances are that we have overlooked a factor (job requirement) in our initial task listing. For example, if past attendance is important to us, then we could have written another factor, adding "Good attendance record," given it a factor weight (say, "7"), and evaluated all three of the administrative assistant candidates in terms of it.

Now let's look at the risks in hiring Edith. What could go wrong if we hire her for this position?

Candidate: Edith

Risk	*P*	*S*	*P X S =*
She made a number of errors in the typing test. She said it was because she had not had an opportunity to keep up her typing skills in her old job. There is some concern that she will not be able to improve these skills on the job.	1 X	10	10
		Total composite risk:	10

Note that we do not subtract a candidate's risk score from the factor score. We only compare our candidates' risk scores to help us make a balanced decision, e.g., Sam's risk score of 31 is well above Edith's score of 10.

So the final result of our decision-making process to select the best candidate for the administrative assistant's position is that Edith appears to be the strongest candidate—leading the second-ranked candidate, Sam, in both job task qualifications (414 to 389) and lack of risk (10 to 31).

☑ **3. Promptly notify all candidates of our decision.**

I would like to emphasize the importance of *promptly* notifying all candidates of our hiring decision. It is completely improper—and too often done—to keep job candidates who are not selected hanging on for days and even weeks. Candidates may well have other job offers pending that they don't want to accept until they hear from us. And regardless, they normally are quite anxious to hear whether they were selected or not. Not knowing the result of a job application can be even more stressful than learning that we have not been selected. Certainly we would feel very frustrated if we really wanted a job and the employer put off contacting us about the outcome of our application.

So it is quite unfair not to notify job candidates promptly, within a week at the most. When we don't let them know our decision, they are placed in the dilemma of whether or not to call us, a difficult decision for many candidates. If they call, they may feel they will be seen as "pushy." And if they don't call, they have no idea as to when, if ever, they will find out how well they did.

If we plan to contact unsuccessful interview candidates by phone, we may also want to write what we will say prior to calling them. If letters are to be mailed, we avoid sending one that looks like a form letter, such as:

Dear Sir/Madam:

We regret to inform you that you were not selected for the ___*sales*___ job. Thank you for your interest in our organization.

Sincerely yours,

Mr./Ms./Dr. ___*I. M. Lazie*___

Also, we should try not to give unsuccessful candidates the impression that there was something "wrong" with them because they were not selected. We need to keep our focus on the positives, as in the following example:

Dear Sue,

Thanks for all your efforts in applying for the computer programming position here at ITC. I know that the day you spent in interviewing would have been strenuous for anyone.

Sue, you were asked to come in for an interview because of your excellent qualifications. And although you were not chosen for this position, you had many strengths. The person we selected, however, was slightly more qualified for this particular job.

I am keeping your application on file in case we have additional needs in the future. Thanks for your interest in our organization.

Sincerely yours,

Dick Leatherman

Whether or not you give specific information to candidates as to why they weren't selected is up to your management or personnel department. My preference is to provide feedback if requested. But I also recognize that because of possible litigation concerning selection, it is often more prudent not to offer such feedback unless it is asked for.

Finally, in a letter of notification to a candidate, the specific job applied for should be referenced, and you (or the interviewer, if it was not you) should sign it.

☑ 4. File all information on candidates who were qualified, but not selected, for later use.

Remember that the candidate whom we hire may not work out, or may quit shortly after being hired. Sometimes in spite of our best efforts, the candidate is not happy with the new job, or we aren't happy with the candidate. Or we may soon need to hire another person for a similar job. For these reasons and others, it is wise to keep information on file that we have obtained in interviews with unsuccessful candidates. This information was very expensive to obtain and keeping it could save us a great deal of time and money if it reduces our need to interview additional candidates in the near future.

In addition, if we are ever asked to justify our selection, we will have the data to establish that our decision was fair, objective, and impartial (as it should be). So we need to keep on file the *Interview Planning Worksheet* we used to determine the job requirements and questions to be asked. And we should save any worksheet we used to make our final selection (e.g., KT grid, etc.). These records, on both successful and unsuccessful candidates, will be very important and useful to our organization in case of future litigation.

Here we should note again that various acts and laws relating to discriminatory practices require us to keep our interviewing and selection records and notes for specified periods of time. These time periods vary, depending on the legislation and the type of job applicant. If we keep them at least two years, we will normally be within the law. But it is best to check with your organization's attorney to make sure you are complying with existing laws.

Summary

Much information has been presented in this chapter. But as we have seen, the processes of preparing for job interviews, prescreening the applicants, conducting interviews, selecting the best candidate, and following up require thought, time, and effort. And there are really no shortcuts. The amount of time devoted to preparing for our interviews directly affects the quality of those interviews—which in turn determines the quality of the information we have available to use in the selection process. The selection process we decide to use will determine the quality of our final candidate choice. And surrounding this entire process are legal requirements concerning discrimination.

But the benefits to our organization of making good "million dollar decisions" make all of our efforts worthwhile. When we take the time to prepare and conduct quality interviewing and selection meetings, we will have more confidence that those who

1. Get job offers have the skills to do the job, a genuine interest in the job, and the information needed to accept or reject our job offer

2. Accept job offers will perform well on the job and stay with the organization

3. Are not made offers will feel the process was thorough and fair and feel favorable about applying for other jobs with our organization

4. Make informal (or legal) challenges of decisions made can be answered with supporting evidence

In closing, I would like to offer two basic principles that will affect the quality of what we do throughout the entire interviewing and selection process:

Treat others as we would want to be treated. There are few activities harder than looking for a job—especially if we don't currently have one. So we should have compassion! We treat job applicants with courtesy, respect, and consideration. I firmly believe that what goes out comes back. The way we treat others is the way we in turn will be treated in life.

Spend sufficient time to prepare properly for interviews. The time we spend in preparation will 1) save time through good prescreening of applicants; 2) help us be more comfortable in interviewing candidates, because we will know what to ask; and 3) greatly increase our chances of hiring the best employee for the job.

Instructions for the Selection Worksheet

1. Write a decision statement (e.g., "Select the best candidate for the job").

2. List all important factors (job task requirements).
   - Identify must factors (label "M").
   - Numerically weight the remaining factors from 1 to 10 ("10" = most important).

3. List candidates (finalists).
   - Select only three or four best candidates for analysis.
   - Write candidate data for must factors.
   - Eliminate any candidate who doesn't meet every must requirement.
   - Write candidate data for remaining factors using specific facts, figures, opinions, and impressions (*not* simply "Yes," "No," "Poor," "Good," "Better," "Best," etc.).
   - Numerically rate each candidate on each factor. (Do not rate must factors.) Assign a "10" to the best candidate concerning each factor, and an appropriate lower score to the other candidates.
   - Multiply each factor weight by each candidate rating and record the results.
   - Add column scores for each candidate and compare totals.

4. Taking the top candidates, evaluate the risks.
   - Assign *probability* and *seriousness* values (10 to 1 scale, "10" = highest probability, greatest seriousness).
   - Multiply probability and seriousness ratings, add resulting risk totals for each candidate, and compare.
   - Make selection based on final comparison of candidates' factor (job task) scores and risk scores.

Selection Worksheet

Decision Statement:				
Factors (Job tasks requirements)	Weights	Candidate 1 _____ _____ _____	Candidate 2 _____ _____ _____	Candidate 3 _____ _____ _____
		Data & Rating (10 – 1)	Data & Rating (10 – 1)	Data & Rating (10 – 1)
Total Scores:				

Risk for Candidate 1:	P	S	
	x		
	x		
	x		
	x		
	x		
	x		
	x		
	x		
Total Risk:			

Risk for Candidate 2:	P	S	
	x		
	x		
	x		
	x		
	x		
	x		
	x		
	x		
Total Risk:			

Note: "P" = Probability (10 – 1 scale); "S" = Seriousness (10 – 1 scale)

Leading Transitions

18

Leadership
Employee
Career Counseling

To live means to experience—through doing, feeling, thinking. Experience takes place in time, so time is the ultimate scarce resource we have. Over the years, the content of experience will determine the quality of life. Therefore one of the most essential decisions any of us can make is about how one's time is allocated or invested.

Mihaly Csikszentmihalyi
Finding Flow

At the turn of the century, an entire generation of young people grew up reading a series of novels written by Horatio Alger. The books were titled *Strive and Succeed, Making His Way, Struggling Upward, Do and Dare,* and *Helping Himself.*

In almost every case, these books had a plot that went as follows: A young boy had either an absent father, or a father (often a minister) who was kind and good, but not concerned with the practical side of life. The family was always poor. And there was usually a rich villain who was going to foreclose on the mortgage—a princely sum like $500, in a day when we could buy a house for $600.

But the ending always turned out happily. In the Horatio Alger stories, "happy" meant that the boy earned the money to pay the mortgage because he was honest, hard working, kind, and loved God, his mother, and his country. The central theme was "If you are willing to work hard, success will come automatically because of the grand opportunities that exist in this country."

Today the Horatio Alger story is, unfortunately, largely untrue. This is so because the facts of life in the business world are quite changed. We still view the individual as fundamentally responsible for his or her success or failure. But the maxim "Hard work will ensure success" has by now become more myth than truth. Look at the facts. Only a few decades ago, the chances of being promoted were one in five. Today the odds are one in thirty. In other words, employees are six times less likely to be promoted to leadership positions today than they would have been in the recent past.

Future expectations are formed by past experiences. A whole generation— our parents—grew up with remarkable opportunities. Their children are now our employees, and they have similarly high expectations. They were told, "Work hard. Stay in school. Go to college. Get your degree. Do these things, and you will succeed!" As a result, they expect responsible jobs with opportunities for advancement. The truth is, however, that they are not going to find the same opportunities that our parents did in the past. We need to manage differently! And one solution is a career development system that can greatly help our employees overcome career obstacles and achieve success.

Career Development Systems

Good organizations know that their employees are their strength. Today we will find such organizations helping their employees build careers that make them more and more valuable to the organization.

Here is a picture of the way the parts of a modern career system fit together. As you can see, the central focus is on career counseling and career action plans.

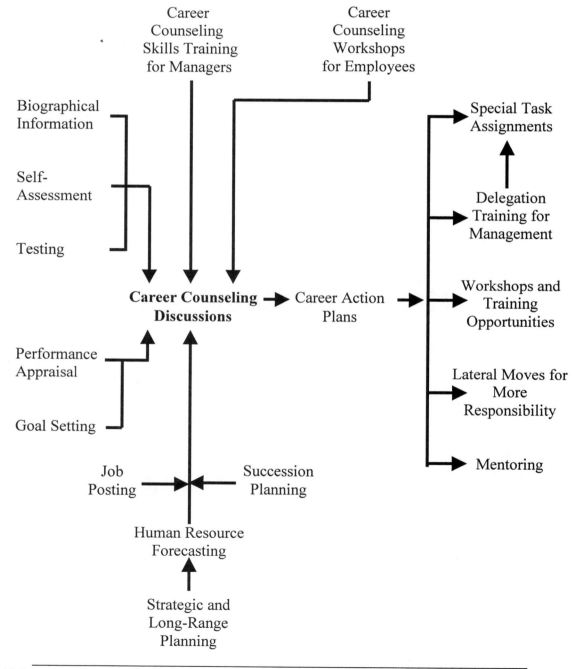

Organizational Strategies

Organizations are built on a foundation of strategic planning. Top management usually conducts this planning in order to define the organization's mission or vision. From the organization's definition of what it is about—its mission—a long-range plan is developed.

After the organization completes its long-range planning, it can then forecast its human resource needs. When the forecasting is complete, the organization can then do succession planning to determine who needs to be trained to do what in future jobs. Finally, the organization communicates its human resource needs to its employees by job posting.

Even if our organization does not do forecasting or succession planning, we can still take responsibility for our employee's career development. The first step is to help our employees figure out where they are going, what knowledge and skills will be required, and then determine what they need to get there.

Useful Strategies for Determining Employee Needs

To explore employee developmental needs, we need to analyze their past experience to determine their strengths, knowledge, skills, and values. This information will be very useful in helping them make sound career development decisions.

For example, if you look at my background you will discover that in nearly every job I've had, I have enjoyed making presentations. Even in high school, my only A was in Public Speaking. (Where I went to school, it was socially unacceptable to make too many A's!) Therefore, if you were assisting me in my career planning, you would focus on my strength and skills in making presentations.

Job History Form. One way to organize information about employees is to ask them to fill out a *Job History Form.* They will begin by listing each job they have held (a maximum of five), starting with their present position. A major job change within one organization is counted as a new job.

Next, the employees break down each job into its major tasks, and enter the details on the form. Then they show their level of personal satisfaction for each task. Finally, for those tasks rated very high or very low in satisfaction, they note the reasons why they liked or disliked each one.

This list will provide clues and themes to the key things they want in a career, as well as to the things they wish to avoid. The following is an example of a job history describing one of my past positions:

Job History

1. Job	2. Major Tasks	3. Satisfaction 5 = High Level 1 = Low Level	4. Why did I like or dislike each task (1's or 5's)?
Department Manager	*Team leader*	*3*	
	Long-range planning	*4*	
	Handling budgets	*1*	*I hate dealing with budgets because I am not very good at it!*
	Writing and creating new programs	*3*	
	Making presentations to executives	*2*	
	Acting as a resource person for technical questions	*5*	*I enjoy being the "expert" and helping people.*
	Speaking at local and national conventions	*5*	*The recognition I receive feels good to me.* *I also like feeling competent.*

5. What generalizations (themes) can you make about yourself from your job history analysis? What are the key things you want in a job, and what things do you wish to avoid?

    1. I like the mentoring role.
    2. Recognition for work well done is important for me.
    3. I would strongly dislike working with numbers.

On the next two pages is a *Job History Form* that you may copy and use.

Job History Form: Page 1

Your Name: _____ Date: _____

1. Job: List each job you have had (max 5), starting with your present job.	2. Major Tasks: List the major tasks in each of the jobs you now hold and have held in the past.	3. Satisfaction Level 5 = High Level 1 = Low Level	4. Why did you like or dislike that specific task? Note reasons for only the highest (5) and lowest (1) satisfaction levels.
Present Job Title:			
Previous Job:			
Previous Job:			

Job History Form: Page 2

1. Job: List each job you have had (max 5), starting with your present job.	2. Major Tasks: List the major tasks in each of the jobs you now hold and have held in the past.	3. Satisfaction Level 5 = High Level 1 = Low Level	4. Why did you like or dislike that specific task? Note reasons for only the highest (5) and lowest (1) satisfaction levels.
Previous Job:			
Previous Job:			

Themes: From your analysis, list the key things you want in a job and the things you want to avoid.

Life History Form. In addition to the *Job History Form*, the employee should also fill out a *Life History Form*. This form will also ask him or her to identify major skills and interests.

To use a *Life History Form*, employees begin by listing five key positive events in their lives, either job-related or personal, that resulted mostly from their own efforts. For each event, they list the skills or abilities they used. Then, the employees honestly indicate specific reasons why each of the events was important to them. Next, they examine each of their skills and abilities, and make a new list of the most important ones. Finally, they analyze the reasons why each positive event was personally important to them, and list the underlying values shown in the event. That is, what did the employee like or enjoy about each situation?

To illustrate the use of this form, let's look at a life event that was significant to me. The teachers in my elementary school thought I was strange. I could read at an astonishing speed. But I absolutely could not spell. As a matter of fact, after failing the sixth grade, I almost became a grammar school dropout.

It wasn't until I was in college that I learned I had a condition referred to as "dyslexia." Many years later I felt honored when I was asked to give the commencement address to a special high school graduating class of twelve students—who were all dyslexic! Here is the way I analyzed this positive event in the format described above.

Life History

1. Positive Event	2. List your skills/abilities that resulted in this event	3. Why was this event important?
I gave the commencement address to a high school class of dyslexic students.	*Speaking before groups*	*Recognition: I felt needed*
	Writing skills (not spelling!)	
	Knowledge of how to conduct a needs assessment (I interviewed each of the 12 students prior to writing the speech)	*Deep satisfaction in helping others personally*
4. From #2 above, list your most important skills and abilities.		5. Identify your underlying values.
Speaking before groups		*I like being in a situation where I can help others and am perceived as being exceptional.*
		I enjoy the resulting recognition.

It is difficult to perceive the power of the *Life History Form* and *Job History Form* until your employees have had an opportunity to experience them. On the following two pages is a *Life History Form* that you may copy and use with your employees.

Life History Form: Page 1

Your Name: _____ Date: _____

1. **Positive Event:** List a minimum of five positive events in your life.	2. **Skills and Abilities:** List your skills and abilities (that you enjoy) that resulted in the event.	3. **Reasons:** Why was the event important to you? Be very honest and specific.
Positive event #1:		
Positive event #2:		
Positive event #3:		

Life History Form: Page 2

1. Positive Event: List a minimum of five positive events in your life.	2. Skills and Abilities: List your skills and abilities (that you enjoy) that resulted in the event.	3. Reasons: Why was the event important to you? Be very honest and specific.
Positive event #4:		
Positive event #5:		

4. From Column 2: List your most important skills and abilities.	5. From Column 3: Analyze the reasons why the event was personally important to you, and see if you can determine your underlying values.

Testing

There are a number of tests or questionnaires that can help us to determine our employee's career interests and needs. Examples of such tests are John Holland's Self-Directed Search, the Myers-Briggs Type Indicator, the Enneagram personality type indicator, and, for supervisory or management positions, the Leatherman Leadership Questionnaire. We can usually obtain tests such as these through our organization's human resource department.

There are two main kinds of tests to help people determine career interest and needs. The more common tests are called *perception* questionnaires. *Knowledge-based* questionnaires are less common.

Perception Questionnaires. Perception questionnaires are used to determine which topics in a list are perceived as being career development needs. For example, a questionnaire that begins by asking the employee, "Which of the following topics do you feel are important for your future development?" belongs to this class of questionnaire.

Perception questionnaires are easy and quick to complete. They can be filled out by the person being tested, the boss, a peer, or even a client or customer.

Unfortunately, perception questionnaires also have very serious limitations. For example, some topics from a career development questionnaire might be selected as important when, in fact, they are not truly the employee's needs. When topics such as "communications," or "time management" appear in a list, they are almost guaranteed to be selected as critical. This is because they are what we call "umbrella" terms. In other words, terms like "time management" are labels that cover a number of different subtopics. If any of the sub-parts are important to us, we will usually mark "time management" as important, even if the other parts are not important to us at all.

Also, what people think they need, and what they really need, may be quite different. For example, I may have little competence in managing my performance appraisal interviews, and yet not know that I need help in this area. It often happens that entire organizations don't know that they don't know how to conduct performance appraisals effectively!

Knowledge-Based Questionnaires. Knowledge-based tests, on the other hand, are used to determine our employees' actual knowledge in specific job task areas. For example, the following is a typical knowledge-based question:

The primary responsibility for career development rests with the

A. Employee's immediate supervisor
B. Human resource's establishment of career development programs and procedures (e.g., mentoring, training programs, career planning systems)
C. Employee
D. Chief executive of the organization, since his or her support is essential for the success of any career development program

As with perception questionnaires, knowledge-based tests are easy to administer. But unlike perception questionnaires, knowledge-based tests, when properly developed, provide very accurate information. Also, they reveal exactly what the person knows, rather than what the individual thinks he or she knows.

Performance Appraisal Systems

Another source that can help us identify our employees' needs and strengths is a performance appraisal—when it is properly done. If we are honest and accurate in our feedback to our employees, if the appraisal system is designed to allow the employee to be a part of the discussion, and if the performance appraisal form includes information about their future, then good career development information can be obtained.

In order for the performance appraisal interview to be meaningful for the employee—and the organization—the employees must have an opportunity well in advance to discuss their job responsibilities with their leader (as much as one year prior to the interview, if possible). This pre-interview discussion is important in order to reduce the chances that employees are appraised on issues or factors they didn't know were going to be included. Here, there should be a full discussion of the job's tasks, the standards for each task, the employees' authority level for the task, and a careful analysis made of any problems that might impede performance.

In addition, leaders must be able to give their employees honest and straightforward feedback when appraising them. Leaders must also be willing to spend time in the appraisal interview discussing not only employees' past and present performance, but their job future as well. And last, the performance appraisal form that is used should address such issues as career planning and setting future developmental goals and objectives.

As a part of a well-rounded performance management system, some organizations use a formal goal-setting process where employees, with their leader's help, write job-related goals and objectives, and then create plans to reach their objectives. This type of information, even though it is focused on an employee's present job tasks, can provide further career development data.

Career Development Workshops

Most performance appraisal systems fall short of the desired standard. Therefore, many organizations have encouraged the employee to accept responsibility for his or her own career development by setting up career development workshops for them. In these workshops, employees complete worksheets much like the *Job History Form* and *Life History Form* presented earlier, and design action plans for their personal development.

Such workshops not only assist employees in identifying their knowledge, skills, and values, but also show them that they are not alone in their career development needs. A payoff for the organization is that employees often find that they have far better opportunities within their organization than outside of it.

Leader-Employee Career Counseling Sessions

One of the best ways we can help our employees with their career development is to conduct individual career counseling sessions. In these interviews, we can help employees to

1. Determine whether their organizational goals are realistic.

2. Identify their strengths and determine whether they are important for future positions.

3. Identify areas of needed improvement.

4. Become knowledgeable about career alternatives.

5. Create action plans for continued development covering both strengths and needs.

Now let's consider some important strategies to guide us in conducting a career counseling session with our employee. First, we'll look at an eight-step procedure for conducting a career counseling session with an employee, and then we'll describe each step in detail. The eight key steps are as follows:

☑ 1. Prepare for the meeting.

☑ 2. Open the interview.

☑ 3. Obtain the employee's perceptions of his or her knowledge, skills, and values.

☑ 4. Discuss the employee's perceptions.

☑ 5. Explore career choice alternatives.

☑ 6. Create an action plan.

☑ 7. Conclude the interview.

☑ 8. Follow up.

Here are the eight key steps in detail.

☑ 1. Prepare for the meeting.

Make an Appointment with the Employee. Not only should a leader prepare for a career-counseling meeting, but so should the employee. Therefore, we should meet briefly with each employee well in advance of the session and advise him or her of the date, time, location, and meeting objectives. We tell him or her that we would like to discuss career goals and share ideas on the kinds of developmental activities that he or she should undertake.

If appropriate, we can encourage the employee to consider all possible alternatives for his or her career development. In other words, the focus should not be just on promotional opportunities, but also on such issues as job enrichment, special projects or assignments, and lateral moves. For example, we might say something like,

> *I'd like to meet with you in two weeks and spend some quality time reviewing the jobs you have held in the past, where you are today, what you might want to do in the future, and how you might get there. In short, one of the objectives of this meeting is to create a written action plan that can help you reach your own realistic career objectives.*

> *A word of caution: the purpose of this meeting is to help you explore your own career goals, not to announce some sort of promotion. So, between now and when we meet I'd like to encourage you to think of a wide range of career alternatives. That is, consider things like how we can make your present job more challenging. Are there special jobs or tasks that you would like to take on? And what kinds of training do you feel you need to prepare you better for your future? It's important for you to consider a wide variety of possible goals, because it's a statistical fact that there are more and more highly qualified people available for fewer and fewer openings.*

> *In most organizations, the chances of being promoted today are about six times less than they were a decade ago. It used to be that a promotion was the only measure of success on the job. But today we need to measure success in other ways—like how happy we are doing what we have chosen to do. Or how productive we are. We can no longer use promotions as the major measure of whether or not an employee is successful. So it seems to me that the astute employee will explore a wide range of possible career outcomes, rather than be limited simply to the idea of "promotions."*

Then, we can give the employee a copy of the *Job History Form* and the *Life History Form* and ask him or her to complete them in advance of the meeting. We could say,

> *Now to prepare for this meeting, I'd like you to fill out these forms. They will help you identify the knowledge, skills, and abilities you have, and also enable you to determine the kinds of things you really enjoy doing, as well as the things you don't like doing. I think you'll find that they will give you an even better understanding of yourself—and also give us good information for our meeting.*
>
> *On the* Job History Form, *list five jobs or positions you've held in the past, starting with your present job and working backward. The* Life History Form *focuses more on significant events you have experienced, not only on the job, but in other areas of your life as well. See what you can do. And if you have any questions, come see me.*

We will also need to determine if the employee already has a career development action plan (few employees do). If so, we can ask him or her to bring it to the meeting. It is also advisable to urge the employee to come prepared to do most of the talking, since the responsibility for career planning is the employee's, not ours. We might say,

> *Please come prepared to do most of the talking in this meeting, since it will be a discussion of your career. My role will be to listen, ask questions, and offer suggestions to help you develop a written career plan.*

Taking time to properly prepare the employee for such a meeting is essential. If we expect the employee to do most of the talking, he or she needs time to reflect on the topics that will be discussed. Last, it is a good idea to reserve a private area where interruptions can be controlled.

On the following pages is a handout that can be reproduced and given to your employee to aid in preparing for the career-counseling interview.

**Employee Guide to Use in Preparing
for a Career Counseling Interview**

The *Job* and *Life History Forms* help you to identify your knowledge, skills, and abilities and enable you to determine the kinds of things you really enjoy doing as well as those you don't.

Use the *Job History Form* to list five jobs or positions you have held, starting with your present job and working backward. Use the *Life History Form* to list significant events in your experience.

Develop Alternative Career Goals. Then, considering your talents and skills, as well as the things you like and don't like doing, try to identify where you want to be in the future. Within reason, the more alternative career goals you bring to your counseling session to examine, the better your decisions will be. This means looking ahead at many possibilities, including job enrichment in your present job, special projects, or lateral moves for more exposure or challenge.

A good strategy is to brainstorm a list of possible career goals. The idea is to create a list of goals on paper—without judging whether or not they can be achieved. When your list is complete, delete those goals that seem impractical, combine the remaining ones where possible, and add to the list new ideas that come to mind.

Create a Career Plan. When you have identified the direction you would like to go (even a tentative one), begin to develop a step-by-step plan to reach your goal. A useful *Career Goal Planning Worksheet* is found on the next page of this handout. Make several copies of this worksheet for use in your planning.

Analyze Risk. A key question in planning is to ask, "If I do this, what can go wrong?" This is an important question you need to ask yourself—and others—as you prepare your plan. The idea is to try to develop preventive and contingency actions you can take if problems do occur. Preventive action includes those things you can do now to reduce the possibility that a problem will occur. Contingency action is what you will do to stabilize your plan if the problem occurs anyway.

You may wish to develop several possible career plans for your meeting with your leader. One is your primary plan. The others can be used if your primary plan proves to be unrealistic for your organization. Your career plan is tentative at this point. To implement a plan, it must meet not only your needs, but the organization's needs as well. Therefore, after completing your forms, set up a time with your leader to review your plans and obtain his or her input.

Career Goal Planning Worksheet

1. Write your goal statement: _____

    _____

    _____

2. List the steps in your plan to achieve this goal (do not number or date the steps yet).

Step Number	Step	Completion Date
____	_____	_____
____	_____	_____
____	_____	_____
____	_____	_____
____	_____	_____
____	_____	_____
____	_____	_____
____	_____	_____
____	_____	_____
____	_____	_____
____	_____	_____
____	_____	_____
____	_____	_____
____	_____	_____
____	_____	_____
____	_____	_____
____	_____	_____
____	_____	_____

3. Identify potential problems with your plan by asking, "What can go wrong?"

    _____

    _____

    _____

    _____

    _____

4. If possible, develop solutions (preventive and/or contingency actions) for any identified potential problems and incorporate these solutions into your plan as new steps.

    _____

    _____

    _____

5. Finally, number the steps in your plan, determine a completion date for each step, and then review with your leader.

The day of the interview with our employee has arrived. The next step for us as the leader is to

☑ **2. Open the interview.**

Before meeting with the employee, we need to arrange the meeting area so that the employee feels as comfortable as possible. If we use our office, we can seat both of us in front of the desk. An even better place to hold the interview is in a neutral meeting area such as a conference room. Our intent should be to put the employee at ease by reducing the physical barriers to communication.

When the employee arrives for the meeting, we should greet him or her warmly. Then again westate our role, time constraints (if appropriate), and the meeting objectives. An illustration of what could be said follows:

> *I'm pleased to have this opportunity to discuss with you your career goals. In today's meeting, I see myself as being a coach, a listener, and a possible resource for you as you explore your alternatives. This is your meeting, and you're in charge.*

> *As I see it, your objective is to explore your strengths, as well as areas where some improvement may be helpful, and to discover what you like to do and don't like to do. We also need to look at career alternatives and to create an action plan for implementation.*

In addition to explaining our role and the meeting objectives, we should also stress that there are no guarantees that what is planned will actually happen. However, by creating a well-conceived, written action plan, the employee can increase the probability of reaching his or her goal.

Last, unless we have a photographic memory, we may need to take notes so that we don't forget important ideas that are discussed. It is courteous to ask the employee's permission to take such notes during the meeting.

☑ **3. Obtain the employee's perceptions of his or her knowledge, skills, and values.**

In this step, we begin the process of obtaining information from the employee. A good way to start is to ask the employee to summarize the strengths highlighted by his or her *Job History Form* and determine the types of tasks that have been satisfying and dissatisfying. Then we ask for a summary of knowledge, skills, and values highlighted by the life history analysis.

It is important that we help the employee do most of the talking by maintaining eye contact, listening carefully, and not interrupting. We rephrase the employee's comments throughout the meeting, which not only ensures that we understand what the employee said but also demonstrates to the employee that we are listening carefully. In addition, we can encourage the employee by giving verbal prompts as he or she is speaking: "That's interesting," "Please continue," and "Could you give me an example?"

☑ **4. Discuss the employee's perceptions.**

Here we need to provide feedback on what the employee has said. For example, we might wish to reinforce any areas of agreement on the employee's perceptions of his or her strengths, as well as to state (rephrase) areas of needed improvement. We may also need to provide our honest observations on areas of need—and strengths—that the employee did not mention.

Last, we don't challenge the employee's values. If the employee says, "Money is the most important thing to me!" we don't respond, "You mean that money is even more important than your family?" Determining what the employee values is the objective, so it is not appropriate here to challenge his or her values.

☑ **5. Explore career choice alternatives.**

Within reason, the more alternatives the employee has available to examine, the better will be the final decision. This means that the employee should be encouraged to look at many different possibilities, such as job enrichment of his or her present job, special projects, and/or lateral moves for more exposure or challenge. It may even be appropriate for us to assist the employee in exploring opportunities outside the organization.

A good strategy is to help the employee brainstorm a list of possible career alternatives. The idea is to create a list of alternatives on paper without judging their viability. When the list is complete, we then delete those alternatives that seem impractical, combine the remaining ones where possible, and even add new ideas that come to mind. Last, we help the employee select an alternative (or alternatives) that best meets the needs of both the employee and the organization.

☑ 6. Create an action plan.

After selecting one or more appropriate career alternatives, the next step is to assist the employee in writing an action plan. But we need to be careful and watch out who holds the pencil! If the leader writes the action plan, it will be the leader's, not the employee's. We can begin this step by saying,

> *Why don't you start by writing out a general goal statement that includes one of your key alternatives? This statement should clearly describe what you want to become, or to do, and in what length of time you hope to accomplish this.*

If the employee has more than one career choice alternative, then he or she may need to write out a goal statement for each. And in some cases, there is one major alternative for which other alternatives become sub-steps, or sub-goals, in the final action plan.

After writing a goal statement, the employee should develop a list of actions that need to be taken to reach the goal. Again, the employee should explore, with our help, a number of different types of actions, such as mentoring opportunities, training programs, coaching by us, special task assignments, and even temporary lateral moves where necessary. Each of these actions or steps can then be dated and listed in sequential order. At this point, it may be necessary to revise the original goal date to meet the time requirements of the individual action (activities). For example, we could say to our employee,

> *Why don't you start by writing out a general goal statement for now. Then, after you finish the plan you will have a better feel for how long this will take to achieve and can write in a date by which you would like to accomplish your main goal.*

Before finalizing the plan, we should look for potential problems by analyzing the list of activities or actions. It is important to do this with the employee, because if we can identify potential problems now, we can anticipate likely causes and solutions.

We can develop solutions of two kinds: 1) preventive solutions, which will reduce the probability of the problem ever occurring, and 2) contingency solutions, which will reduce the severity of the problem if it does occur. These preventive and contingency actions can then be included as a part of the original plan. The time to consider problems and solutions is in the planning stage, where it will greatly increase the chances of successfully reaching the goal. When the plan is complete, it may be necessary for us to establish follow-up meetings with the employee. We can select key milestones and use these dates to plan meetings to review the employee's progress toward completing his or her goal.

 7. Conclude the interview.

In this step, we need to encourage the employee to continue to accept responsibility for his or her career development. In addition, we can check for any unasked or unanswered questions, and offer to answer any questions arising in the future. Last, if it fits your management style, you might thank the employee for his or her efforts in creating the career plan.

We could say,

> *This is your plan, and its success is primarily dependent on you. I'll help in any way that I can. But for the most part, you're going to have to make it happen. I have confidence in you and know that you will give it your best effort.*

> *Is there anything you have not asked, or that we have not considered?*

> *I appreciate the work you did in filling out the <u>Job History</u> and <u>Life History</u> forms and the time you've spent with me today. I feel very good about what we have accomplished together.*

 8. Follow up.

Sometimes we get so busy in our leadership job that we don't make time to follow up with the employee. Understandable—but a potential disaster! We have seen that today it is necessary to do career counseling with our employees. Career counseling is now something that is not just "nice to do" but is mandatory.

In addition, if we do spend the time necessary to help the employee develop an action plan and then ignore the employee's future efforts, the employee will have a legitimate reason to believe that we don't really care. We can't "talk a good game," and then fail to follow through with what needs to be done. Career counseling is too important for the productivity and future of our employees, our organization, and us!

19

Leadership

Leading Change

After a major change there is often a decline in productivity, quality, and innovation—precisely those things the action was designed to improve! Experts agree that the key to better results is helping employees see that the new situation is not the end of the world, and that with some readjustments—however painful—the organization can become healthier and stronger than ever before. Doing this requires that we first understand what employees are experiencing after change and why.

Anthony J. Mulkern
Transition and Recovery from Organizational Change

Change causes problems. In fact, Peter Drucker states that all problems result from change. Not only do we have to deal with external problems resulting from change, we also need to deal with our emotions. Fear, anxiety, and worry can all occur from changes.

These emotions usually come from apprehension about the unknown. We're not certain what's coming, or whether we can handle it. We're not sure we want to give up where we are. We may fear that we are going to be less comfortable with the future than we are with the present.

Human beings tolerate change in different ways. While some feel overwhelmed even by the thought of making a change, others seem to thrive on it. Whatever our tolerance, this chapter is for those who must cope with change. This chapter will cover how to increase our tolerance for change—and how to manage it to our employees' benefit.

Many changes are positive, though some changes don't seem to benefit us directly. We may feel that a change leaves us with fewer benefits, and that it is something we will have to suffer through.

Our ability to manage change is linked to our feeling of being in control, and to the personal benefits we see in making the change. Our challenge is to discover the ways that a change will benefit us—and our employees. Or, if there are no apparent benefits, we will need to find strategies to control the negative effects of the change.

Let's first look at the major causes of change and then examine some strategies that can help us manage changes that affect our lives.

Causes of Change

There are two major categories of change, external and internal. External changes are those that originate outside our organization. These are the ones that can cause us the most mental distress because they often create a feeling of loss of control. For example, if the economy turns downward and our organization starts to lay off workers, it may be difficult for us to maintain the morale of our employees.

Internal changes are those that result from an organization's own initiatives. For instance, if your organization decides to relocate its operations, you can be assured that you and your employees will deal with major changes.

External Changes

There are seven major causes of external change:

1. New technology

2. Governmental regulations

3. Variable economy

4. Job mobility

5. Constant increases in wage levels

6. Union activity

7. Personal relationships

These external changes cause major problems. But they can also create positive opportunities—opportunities to do things differently, and better. Let's examine each of these causes.

New technology can create havoc within any organization. Although it is rare that new technology results in industry-wide disruption, it may cause great distress in a particular organization. Even if our employees don't lose their jobs, they may feel anxiety over the possibility of being retrained or moved to another job.

New technology, however, can also result in jobs that are even more secure. Suppose our organization decides to reorganize its reporting procedures and therefore installs a new system to speed the flow of information. As a result, our employees must be given hundreds of hours of training to teach them how to use the new equipment. This additional training and their new skills will make them even more valuable to the organization.

Governmental regulations can also have a great impact on organizations. The Americans with Disability Act, tax regulations, automotive emission and gas consumption regulations, waste water disposal guidelines, and safety regulations are all examples of laws and regulations that have created major changes, resulting in problems within organizations.

But even changes in governmental regulations can produce opportunities. For example, look at what has happened to the automobile industry. Continued change in the government's regulations concerning automotive gasoline resulted in the development of high-efficiency engines that are among the best in the world. The net effect of this has been to help save jobs by making the U.S. more competitive in world markets.

Variable economy creates inflation, stagnation, and depression. Third World debt, balance of payments, national debt, wars, and competition from a world market are all economic realities of our time. Since we have little chance of preventing these problems, we can reduce our anxiety when they occur by taking action ahead of time to protect ourselves.

Note that I said "when," not "if," they occur. Large-scale economic changes have happened, are happening, and will continue to happen. You know that you will experience some, or even all, of the global economic problems mentioned above, and that they will have a profound effect upon your organization.

Thus, it is to our benefit to do those things now that will help us cope with such problems when they occur. In our personal lives, for example, we can increase our savings rate, cut back on high-interest charge accounts, and reduce our expenses. On the job, we can make ourselves and our employees ever more valuable to our organization by increasing the quality and quantity of our group's output. The people who survive swings in the economy are those who are the least dispensable to their organization. And it's much easier to make such changes now than after trouble comes.

Job mobility has both positive and negative consequences. It's great to attract high quality applicants from other organizations. It's not so great to lose our people to other organizations. Therefore, it is not enough to attract good people; we have to figure out ways to keep them. For the most part, employees don't leave organizations for financial reasons. There are some people, of course, who are always hungry for more money or simply new "pastures." But even when employees earn fair wages, they may leave because another job offers an opportunity for more responsibility, greater challenge, and better leadership! In other words, today's employees are often more committed to their professions than to their organizations. The leaders of these highly mobile employees may need to implement training programs to help create challenging environments that attract and keep good people.

The challenge for us is to select good people from the mobile market, then keep them by using the strategies outlined in the chapters on training and motivation. For example, we might give our new employees helpful information on the people that they will be working with—i.e., what the existing employees do in their jobs and their hobbies and outside interests. This will help the new employees establish links of interest so that it will be easier to make friends. The more they know about their future jobs, their organization, and the people they will be working with, the more comfortable and effective their transition will be.

Constant increases in wage levels may result in employees who can afford to take frequent unofficial three-day weekends. This will require that we clearly tell our employees the organization's expectations concerning time off, keep careful records of attendance, and immediately deal with problems when they occur.

Union activity is another major external factor that may have high impact upon the way that we carry out our leadership role. Unionization often results from poor management—management that *talks* about leadership, but doesn't do it. This indicates that it is far better to have a proactive stance that reduces the probability of having a union election. In other words, if an organization and its leaders treat their people fairly, the chances are that a union will not successfully win an election.

If the organization already has a union, then stressful changes can occur each time a contract is up for renewal. Here, lack of information about contract issues or how they are to be interpreted can cause stress. The better an organization communicates to its leaders the key issues, the more prepared the leaders will be in handling any changes that may be required.

Personal relationships can be another major external factor causing change— one that we must all cope with. Marital problems, separation, divorce, alcohol or drug-dependent family members, children leaving home, death—all these are examples of external situations that can cause untold stress and change in our lives. The best strategy to deal with such changes is to encourage our employees to get professional help and, if possible, group support. It is far better for our employees to seek help than to try to "tough it out" by themselves. There are many things one can do to cope positively with severe stress in personal relationships, but experience shows that trained resource people outside the situation often make a critical difference.

Internal Changes

External forces can cause internal organizational changes—sometimes sweeping ones. But internal initiatives also cause major changes within an organization. These actions fall into three categories: personnel changes, job changes, and organizational changes. Let's look at each of these in turn.

Personnel changes can have a strong impact on our employees' ability to cope. Suppose you receive a promotion and your employees get a new boss, or one of your group's fellow workers leaves the organization, or you hire a new employee to work in your group. These changes can be difficult to manage.

When bosses change, people become understandably apprehensive. What will the new boss be like? What will be his or her expectations of them? This problem is even more difficult if the employees had an extremely good relationship with their old boss.

There are things we can do to help our employees constructively cope with personnel changes. For example, new bosses have histories—they come from somewhere. The odds are that the new boss was promoted from within the organization. If so, it is often easy to obtain background information on the new leader for our employees.

Special problems can occur if the new boss came from our section and is now the leader of what were his or her co-workers. Here it is especially important that we spend time with both the new leader and the employees to help them manage this transition. If the leader is new to leadership responsibilities, we may need to help him or her understand the difference between the new job and the old one. And we must manage the feelings of other employees who wanted the job. The key here is to be sensitive and aware that both the new leader and the employees will have strong feelings about this change. Our job is to listen—and to help them manage their feelings.

Losing a valued co-worker can also be distressing. Close relationships that develop on the job are normally altered when one individual leaves. We have at least two options to manage the change that occurs when an employee loses a friend through resignation, termination, or transfer. First, we can help the two employees deliberately plan outside activities or develop common interests that have nothing to do with work. This will help them to maintain a continuing relationship, though they no longer work together. Second, if our employee must give up the relationship, it is important to permit him or her to grieve this loss. For example, I once had a wonderful boss, an ex-football player who was a mountain of a man with a heart of gold. And I liked him a great deal. But because our boss-subordinate roles had not allowed for a friendship off the job, we could not maintain our relationship when I resigned my position and took another job. I permitted myself to fully experience the sadness and deep sense of loss that this change caused. And my open acknowledgment of my feelings helped, though I miss him still.

Another type of change occurs when we hire a new employee. Most new employees are anxious about their new jobs, and feel great discomfort about the strangers they will be working with. Our job is to help them overcome their anxiety in order to manage the change as smoothly as possible.

Since we know that this person is probably nervous and anxious about the new job, we don't say, "This job is simple. You'll catch on in no time." Rather than relieving tension, this can make it worse. By stating that the job is easy, we are, in effect, saying that the person is not very smart if he or she has trouble. Better to say something like, "I know that most new jobs appear difficult. But I am confident that you can manage it."

We can also help new employees overcome some of their anxiety by finding out what their outside interests are. Then as we introduce them to others in our section or department, we can suggest links of common interest.

Job changes can also have major effects on employees. Such changes range from the addition of a new job task to a new job due to promotion or transfer. The key word here is "new." The more a new job is unlike the old one, the greater the employee's anxiety will be. So if we assign an employee to a completely new job, we can expect him or her to feel anxious about it.

A key strategy here is to make all of the tasks of the new job clearly visible. That is, we need to take the time to describe the employee's job tasks on paper. Then we can review each task with the employee and devise an on-the-job training plan. This will take some of the mystery out of the unfamiliar assignment and reduce the employee's anxiety. It will help him or her to see that what may at first appear to be an overwhelming job is really a series of particular tasks that he or she can handle successfully.

Organizational changes often cause employees deep concern about their future. Some changes that affect the organization, like external technological or economic ones, have already been discussed. But there are also internally caused changes that organizations make. They may want to be more competitive, introduce a new product or service, increase their profits, reduce operational expenses, or pay bigger dividends to their stockholders. Or management simply may want to look good in the eyes of a new administration. As a result, we see mergers, acquisitions, downsizing, rightsizing, and spin-offs. Whatever the organizational change, our employees are almost certain to be affected by it in some way. In the past, workers who were laid off due to changing economic conditions were recalled. With today's reductions in force, the layoffs are permanent—jobs have been eliminated! In the past, these changes usually affected a specific industry. Today, they affect all industries! Yesterday, these changes were caused by economic downturn. Today, new equipment, new technology, new processes, and new policies and procedures cause them. These major changes affect all our employees—and us.

A major problem occurs because high-level decisions are usually made in secret (often for good reasons). Major decisions are argued, fought over, discussed, and finally accepted at the executive level, and then presented to the organization's employees. Executive management, who have often had months to come to grips with their momentous decisions and iron out all the details, expect the announced changes to be reasonably well received by the rank-and-file employees. Sure, they expect some minor disruptions, but nothing that middle management can't handle. Much to their surprise, the very things they wanted to have happen—things like lower production cost, better quality, greater effectiveness, and increased earnings—don't! Good people, the very ones they want to keep, are the first to put their résumés on the street. Turnover is up. Morale is in the "flusher"! Production falls. Quality is out the window. Creativity disappears. Loyalty to the organization vanishes. And executive management wrings their hands and wonders what happened.

Changes like these must be managed. And to manage change requires leaders! It requires leaders who know the best way to help their employees is 1) to communicate, communicate, communicate, 2) to know that the employees will need time to adjust to what they see as cataclysmic changes, and 3) to listen to their employees. Competent leaders know that employees are going to experience strong emotions such as anger, guilt (they still have a job and their friends don't), anxiety, and fear! In short, the employees feel betrayed.

Therefore, leaders will need to spend most of their time communicating with their employees one-on-one and in group meetings. And when they do, they need to tell the truth! They need to tell what has happened, why it really happened, what other changes are planned, and what changes will not happen.

Unfortunately, the employees' direct leader often doesn't know the information that he or she needs to communicate. Therefore, leaders need to be assertive about their right to know what is going on. They can speak with their boss, the human resource department, or even their boss's boss. Most of their employees' concerns about organizational changes are due to not being kept informed. The more employees can find out the specifics of a change from informed people, the better they will feel and function.

Here, of course, we must be careful about the "rumor mill." Since organizational changes tend to produce strange rumors, we need to make every effort to obtain our information from those people who, in fact, know the facts—and then communicate what we find to our employees.

Guidelines for Managing Change

Several guidelines stand out clearly when we consider how to manage change well.

- First, we need to give the employees an opportunity to express their feelings. When employees appear angry, we can't react by becoming defensive. We listen and let them talk.

- Second, changes frequently involve significant personal benefits. Our job is to identify those benefits and to discuss them with our employees in order to create within them a genuine acceptance of the change.

- Third, we as leaders cannot become paralyzed by change. We need to determine what aspects of the situation we can control and take positive action on these parts. Even the effects of a change that appear most negative can sometimes be turned to our advantage when we creatively take charge in the areas we still control.

- Finally, we can seek the assistance of others. The simple act of talking to someone who is a good listener is sometimes enough to reduce our anxiety to a manageable level and free our energy.

Above all, even if an organizational change seems overwhelming or impossible for a specific employee to accept, don't let him or her quit in a huff! Ask that he or she take time to think through the reasons for staying with the organization. If the employee still wants to leave, we encourage him or her to find another job before resigning. We can also remind this employee that it is much easier to obtain another job while still holding one. The plain fact is that prospective employers see an employee as more valuable if he or she has a job than if not.

I know that many leaders would allow an upset employee to go ahead and quit, especially if the employee was only an average performer. But the best policy is always to treat employees the way we would wish to be treated. We need to remember two things: it may be easier to turn the employee around than to hire and train a replacement. And if the employee leaves anyway, we want him or her to say good things about the organization and us.

Using "Force Field Analysis" to Manage Change

Many years ago, I used to write books in longhand. And then came computers. Talk about major change! So I bought the simplest word-processing program I could find, and sat down to use it. A computer expert obviously wrote the instructions, using words I had never heard of to explain things I couldn't picture. I became so frustrated that I almost gave up. The fact that the word processing program had a built-in word speller to help me overcome my spelling problem was the only reason I stuck with it. And I finally learned how to use it.

Let's look at this example to illustrate the use of what is called *force field analysis*. Force field analysis is a tool that helps analyze change in order to 1) gain personal control over changes and 2) bring possible benefits of change, sometimes unperceived at first, into the present.

The first step in force field analysis is to list on one side of a vertical line all the reasons—or *forces*—that support the change. The next step is to list all the opposing forces—reasons against changing—on the other side of the line. The final step is to draw opposing arrows to represent the competing forces, with longer arrows indicating stronger forces.

Force Field Analysis
Changing from Longhand to a Word Processor

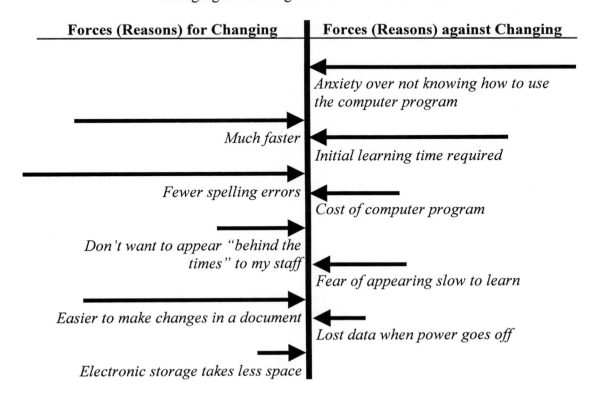

Forces (Reasons) for Changing	Forces (Reasons) against Changing
	Anxiety over not knowing how to use the computer program
Much faster	*Initial learning time required*
Fewer spelling errors	*Cost of computer program*
Don't want to appear "behind the times" to my staff	*Fear of appearing slow to learn*
Easier to make changes in a document	*Lost data when power goes off*
Electronic storage takes less space	

Now that I've learned how to use a word processor, I'll never go back to writing in longhand. But notice that I had an overwhelming reason (my need for a spell-checker) to continue my efforts to master this new process.

Force field analysis helped me decide to make this change by graphically showing me the factors that were influencing my feelings about the change. I could see at a glance all the positive reasons for accepting this change as well as the ones against it. Next, I could begin to minimize the effects of the opposing forces through specific actions. For example, I could reduce the required learning time by having someone who knew the program instruct me. His help also could reduce my anxiety over not knowing how to use this new program and my fear of appearing to be a slow learner. Purchasing a non-interruptible power source took care of the "lost data when the power goes off" problem. In the final analysis, the reasons for learning how to use the program far outweighed the reasons against it.

A force field chart will help us and our employees deal openly with feelings about change. It can also increase our employees' acceptance of the need for change. This technique is especially helpful if the employee must cope with changes that appear to have little value. If we can show our employees factors in favor of change, then they can more easily accept the possibility that the organization (or others) had what it believed were good reasons for the change— no matter how idiotic it might seem initially! Our job is to help our employees discover the reasons for change—and its possible benefits.

To analyze a specific change, we can start by sketching a force field chart as just shown. Then, with our employee(s), we list as many benefits and disadvantages as we can. If the benefits side looks sparse at first, we may need to uncover additional reasons why the change was introduced. We can ask our boss or ask peers whose opinions we respect. We can talk to others outside our organization, if the change is not confidential, to get their views.

When we talk with our employees, we need to remember our goal is to discover with our employees other positive reasons for the change—not to affirm our present discomfort with it. We need to find out the reasons for change so that we can better support it from a knowledgeable position. If our employees can support, or at least accept, the need for a change, our next step is to help them look for ways to control the opposing forces (negative effects) coming from the change. This will enable them to cope with change constructively, creatively, and, as is often done, to their advantage.

We need to also remember the major strategies in managing change with our employees: 1) communicate, 2) listen, 3) take care of ourselves, 4) help the employees look for the benefits, and 5) help them take control.

On the following page is a worksheet to use for managing the changes that affect you and your employees.

Managing Change Worksheet

1. Write a brief description of the change that concerns you or your employees.

   _____

   _____

   _____

   _____

2. Using the force field chart below (use easel paper if you are working with a group), list the reasons, or forces, that support the change on the left side and the opposing forces on the right. Place an arrow over each force, with the length indicating the strength of the force (reason).

Forces for Change	*Forces against Change*

3. What information do you need to complete the chart further?

   _____

   _____

   _____

   _____

   _____

4. Who has the needed information?

   _____

   _____

   _____

5. What are the major benefits of this change for you or your employees?

_____

_____

_____

_____

_____

_____

_____

_____

6. What specific actions can you take toward the opposing forces (negative results) that will minimize, or even reverse, their effects, putting you or your employees in better control?

_____

_____

_____

_____

_____

_____

7. What additional actions will you or your employees need to take to make this a beneficial change?

_____

_____

_____

_____

_____

_____

The Close

20

Leadership
Leading
Your Employees

One reason corporate and governmental bureaucracies stagnate is the assumption by line executives that, given their rank and authority, they can lead without being leaders. They cannot. They can be given subordinates, but they cannot be given a following. A following must be earned. Surprisingly, many of them do not even know they are not leading. They mistake the exercise of authority for leadership, and as long as they persist in that mistake they will never learn the art of turning subordinates into followers.

John W. Gardner
Leaders and Followers

Times are changing! In a world of global markets, scarce resources, and tougher competition, the winds of change are being felt everywhere. Our employees are changing too. They are better educated, more highly specialized, and have gained greater mobility. And they cost more—more to find, more to train, more to replace.

And how about you? Are *you* moving with today's changes? Do you understand what's happening in our organizations? Do you know your employees real needs? Do you know about leading your employees effectively in the often-bewildering tasks they face? And do you really understand that every change is an opportunity to do something better—a chance to grow in your leadership skills?

This book was written for you! As it states at the beginning, it is for leaders who are looking for common sense, down-to-earth techniques for handling the great variety of employee needs that occur every day. It is a very special how-to book, with step-by-step instructions on how to lead our employees. It provides practical suggestions, tested strategies, proven methods.

So this book is not about theories that don't relate to the job, or about leadership styles and personality. Instead, it is written to show exactly what to do to lead effectively. Its twenty chapters cover virtually every important employee problem situation—your needs as well as theirs. And detailed, reproducible on-the-job worksheets are presented throughout to help you apply what you have learned.

We have seen a number of key principles running throughout this book. I would like to end by listing, as simply and clearly as possible, some of the most important ones.

If you want to be a truly effective, helpful leader,

1. Prepare before every important interaction with your employees. (In nearly all of the step-by-step leadership models I have presented, step one is to *prepare*!)

2. Do the job *with* your employees, not by yourself.

3. Lead your employees—don't order them around.

4. Keep everyone informed.

5. Talk *with* employees, not *at* them.

6. Trust your employees with responsibility. They want to be challenged.

7. Set high standards, for employees tend to fulfill their leader's expectations.

8. Involve your employees. It will raise their morale, stimulate their creativity, and increase their commitment.

9. Look for what was done well, not always for what was done wrong.

10. Make your feedback specific, not general, and positive, as well as corrective.

11. Follow up to provide needed, timely guidance, to ensure that what is planned happens, and to make performance matter.

If you will follow these principles, you will succeed in leading your employees. And they and your organization will thank you!

Quality Leadership Skills
Standards of Leadership Behavior

About the Author: Dick Leatherman, Ph.D., SPHR

Dick Leatherman served as Manager of Education and Training for the 3M Company, and then spent twenty-five years as the CEO of International Training Consultants, Inc. (ITC). He successfully grew ITC from a one-person organization to a major producer of training packages, videos, and assessment instrumentation and now serves as the Chairman of the Board. He also teaches full time at the University of Richmond, where he is the Academic Program Director of Human Resource Management for the School of Continuing Studies.

Dick is widely recognized for his pioneering work in the areas of trainer training, employee development, and needs assessment instrumentation. His published instrument, the Leatherman Leadership Questionnaire (LLQ) is the premiere test for measuring leadership knowledge. He is the author of several books, including *The Training Trilogy* and *Is Coffee Break the Best Part of Your Day?*

He attended the University of Minnesota, and holds his M.A. and Ph.D. from Virginia Commonwealth University.

Second Edition

ISBN 0-9674325-1-0